STREET
SCRIPTURES

STREET
SCRIPTURES

Between God and Hip-Hop

Alejandro Nava

The University of Chicago Press

Chicago and London

The University of Chicago Press, Chicago 60637
The University of Chicago Press, Ltd., London
© 2022 by The University of Chicago
Published 2022
Printed in the United States of America
31 30 29 28 27 26 25 24 23 22   1 2 3 4 5

ISBN-13: 978-0-226-81914-3 (cloth)
ISBN-13: 978-0-226-81916-7 (paper)
ISBN-13: 978-0-226-81915-0 (e-book)
DOI: https://doi.org/10.7208/chicago/9780226819150.001.0001

Library of Congress Cataloging-in-Publication Data

Names: Nava, Alejandro (Author on hip hop), author.
Title: Street scriptures : between God and hip-hop / Alejandro Nava.
Description: Chicago : University of Chicago Press, 2022. | Includes
     bibliographical references and index.
Identifiers: LCCN 2021041772 | ISBN 9780226819143 (cloth) |
     ISBN 9780226819167 (paperback) | ISBN 9780226819150 (ebook)
Subjects: LCSH: Rap (Music)—Religious aspects. | Rap (Music)—History
     and criticism. | Hip-hop—United States—Religious aspects. | Popular
     music—Latin America—History and criticism.
Classification: LCC ML3921.8.R36 N38 2022 | DDC 782.421649—dc23
LC record available at https://lccn.loc.gov/2021041772

♾ This paper meets the requirements of ANSI/NISO Z39.48-1992
(Permanence of Paper).

a mi familia

CONTENTS

Introduction

If I keep my ear to the streets, I will hear the entire world.

DMX

In both religious studies and hip-hop studies, a noticeable sea change occurred in the waning years of the twentieth century, the time of my graduate studies at the University of Chicago. From where I stood, the approaching millennium seemed to bring about a change in the prevailing wind patterns of academic life, the currents now turning and spinning like a whirling dervish around questions of style, grace, form, elegance, and, in a word, aesthetics. While I found my way to the study of religion through the jarring and galvanizing work of liberation theologians, by the time I began my graduate studies the sun appeared to be setting on prophetic-oriented approaches to religion, now pushed to the shadows and eclipsed by rising concerns for style, form, and beauty. Perhaps, I thought, the heyday of liberation theology had come and gone. Perhaps it was played out, and I was joining the game as the clock was expiring.

Take the concept of "liberation": once the inspiration for dreams of equality and justice, and synonymous with ethical-political struggles, the term started to lose some of its air by the late 1990s and early aughts, a sudden tumble into obsolescence. If it didn't disappear altogether, "liberation" was often spiritualized and aestheticized, stripped of the communal and political connotations that once prevailed in the civil rights and black power generations. It lost the clout that it once had in the 1970s and 1980s.[1] To some, as Daniel Groody chronicled in a volume on liberation theology's legacy, it became passé and moribund, smoke without fire: "The fire that ignited such

1

passion a few decades ago has burned low, and as the coals of liberation begin to lose their heat some wonder whether it will simply die out all together or be just an occasional spark here and there."[2]

With "liberation" suddenly sounding tired, many critics turned to other symbols and experiences in the study of religion. In theological circles, mysticism and aesthetics became appealing topics of conversation. Since prophetic-oriented theologies (liberation theology, black theology, mujerista and womanist theologies, etc.) were widely influential in the 1970s and 1980s, driven by a blistering ethical-political consciousness, theological aesthetics seemed to emerge in the later years of the twentieth century as a necessary corrective to liberationist politics, a reminder that religion has a rich surplus of meanings that cannot be reduced to a matter of ethics or politics alone. As apologists for the seductive pleasures of visual, sensual, and auditory beauty, apart from any pragmatic or utilitarian end, these voices emphasized the value of religion or the arts as ends in themselves, beauty for the sake of beauty. When religion is stripped of aesthetics and spirituality, reduced to a barren ethical or political platform, they argued, it loses its radiance and glory, its exuberance and splashes of pageantry. You end up, as Kant did, with a religion within the limits of reason and morals alone, a view of the sacred that has been shorn of all beauty, looking gaunt and pale, drained of style, grace, and wonder. You end up with a desolate and bland religion, a rainbow without color, a flower without fragrance or bloom.

While liberation theology never reached such a dull position, I think it's fair to say that it tended to be primarily deconstructive and iconoclastic in spirit, suspicious of the trappings and frills of popular religion. Aesthetical extravagances—architecture, statues, images, relics, dances, paintings, liturgical fashions, music, rituals, festivities, ceremonies, carnivals, and so on—were seen as the outer layers and trimmings of religion, like a piñata with bright, colorful ruffles but empty within. If pleasing to the senses, and catching to the eyes, so much ornament can blind us to the desperate needs of the poor all around us. In order to keep our eyes and ears fixed on the kingdom, liberation theologians used their words like a cudgel to smash material and aesthetic idols, and this included all beliefs, practices, rites, or myths that would replace allegiance to God with mammon, power, pleasure, and ego. They targeted the escapist and pacifying consolations of religion in particular, their opiate-like tendency to soothe the spirit while stifling resistance and rebellion. Charming and mesmerizing, the delights and pleasures of religion were seen as calming sedatives, turning the drumroll of revolt into a soft and soothing lullaby, pleasing but hardly defiant. Easily lost in the delights of beauty—the rapture of music, the lighting of candles, the solace of ritual, the touch of a relic, the sublimity of art, and so on—are the biblical injunctions to live in solidarity with the poor and mistreated. Lost is moral vigilance, the gospel truths that inspire acts of justice and rouse us to action. The prophet Amos, a feverish messenger of such things, prepared the way for this outlook: "Take away from me the noise of your songs; I will not listen to the melody of your harps. But let justice roll down like waters, and righteousness like an ever-flowing stream" (Amos 5:23–24).[3]

For myself and many others, Archbishop Óscar Romero (1917–1980) was the patron saint of this vision. In his last homily, just before he was shot at the altar while celebrating Mass, his body broken and sacrificed for others like the Eucharist, he took the occasion to consider the meaning of liberation, extolling the life of a martyred woman as a shining example of the concept: "In particular, I can glimpse her noble spirit, how she placed all of her refined education, her graciousness, at the service of a cause that is so important to-day: our people's true liberation."[4] This woman's courage and compassion for the poor and vulnerable, he exhorted the church, was the clearest illustration of the meaning of liberation, apparent in her life as much as in her words.

I myself was drawn to liberation theology for this single-minded purpose, its siren-like blasts of prophecy, its seething voices speaking on behalf of the desperate, huddled masses of the world. It was this vision that first fired my imagination when I was an undergraduate at the University of Arizona. I had a budding social conscience as a child—regular family trips to some of the makeshift shanties and colonias across the border in Nogales were eye-opening, formative experiences—but the Latin American theologians were the first to put words on paper for me, articulating something that I felt but couldn't quite verbalize. They mapped a world of theology that was unknown to me, and the discovery was akin to a continent seen for the first time, a new world suddenly materializing before my gaze.

Though only a faint outline or silhouette at this point, the ideas of liberation theology really started to take on flesh and blood in my life as refugees from Central America started to reach the US-Mexico border to request asylum, fleeing oppressive governments, funded and backed by the United States that left dead not only Archbishop Romero but thousands of ordinary workers and peasants. Beginning in the early 1980s, the Sanctuary Movement in Tucson, established by Rev. John Fife and Jim Corbett, emerged as a response to these events, providing protection and aid for displaced and desperate lives.[5] Facing some of the same dangers as nineteenth-century abolitionists when helping runaway slaves, churches and synagogues would eventually be criminalized for their humanitarian work, "guilty of the gospel," to recall the words of Sr. Darlene Nicgorski, one of the religious leaders indicted on federal charges—along with Rev. John Fife, Jim Corbett, Fr. Anthony Clark, Fr. Ramon Quiñones, and others. The Sanctuary Movement, in essence, became the new Underground Railroad of the late twentieth century, and I was inspired by it all, wanting to see if I could follow the trail of the new Harriet Tubmans of our day.

By the time I finished college, my fascination with the question of religion intensified, prompting my interest in graduate school. I went to the University of Chicago to satisfy this hunger for ideas and knowledge, and to see if I could learn more about the history of liberation theology. Besides immersing myself in this stream of thought—I would write my dissertation on Gustavo Gutiérrez, one of the founding fathers of the movement—I also discovered other facets of religion that exceeded the boundaries of ethical and social concerns, running over their banks like a swollen river. Much of it had to do with the role of beauty in the study of theology, how the mystics, poets, and artists in the Christian tradition—a Pseudo-Dionysius, Dante, John of the Cross, Teresa of Ávila, Sor Juana Inés de la Cruz, Michelangelo, or T. S. Eliot—seduced their readers with mystical and aesthetical flourishes: the musical rhythms of poetry, the perfumed pulses and repetitions of ritual, the marvels and spectacles of nature, the visual inspirations of art and architecture, the blossoming of the senses in a mystic's shudders and swoons, or the stabs at naming God that inevitably turn to dust and silence when words no longer suffice.

David Tracy's notion of a "public theology" was decisive in these matters, a school of theology that defended liberation theology's "preferential option for the poor" but also drew upon the resources of art, culture, philosophy, and spirituality for naming and thinking about God. Theology was bigger and brighter in this portrait, encompassing mystics and artists as well as prophets, joining them together in a formulation—"mystical-prophetic"—that was faithful to the rich plurality of the Christian tradition. Not unlike the way a deejay would juggle beats and samples together, Tracy, a Catholic theologian, was particularly skilled at interweaving divergent fragments, threading them together into a colorful quilt of ideas. If there was an Achilles' heel in liberation theology, I came to believe, it tended to be its neglect of the meaningful, even liberating, role that the arts, beauty, and popular religion play in the lives of the poor. In liberation theology, ethical and political concerns almost always outpaced aesthetical concerns, like the thunder before the rain, but this perspective can result in a dry and desolate landscape, ethics without beauty. Prophetic voices like Amos are too quick to silence the noise of song or the melody of harps, their dreams of justice too stark. Sometimes, as Jeremiah suggests, we need "skilled women" (poets/singers, they must have been) to "raise for us a dirge/ that our eyes may run with tears/ our pupils flow with water" (Jeremiah 9:17–18). Learning of the potential of the arts for theological inquiry, at any rate, led me down unexpected roads in graduate school. I was swept up by the strong aesthetic currents of the time, wanting to learn more about the sensual and embodied forms of religious thought in poetry, music, painting, mysticism, ritual, and dance. In a seminar with Anne Carr, complementing my reading of David Tracy's theology, I studied Hans Urs von Balthasar for the first time, the theologian who pioneered the modern project of theological aesthetics, and who had a perceptive eye for the stuff of visual beauty, as well as a fine and sensitive ear for music.

While I found the erudition thrilling, Balthasar's cultural and musical tastes were nothing like mine, however. He preferred classical, genteel, and elegant compositions, palaces of sound; I was drawn, instead, to shanties of sound, music that emerged from street corners and spoke to the struggles of the underdogs of the world. Hip-hop was my thing, its spine-tingling beats and absorbing rhymes speaking to me in a language that I understood and relished. With these sounds playing alongside my studies of Black, Public, and Latin American theologies, I would find Balthasar's almost exclusive interest in European arts and cultures to be extremely cloistered, a vision that spoke from privileged and parochial settings, not from the underground. I recall heading to class with Tupac, Public Enemy, Nas, OutKast, and Cypress Hill ringing in my ears and rattling my bones, and part of the lure, I see now, was the way their beats and rhymes not only complemented my interest in Afro-Latin theologies, but acknowledged, and even reveled in, underprivileged backgrounds, lending dignity to places and peoples that had been routinely demeaned in American history. The swagger and sonic booms of hip-hop made this shy Latino kid feel bigger, and for someone who didn't feel like he belonged at this great university, this was important for my success.

As much as I cherished rap music, though, it was a private pleasure at the time; it didn't immediately occur to me that my musical tastes and academic interests might intersect. They harmonized and rhymed with each other in many ways, but hip-hop was generally beneath the radar of the academic vision of the University of Chicago, only a distant rumble that could be heard out of the shaking, thumping car speakers cruising down Fifty-Third Street. It wasn't relevant, a voice seemed to whisper, to the serious philosophizing that took place within the gargoyle-festooned walls of the university. The truth is, even though I fell hard as a child for the beats and rhymes exploding out of boom boxes and rumbling car stereos, and followed my brother around the city when his breaking crew was competing, I underestimated hip-hop's potential. It wasn't until I stumbled into a guest lecture on campus by Michael Eric Dyson, circa 1995 or 1996—on the subject of religion and hip-hop, when he was writing, I believe, *Between God and Gangsta Rap* (Oxford, 1997)—that I began to think differently. I don't recall everything that was said, but I know that it shook my mind, and got me to think more about hip-hop's lyrical and spiritual virtues.

As the years went by and I became a professor in the early 2000s, I created a class on hip-hop and religion at the University of Arizona, "Rap, Culture, and God." In the course of teaching the class, scrutinizing the music with my students for its rich deposits of prophecy, lore, and entertainment, one thing began to stand out clearly above the din of the beats: the frequent appeals, invocations, and even prayers directed to God. Religious motifs constantly surfaced in the genre, even when the music was dripping in secular purposes. I had noticed this before—this is what inspired the class, after all—but it was more pervasive than I had presumed. Religious themes were not confined to any one coast, or any one school, but were omnipresent in hip-hop, a fact that led me to see the genre in theological terms, as a form of "street scriptures" or "street theology."

Street Scriptures

Guided by this premise, I will speak of "street scriptures" and "street theology" in a couple different ways throughout this study: first and foremost, the term "scripture" indicates a body of writings considered sacred and spiritual, and I'm interested in the many moments where such emotions and desires, surprisingly hallowed, surface in the genre of hip-hop, the instances, to invoke Lauryn Hill, "where hip-hop meets scripture."[6] The term "street scriptures" thus implies a messy fusion of the sacred and profane, the inclusion of religious desires and imaginings in rap's street-centric repertoire of boasts, disses, commentary, reportage, journaling, hyperbole, exhortation, self-realization, soul-searching, and so on.

But there is also a less obvious reason for the choice of the terms: hip-hop recovers the oral, rhythmic, and melodic nature of ancient scriptural transmission, bringing back language to its oral and performative roots. It reminds us that most scriptures, before becoming frozen on paper, were originally recited, chanted, rhapsodized, incanted, declaimed, and sung in ways that set them apart from ordinary speech. Rhythmic and melodic recitations of poetry were, in fact, the primary modes of reading in the Jewish and Greco-Roman worlds alike.[7] In the ancient world, poetry was a dance with words, a dance with a certain rhythm, tempo, pace, inflection, timbre, accent, and bodily expression. Epic, lyric, and even tragic poetry followed a particular meter, and responded, like a cobra charmed by a wind instrument, to the sound of music through a lyre or pipe-like *aulos*. Synchronized with music, these ancient poetics were "audio-tactile" in nature, the spoken words drumming in the ears, exciting the skin, firing the emotions, and arousing the human senses. Tellingly, as Anne Carson explains, "Homer's word for 'word' (*epos*) includes the meaning of 'speech,' 'tale,' 'song,' 'line of verse,' or 'epic poetry' as a whole."[8] Word is bond for the Greeks because it joins together poetry, song, and story.[9]

And what Carson says about Homer's *epos* holds true for the Greek term *mousike* as well: unlike contemporary understandings of "music," the Greek word implied poetry set to music, a combustible combination of poetry, song, and dance. To do *mousike*, as Socrates describes it in the *Phaedo*, entailed musical and poetic compositions under the spell of the Muses, verses that fused poetry and music together, part word, part song, part rap. Chronicling the last days of Socrates, the *Phaedo* reports, in fact, a startling decision in the life of the philosopher: Socrates, we are told, elected to devote his remaining time on earth to the practice of *mousike*. Instead of spending his last days working on dialogues or treatises or arguments, as we might expect of a philosopher, Socrates paid homage to the arts of the Muses, using his dwindling time and energy to compose poetic/musical arrangements, letting out a long dying note. He becomes a rhapsodist in this, his final hour.[10]

Family resemblances, on this matter of poetry and music, can also be observed between the ancient Greeks and the major scriptural traditions of Judaism, Christianity, and Islam.[11] Before the early modern period, in fact, most Jews and Christians did not have access to a written Bible; they would not have *read* the Bible so much as *listened* to it in liturgies, ceremonies, rituals, and dramas. By the time of Jesus, and especially after the destruction of the Temple in 70 CE, Judaism had increasingly become a religion of the Book, it's true; and yet, this Book was filled with words that came alive only when they were read, recited, and performed, only when the reader or cantor breathed life into the dry bones of the parchment or papyrus. It was meant to be heard. "Our English word 'scripture' implies a written text," explains Karen Armstrong, "but most scriptures began as texts that were composed and transmitted orally.... Even as a scripture became a written text, people often regarded it as inert until it was ignited by a living voice, just as a musical score comes fully alive only when interpreted by an instrument."[12] Whether it was the voice of the priestly Levites (known as musicians and singers in addition to teachers of Israel), Quranic reciters and muezzins (famous for their ability to melt the hardest heart with the very sound of the Quran) or, among early and medieval Christians in church liturgies, the Divine Office, or Gregorian chant, the scriptures reached the ears of listeners by way of aural means, with the reciters amplifying instruction by the twirling of the tongue, throat play, or with a note that billowed through the air like incense.

In Hebrew, revealingly, the standard term for "poem" is *shir*, or song, suggesting a very thin line between poetry and song.[13] Biblical poetry, as such, aspired to the condition of music, taking great delight in the sounds of language itself, playing with the cadences, rhythms, and rhymes of the poetry, as in the use of alliteration and assonance in Song of Songs 8:6: khakhotam ... kakhotam ... kiazah khamavet ... qashah khisheol qin'ah. (While the Hebrew repeats the "k" sound, the English translation chimes together on the letter "s": "Set me as a seal upon your heart, as a seal upon your arm, for strong as death is love ...")[14] If the Song of Songs, traditionally attributed to King Solomon, betrays the hand, or ear, of a poet-singer, the book of Psalms, attributed to the musically gifted David, is a kindred composition, orchestrated like a musical score. From the Greek *psalmos*, a song sung to a plucked instrument, many of the psalms, suggests Robert Alter, were liturgical songs intended to be intoned to the accompaniment of the lyre, drum, harp, flute, cymbals, and other instruments (see Psalm 150, for example).[15] It is likely, then, that musical instruments accompanied biblical recitations, even though instruments were eventually excluded from liturgies (banished in mourning, some say, for the fall of the Temple in 70 CE).[16] With or without instruments, in any case, by the Middle Ages, diacritic marks and accents in the Masoretic Bible provided readers/cantors with direction in the pronunciation and cantillation of the text, telling them how to recite or sing a particular letter, syllable, or vowel.[17] (Cantillation, the art of chanting the Bible, derives from the Latin *cantare*, "to sing.") In the process, the spoken word was imbued with rhythm, prosody, and melody, helping the listener fully feel and absorb the meaning of a text. More than just decorative curlicues, irrelevant to the meaning of the text, the cantillation marks (*ta'am* in Hebrew, meaning "taste" or "sense") were commentaries on the text itself, interpreting the meaning of the text musically, bringing out the "sense" of the passage and giving the listener a "taste" of its meaning, evoking, in short, the "sense and taste of the Infinite" that Schleiermacher famously defined as the essence of religion.[18]

Bearing the musical qualities of the Torah in mind, for example, the Egyptian Jew Artapanus (third to second century BCE) claimed that Moses, author of the Torah in his view, was not only a lawgiver but an inspired musician to boot, his musical skills so prodigious that the Greek Orpheus, famous for his own musical prowess, cut his teeth at the feet of Moses. Whatever is meant by the colorful contention, it is, at minimum, intriguing for painting the tongue-tied Moses as a singer of sorts, his great opus fashioned with rhythmic, lyrical, and sonorous qualities.[19] And Rabbi Yehudah He-Hasid, now in the twelfth century CE, shared a similar opinion, claiming not only that Moses himself chanted and sang the Torah, but, more provocatively, that the original Sinai revelation was itself sung by God, in a melody commensurate with the sublime and awesome nature of the event: "With the melody that Moses heard from God, in that same melody he spoke to the Israelites."[20] No wonder that Rabbi Johanan, in the Talmud, criticized anyone who "reads the scriptures without tunefulness": such a person would sap the Torah of its original lyrical, melodic, and mystical power.[21] They would mute the message and dull the delivery, giving the audience a story without emotion, words without rhythm, logos without pathos. Thus, a first-century Jew like Jesus of Nazareth, when summoned to read from the book of Isaiah, in an episode recounted in Luke's gospel, would not have "read" it in a prosaic dialect (Luke 4:18). Instead, he "would have chanted the passage in an elevated, melodic style," says the biblical scholar Timothy Beal, "he would have sung it into speech."[22] Jesus would have rapped the Bible.

If we jump to the modern period, however, words and readers have become increasingly "desensorialized"—oral cultures have given way to written cultures.[23] Now divorced from the body and music, with the visual imagination overtaking the audio-tactile imagination, modern poetry, and even many religious texts, have become more and more disembodied. "Gone is drum, lyre, or other musical accompaniment," writes Michael Schmidt, "along with the voice or voices of recitation and performance, inflections denoting pace and response. . . . If we were dancing with a human form before, with voice and body and expression, we find ourselves now embracing an absence, less than a skeleton, and having ourselves to provide the warmth and motion, even the flesh."[24]

Hip-hop, needless to say, is a reclamation of the ancient tradition of poetics, a return to the time when the spoken word was the vital breath and soul of a culture, its power mysterious and magical. It resurrects the musicality that once swaddled the Word in Jewish, Christian, and Greco-Roman poetics, an eloquence that aimed for the heart as much as the mind.

The plural form of "scriptures" is important for this study as well: the Greek *ta biblia*, after all, is plural and thus should be translated as "little books" or "little scrolls," a library more than a single book. The emphasis on the diversity of scriptures will be important when contemplating hip-hop. It, too, is a library more than a single book, and presents the listener and critic with a wild diversity of approaches and interpretations. I'm reminded of the word *manifestación* in Spanish: the word is rich in meaning, usually leaning in two major directions. First, *manifestación* can mean the act of protest or "taking to the streets," as in a march, rally, riot, or demonstration. It brims with a sense of agitation and rebellion. It can also mean, however, a showing, revelation, or exhibition, bringing something hidden into the light, making something unknown manifest. In this case, *manifestación* is closer to the experience of beauty, whereby something spiritual and spectral suddenly appears in visible or audible form, entrancing as it is unveiled, exhibited, and displayed.

Hip-hop, my point is, epitomizes both senses of *manifestación*, combining acts of protest with impassioned exhibitions of style, color, and festivity. Some artists may privilege the confrontational and political, some the celebratory alone, but in many cases the music and culture include traces of both, the two connotations bleeding into one beautiful and blurred palette.

Hip-Hop Studies

In my first years teaching hip-hop, I may have favored the dissenting political connotation of *manifestación*, but I always valued the playful purposes, too, where the sheer joy of self-expression in dance, music, and art represented, nonverbally, some of the same yearnings for freedom and justice as the conscious rappers. In these cases, hip-hop's rage for order and beauty—its wild arrangements—may be less political than playful, but this can be liberating as well, if only for allowing its devotees to "sweat out all the problems and troubles of the day," as André 3000 once put it.[25] Regardless of the different ways they articulated their joys and sorrows, in other words, the culture of hip-hop thrust lives shrouded by poverty and marginality into the limelight. It was an improbable achievement, especially given hip-hop's emergence out of a landscape that was tantamount to, in the words of a writer for the *New York Times*, a "necropolis—a city of death."[26] With life expectancy lower than in Panama, and infant mortality twice the rate of the rest of the country, it's a wonder that the founders of hip-hop in the South Bronx were able to put so much flesh and life—so much beauty—on the bare skeleton of their neighborhoods. It merits the kind of amazed response put in the mouth of Nathaniel as he tries to square Jesus's origins, raised in a disreputable and impoverished shantytown, with his exalted status. "Can anything good come out of Nazareth?" (John 1:46).

After considering the four elements of hip-hop (deejaying, emceeing, breaking, and graffiti), and after situating hip-hop in the longer arc of black music in the Americas, we turn to the question of exegesis in my class on religion and hip-hop, now trying to make sense of the spirituality of rap music, trying to wring meaning out of what is said. At this point, Afrika Bambaataa's fifth element of hip-hop, "knowledge," commands our attention, the concept just begging for a more critical, spiritual, even theological approach to hip-hop. Less cerebral than existential, less about dry information or rote learning than experiential wisdom, his understanding of "knowledge" is rich and multidimensional, involving traces of self-awareness, social consciousness, and spiritual wakefulness, not to mention an understanding of the history, values, and artistry of hip-hop. A kind of holy grail of hip-hop, Afrika Bambaataa's fifth dimension is, in my view, about the potential of hip-hop for sculpting the human soul, chipping away at its defects while bringing out its underlying beauty; it's about the quest for a more perfect beat, a more perfect union, a more perfect and just world.

In my reading, many early critics, especially in the academy, saw hip-hop as something promising along these lines, playing the "kind of socially reflective and politically prophetic role that largely defined its emergence," as Tricia Rose has written.[27] They greeted it as the latest black musical genre to provide a map of freedom, a map that plotted contemporary urban life the way the spirituals and gospel once plotted the route to the promised land, the way the blues and R&B plotted the route to freer emotions and freer opportunities. Cast as both seer and player, truth-teller and trickster, prophet and entertainer, the emcee gave voice, in their telling, to people in the struggle, people trapped in the underworlds of American life. The public emergence of the rapper represented the sudden eruption of black and brown voices onto the stage of American life. Once invisible, and confined to the corners of the world, ghetto youth suddenly had hip-hop to tell their stories, voice their complaints, verbalize their frustrations, shout their joys, let loose their dreams. Like surfers carving their name on a wave, or graffiti writers tagging and bombing a wall, emcees used their tongues to notch their names on public spaces, claiming territory from which they were commonly excluded, popping off like a firecracker in a stuffy and silent room. Employing linguistic wizardry and musical inventiveness, these youth offered alternative visions of American life, seen from the perspective of the urban poor. They dedicated themselves to art forms that were loud, brash, and impossible to ignore, art forms that made them feel truly alive.

In each instance, hip-hop delivered a message that was, in its purest essence, "defiance through celebration."[28] It was a message that was inventive, boisterous, and revolutionary. Even apart from any scolding on social issues, the big beats and rhetorical extravagance of the rappers' verses were countercultural in themselves, exhibiting the kind of artistic license that allowed urban youth to speak their minds. If nothing else, hip-hop introduced mainstream America to parts of the United States that had suffered from years of government misrule, negligence, and plain old racism.

Though the hip-hop generation, in this portrait, was exploring new treasures of sound, dance, and self-expression, it remained joined at the hip to the civil rights era. Hip-hop, no doubt, defied, interrupted, and modified it—literally cutting, chopping, fragmenting, and scratching the catalogs of soul, funk, and jazz—but it continued to march in step with the hopes of civil rights and black power. And recall that this was an age positively engrossed by dreams of liberation. Nationally and globally, oppressed groups took to the streets under the banner of liberation, fighting and marching on behalf of freedom, justice, and equality. Street-corner orators, shouting preachers, and folk and soul musicians all joined the fight under the banner of liberation: James Brown invoked the notion in "The Whole World Needs Liberation" and "Say It Loud"; the Isley Brothers rallied on behalf of freedom and justice in "Fight the Power"; Jimmy Castor envisioned a world of peace and unity in his widely sampled "It's Just Begun," a song that employs a banging percussion section of Afro-Latin timbales and congos; War addressed global injustices on "The World Is a Ghetto"; Sly and the Family Stone prophesied with fire and brimstone on "There's a Riot Goin' On"; Sam Cooke gave the civil rights movement a masterpiece of an anthem with "A Change Is Gonna Come," adding lush orchestral accompaniment, horns, and kettledrums in order to give the song gravity and majesty; and, of course, Marvin Gaye made the earth tremble with his prophetic tenor voice on numerous joints, most famously with "What's Going On," "Inner City Blues," and "Mercy Mercy Me."

Equally important for hip-hop, the street bards of the age, from the Last Poets and Gil Scott-Heron to Sonia Sanchez and Nina Simone, used street idioms to register the tremors and shocks of the age. When Nina Simone put her hands on the piano, the keys simmered and smoked at her touch, and fire came out of her mouth. As if she was the oracle at Delphi, her words sounded holy and visionary, sonorous and prophetic. Some called for her "to wash and clean my ears/ and talk real fine just like a lady," as she puts it on "Mississippi Goddam," but the times, violent and abusive, called for a more rough, rude, and earthy tongue, a dialect of outrage. "Nina Simone," writes Hanif Abdurraqib, "opens her mouth and an entire history is built before us, where there is nowhere for anyone to hide from the truth as she has lived it."[29] The music, poetry, spirituality, dance, art, and theater of the day, in sum, all joined forces together for social and spiritual revolution; the truths of art were enlisted in the battle for emancipation. Rickey Vincent sizes up the age this way: "Despite the glitzy camouflage of the so-called seventies revival in dress and songs, what was truly visionary of the period was the revolutionary conviction of these particular artists. They dared to imagine complete and total liberation for their people, a theme that fueled the musical exploits of the many great soul groups and funk bands of the mid-1970s."[30]

While these aspirations started to weaken and waver in later years, with the drive for self-advancement gaining the upper hand over concerns for social advancement, hip-hop produced numerous artists who remained anchored in this older vision, who kept on keeping on. Sometimes furious and ominous, sometimes consoling and hopeful, artists in this vein—say Public Enemy or KRS-One or DMX or Ice Cube or Black Star or Rage Against the Machine or Immortal Technique, et al.—continued to play the role of the prophet, even as the crack epidemic, like the horsemen of the apocalypse, ran roughshod over many urban communities. For speaking in frequencies and notes "one octave too high for our ears," as Abraham Joshua Heschel observed about the Hebrew prophets, their proclamations and judgments vexed the conscience, assaulted the mind, and menaced middle-class America.[31] Their words were hot and scalding, churning and burning within their souls until they burst forth in rapped verse.

This is only part of the picture, though: as the late 1990s and early aughts set in, the "shiny suit era" of hip-hop came to power, an era of bling and materialism, merrymaking and unchecked capitalism. More like the dancing and partying Israelites around the golden calf than the thundering voice of Moses, hip-hop started to adorn itself in flashy and grandiose styles, wrapped in glittery and ostentatious fashions. Big pimpin' was in vogue, gangster chic was cool, mammon the god. In the prophetic camp of hip-hop studies, as you can probably guess, this latest fashion represented a betrayal of "real" hip-hop, a salivating for money and power as opposed to spitting the truth. What was once unconventional and subversive had become conventional and conformist, what was countercultural had become commodified. While the OGs of hip-hop had once exposed the collateral damage that inequality, greed, and racism wreaked on communities of color, this generation was "drowning the most heavenly ecstasies of religious fervor in the icy water of egotistical calculation," to quote Marx.[32] It was all about the "benjamins" for Bad Boy Records, "bling, bling" for Cash Money Records, and "Getting Rich or Die Tryin'" for Shady Aftermath and Interscope.

Though it's a valid criticism, this perspective is too cynical, retorted the aesthetic apologists for hip-hop; it misses many of the artistic nuances of the genre. Emerging in the wake of the violent bloodletting of hip-hop's coastal wars, with the death of Tupac and Biggie in 1997, the shiny suit era—or even G-funk in the early 1990s—was a splash of levity in an age heavy on crisis and catastrophe. Instead of wallowing in grief, holding darkness and tragedy close to one's chest, it released grief into the air through loud and showy displays of music and dance, like a New Orleans jazz funeral or Carnival in Brazil. With the bitter taste of death in the mouth of so many, this sweet-tasting and escapist music was a badly needed comfort, the taste of manna for parched throats. Maybe it was pure diversion and escape, but can't joy and celebration—besides the way of the cross—be redemptive too? "This,

too, is a response to grief," writes Hanif Abdurraqib. "Covering yourself in
the spoils of your survival and making music that sent people dancing in the
streets again."[33]

Hip-hop critics at the time, echoing this carnivalesque sentiment, changed
their tune. There was an upsurge in aesthetic-driven approaches, with many
insisting that the artistic virtuosities of hip-hop had been neglected by early
critics.[34] Paralleling the rising tides of aesthetics in religious studies, these
voices took issue with many prophetic accounts of the music and culture, arguing that hip-hop is flattened out and eviscerated when reduced to a matter
of sociology, politics, social justice, or lyrical analysis alone. The prophetic
account of hip-hop, they insisted, leaves out some of the most flamboyant and
exhilarating features of hip-hop, like the language of the body in breaking,
the creative cutting of the deejay, the rhetorical gifts of the emcee, the bold
pieces and throw-ups of graffiti writers, and so on. The search for meaningful
lyrics and political substance—especially by academic critics interested in
deconstruction, post-colonialism, or whatever smacked of "resistance"—led
many scholars to neglect the artistic choices and playful spirit of this youth
culture, to neglect everything that, in their mind, lacked social value. They
reduced hip-hop to a form of literary realism or reportage, ignoring the wild
fantasies in rap, the hypnotic rhymes, the dramatic exuberance and, of course,
the dope, nasty beats that are essential to its magnetism.

Critics began to flip the script. No longer about social change, street knowledge, or spiritual consciousness, hip-hop was now described in simpler terms,
more concerned with style than message, more with entertainment and plain
fun than anything more profound. They reminded readers that hip-hop came
of age during the disco era, after all, an era notorious for escapist and self-
indulgent proclivities. Under this influence, hip-hop would initially shy away
from the social and political activism of the 1960s and 1970s and concentrate
most of its energies on rocking the crowd, exciting the body, burning down
the house. It was dance-centric music concerned with pleasure, diversion,
and amusement. Instead of political renegades, armed with civil rights slogans and chants, citizens of the hip-hop nation described themselves as renegades of music, dance, and art, "renegades of funk," in George Clinton's
famous phrase. Instead of tearing down the building in protest, as in Blind
Willie Johnson's prophetic account of the Samson story (for which he was
arrested by New Orleans police), it was more about tearing the roof off this
sucker, à la Parliament.[35]

The hip-hop revolution, in short, was an aesthetical and cultural achievement more than a political feat, a fact that would be exploited to its fullest by
Southern rap. In fact, some of the richest and creamiest versions of hip-hop,

positively saturated with fat and buttery beats, came out of the "Dirty South" in the late 1990s and early aughts. As if they were intentionally throwing shade at conscious-minded critics and academic nerds, many of the rappers and enthusiasts of this tradition seemed to take particular delight in sounds and styles that were apolitical, epicurean, thrilling, and dirtier than a blues breakdown. Never mind the traumas and tribulations of ghetto life, they concentrated all their energies on making music that was exhilarating and delicious in sound, capable of moving your booty and sending chills up your spine. The joy of the body was treated as a salve for the anxiety of the mind, the ritual of dance as a mode of healing. With raucous percussion, bottom-heavy beats, live instruments, and a lyricism on the border of rap and song, they delivered irresistible, pounding waves of sound, and they stole moments of freedom from a world that was often intent on stifling such things. Up against the imprisoning walls of the ghetto, Southern rap carved out gaps, holes, and small openings to give free rein to its wit, mischief, and musical artistry. Simple, uninhibited, and playful joys were substituted for the serious business of social and political action. James Baldwin could have been speaking of Southern rap when he penned these lines: "Perhaps we were, all of us—pimps, whores, racketeers, church members and children—bound together by the nature of our oppression, the specific and peculiar complex of risks we had to run; if so, within these limits we sometimes achieved with each other a freedom that was close to love. . . . We ate and drank and talked and laughed and danced and forgot all about 'the man.' We had the liquor, the chicken, the music, and each other, and had no need to pretend to be what we were not."[36] If we can speak of "liberation" in the Southern camp of hip-hop, then, it was synonymous with these kinds of sensual and soulful pleasures, manifestations of psychic liberation more than political liberation.

That's not to say that Baldwin saw art in aesthetic and stylistic terms alone, divorced from ethical and prophetic qualities, divorced from substance. Style and substance were both crucial ingredients in art for him, the two qualities providing not only the icing on the cake, but the eggs that give it texture, color, and shape.[37] When missing in binding and leavening ingredients, art will quickly lose its shape, crumbling into a thousand pieces. Beneath the colorful veneer, it can be hollow and empty on the inside, a body without a soul, its senses so lost in pleasure, like the Lotus-Eaters of classic myth, that it becomes oblivious to the outside world, which is the point that many rappers would harp on around 2010 or so. Just as the aesthetic camp seemed triumphant and undeniable, in fact, the winds of change in hip-hop started to change directions once again, breaking the spell of the Lotus-Eaters, interrupting their bliss. Buoyed by Black Lives Matter, #MeToo, March for

Our Lives, and, in general, the resurgence of civil rights activism, hip-hop recovered its prophetic voice around this time, howling and shrieking against the forces of social inequality, sexism, racism, consumerism, and indifference to the poor and vulnerable. The ethical imperative of the day called for everyone to "get woke," a sentiment echoed by countless songs and artists: Erykah Badu's "Master Teacher" (2008); Kendrick Lamar's *Overly Dedicated* (2010); Joey Bada$$'s *1999* (2012); D'Angelo's *Black Messiah* (2014); Rapsody's *Beauty and the Beast* (2014); Janelle Monae's "Hell You Talmbout" (2015); A Tribe Called Quest's "We the People" (2016); Beyoncé's *Lemonade* (2016; including her gripping homage to the Black Panthers during the 2016 Super Bowl halftime show); YG's "FDT" (2016); Chance the Rapper's "First World Problems" (2017); Common's *August Greene* (2018); Noname's "Song 33" (2020); Anderson .Paak's "Lockdown" (2020); Lil Baby's *My Turn* (2020); H.E.R.'s "I Can't Breathe" (2020); Meek Mill's "Otherside of America" (2020); Terrace Martin's "Pig Feet" (2020), and many others.

When A Tribe Called Quest took the stage at the 2017 Grammys, for instance, the hook of "We the People" took aim at all of the strife and problems of our day, mocking in particular the reenergized bigotry: "All you Black folks, you must go/ All you Mexicans, you must go/ And all you poor folks, you must go/ Muslims and gays/ Boy, we hate your ways." It was the perfect performance for the times, building on Kendrick Lamar's performance of "Alright" at the Grammys in 2016. If the pendulum in hip-hop once swung in the late 1990s and early aughts in favor of aesthetics, it's now swinging back toward the urgent proclamations and parables of the prophets. They have become the soundtracks of our times. At the end of A Tribe's performance—without the recently deceased Phife Dawg—Q-Tip, Busta Rhymes, Consequence, and Anderson .Paak stood on stage with their fists raised in the air. And Q-Tip, dressed in black, a shade of the downtrodden, chanted over and over, "Resist, Resist, Resist."

If you cast a wider glance at the global hip-hop scene, as well, similar calls were heard: starting in 2010, hip-hop played a small part in the uprisings known as the Arab Spring, successfully stirring and spreading discontent throughout the Middle East and North Africa.[38] In Russia, opposition voices have embraced hip-hop as an ideal medium for political activism, prompting Putin's repression of the music and lyrics ("Russia's Youth Found Rap. The Kremlin Is Worried," reads a *New York Times* article from 2019).[39] In Cuba, the rap "Patria y Vida" ("Homeland and Life") (2021) appeared on the island like a storm, and soon came to define the unrest and rebellion occurring on the island. A cry for life and liberty, the rap reclaims the slogan from the Cuban revolution, "*Patria o Muerte*" ("Homeland or Death"), and turns it into a cry for change: "*Ya no gritemos patria o muerte sino patria y vida.*" ("We no longer shout homeland or death, but homeland and life instead.") Like something out of Greek myth, the song calls for an uprising that would unseat the generations of old, bringing a fresh breeze, gusting into a tornado, to a government that reeks of stale and stagnant air. (For challenging the regime in this way, the artists involved in the making of the song have been accused of crimes of "resistance" and "contempt," and Maykel Osorbo, one of the song's architects still living in Cuba, was arrested and imprisoned at the Pinar del Río prison in Havana.) Throughout the Caribbean and Latin America, various Indigenous, Afro-Latin@, and mestizo rappers, including reggaeton figures known for carefree and escapist pleasures, are wielding the mic like an arrow or sword, their words increasingly dangerous and prophetic. And this continues in 2020 with the tempest that was unleashed by the death of George Floyd in the United States, the protests thrusting hip-hop artists into the eye of the storm.

As for myself, I'm back in Tucson where I was born and went to college and the Sanctuary Movement of the 1980s, once seemingly dead, has been reborn. Resist, resist, resist is the mantra again. It was the Sanctuary Movement and liberation theology, as I mentioned, that roused me from my dogmatic slumber, their voices like shrill trumpets awakening my conscience, schooling my intelligence. Inspired by this legacy, I volunteer with various human rights and border organizations, from the Somali Bantu Association to Casa Alitas, a shelter in Tucson that supports Latin American and Caribbean immigrants seeking asylum. I am involved with the transportation of refugees, picking up asylum seekers at Casa Alitas and taking them to the bus station or airport, where they travel to stay with their sponsors. For the duration of the time, I listen to their stories and always marvel at the calm and cool that they exhibit in the face of their sojourn, a difficult trek across burning deserts, raging rivers, and ICE detention facilities ("Ice," ironically, is an apt description for the frigid rooms in which immigrants are caged). The majority of them are Indigenous and mestizo women, children, and young men, fleeing barrios and slums that are plagued by circumstances familiar to the narratives of hip-hop: desperate poverty, gang and cartel violence, failed governments, blighted and deindustrialized cityscapes, exploitive factories and farms, unjust authorities, broken infrastructures, and so on. Driven by pressures beyond their control, and inclined to risk it all, the flight of migrants and refugees is almost always undertaken under various forms of duress, a coercion that once compelled Abraham, Isaac, Jacob, and Jesus to migrate to Egypt and other lands.

I realize I'm digressing here, and violating the unspoken rules of academia, but I want to make the simple point that the stuff of scholarship is always mixed up with one's values, beliefs, and politics, and that our personal experiences and sympathies impinge on our fields of study. I can't speak for others, but books, music, and religion have always been matters of the soul as much as the intellect to me, personal and existential matters as much as academic ones. These things have carved and shaped my being, giving a meaningful contour and direction to my life. Sometimes still voices and sometimes whirlwinds, they have inspired and lifted me, becoming a part of me. I study and teach and write and volunteer, consequently, not only as a way of interpreting the world but in the small hope, however quixotic, of changing it—and, if nothing else, of changing myself. W. E. B. Du Bois's conclusion is close to my own feelings: "I faced the great decision. What with all my dreaming, studying, and teaching was I going to do in this fierce fight . . . One could not be a calm, cool, and detached scientist while Negroes were lynched, murdered, and starved."[40]

We all face a similar decision, as momentous and unavoidable as the one that Du Bois posed to himself and others. If there is any value to the notion of street theology, therefore, it includes, besides the focus on popular culture, the disruption of academic norms that presume impartiality, objectivity, and dispassionate analysis. Whether channeling the fundamentals of liberation theology, which was always quick to spot the biases of power, class, and race lurking in such claims, or drawing from contemporary approaches to popular religion, which according to Tomoko Masuzawa not only fills the gap left by traditional scholarship fixated on high culture but also contests and exposes the "unavowed interests inherent in the established organization of knowledge," a street theology aims for an engaged knowledge, somewhere on the border of theory and practice.[41]

But now that I have made my sympathy for a prophetic orientation obvious, it should also be known that the arc of a street theology, as I see it, bends not only toward justice, but toward art, music, and spirituality as well. There are times, in fact, when music, literature, dance, theater, or painting lack a fundamental purpose altogether, when they are ends in themselves, when they bestow their rewards immediately and directly. (Kant described beauty, for this reason, as a "finality which involves no objective.")[42] I'm interested in these moments, too, the small and fleeting experiences of liberation in addition to the big and grand, the ordinary in addition to the revolutionary. If I appeal to the concept of "resistance" in this study, therefore, I will insist on this more inclusive meaning, aesthetical and ethical, spiritual and sociopolitical, personal and communal.

I admit that it can be tricky to do justice to both dimensions of art and religion. Since the prophets are not known for compromise and the aesthetes are frequently satisfied with "art for its own sake," there are many occasions when insurmountable walls are built between the two. Is it possible, absent a unifying Pentecostal wind, to bring them together in one room? In some cases, the disagreements seem irreconcilable: Should art seek to change the world, or just echo it? Is art a matter of beauty and pleasure alone, or should these purposes be tied to what is good and just? With hip-hop, specifically, must it always sound like a fist in the air, as Jon Pareles once described Public Enemy's music, or is it enough for it to deliver a dance-driven stomp, a smooth groove, exhilarating shout, festive holler, or perfectly calibrated bar of rhymes?[43] What should we privilege in our appraisal of the music: sonic qualities or social insight, style or substance, form or content, dance rhythms or pensive rhythms, the meaning of the lyrics or their manner of delivery? Is hip-hop food for the mind and spirit, as so-called conscious rap might have it, or music for the body, as Southern rap, reggaeton/crunkiao/Latin trap might argue? Similar questions haunt religious studies: Should we give more weight to beauty or justice; Hans Urs von Balthasar's theological aesthetics, or Gustavo Gutiérrez's theology of liberation; Sor Juana's Baroque poetry, drama, and mysticism, or Las Casas's furious prophecy on behalf of battered and colonized communities; Nietzsche's conviction that life is justified by beauty, or Marx's imperative to change the world?[44]

Needless to say, both worldviews have their merits. In the Christian tradition, as a matter of fact, these outlooks are rarely so neatly and starkly delineated. Ever since Christianity began baptizing pagan forms of beauty ("despoiling the Egyptians," in Augustine's phrase), theology developed an affection, even reverence, for visible and aural manifestations of beauty. Whether in visual forms—icons, statues, churches, rituals, relics, paintings, nature itself—or in aural forms—music, preaching, grammar, rhetoric, the Word of Scripture—beauty was increasingly seen by the early church fathers as a medium of God's incarnate presence in the stuff of creation, as a form of revelation. In the post-Constantine church, a rapprochement was established between Athens and Jerusalem, between the rich aesthetics of Late Antiquity and the messianic ethics of the Bible.[45] Even in these cases, however, the prophetic Word always served as an interruptive and unsettling force. When the glistening and gaudy forms of beauty, like some bejeweled golden calf, distracted the church from its responsibilities to the poor and needy, or when the temptations of worldly pleasures and indulgences became too great and the church was prone to sellout, prophetic voices would arise—a St. Anthony of Egypt, St. Francis, Savonarola, or St. Óscar Romero, say—to defend the things of the soul against all manner of idolatry.[46]

We can learn something from each perspective, in any event: the aesthetic orientation in hip-hop studies has the advantage when it comes to exploring the deejay's collages of sound, the emcee's flows and rhymes, the vocal textures and tones, the dance and clothing fashions, and all the vibes and beats that can exhilarate the body and soul. Because aesthetics on its own can be used to lie, flatter, deceive, and degrade, however—the Nazi Party's use of art and music is a glaring example—the prophetic orientation might serve as a criterion and test of hip-hop's authenticity, a reality check. Instead of sonic norms alone, this school of criticism is driven by deeper questions of meaning and purpose. To only focus on the surface aesthetics and form of the music, at the expense of meaning, can be an evasion of the urgent questions of truth and justice that are relevant for any study of art. Tom Piazza says it well: "An admiration for the technique itself can override or anesthetize an ability to evaluate or even to see the human dimension of what the artist is saying."[47] Once anesthetized in this way, the mind and conscience can become so thoroughly distracted, even numb, that it misses the human dimensions of music, how it might uplift or degrade, enrich or harm a group of people. Thus, the prophetic orientation—more biblical than Dionysian—is not satisfied with pleasure principles alone. It asks more of art, and considers the question of justice and human rights as important norms for the scrutiny of any work.

We will examine many examples of these two types, but I lean in this study on artists and critics who teeter on the edges of aesthetics and ethics, festivity and prophecy. There will be times when I defend some of the most exuberant and lavish schools of hip-hop—US Southern rap and reggaeton/Latin trap, for instance—but without sheltering them from prophetic criticism, without fully absolving them of bad taste or poor morals. Even when delighting in the joyful, carnal, boisterous schools of hip-hop, where the party is king, we should allow the prophetic voices, like a shrill and unnerving scream, to threaten our pleasures and remind us of the struggles and dreams of others beyond the circumscribed borders of our lives.

Plan of the Book

Now that I've said a little about the personal route and journey that brought me to this study, allow me a few words about the direction of the book. In a way, this book picks up a thread that I felt in my graduate school years but which slipped through my fingers: the corresponding patterns and kinships— sometimes congruent, sometimes dissonant—between hip-hop and theology. Like its ancestors in the blues, gospel, jazz, R&B, and funk, the sacred and profane are less opposites than knotted threads in hip-hop, less parallel streets than crossroads. Religious themes are omnipresent in the genre, surfacing in the oratory and rhetoric, the beats and lyrics, the longings for freedom and justice, the explosive and frenzied joy. It's not hard to detect, in fact, traces of the rich bloodline of the black churches in hip-hop. If Henry Louis Gates is right, we need to "give the church its due as a source of our ancestors' unfathomable resiliency and perhaps the first formalized site for the collective fashioning and development of so many African American aesthetic forms."[48]

The black church, in his reading, has been the bright, crackling fire around which generations have warmed themselves, sought enlightenment and salvation, and dared to envision, like Moses at the burning bush, the path to freedom and equality in the Americas. It has been this nation's moral conscience, vexing and troubling it when it has forsaken its most noble principles, exhorting and guiding it when it blazes a path of justice. It has created liminal spaces, he remarks, "brimming with subversive features," and making possible spiritual expressions that have been remarkably inventive, experimental, and artistic.[49] None of the great musical and artistic creations in African American life, his point is, have been outside the influence of the church, and this continues to hold true, it seems to me, with the culture of hip-hop. Prophetic judgments; chanted and singsong preaching; signifying practices; theatrical displays; mystical fits of emotion; expressions of pathos and sorrow; bodily convulsions and tremors; stomping, shouting, shrieking; call-and-response patterns; rhythmic breaths, grunts, and whoops; low murmurs and half-whispered moans, all of these things were passed on to hip-hop by the mighty Mississippi that has been the black church.

Seen in the broader context of global trends, too, there is a certain logic to the persistence of religion in hip-hop. Just as religious affiliation in the Global North is declining, religion in the Global South (sub-Saharan Africa, Latin America, China) is flourishing. The great majority of Christians now live in the Southern Hemisphere, or else in the fringes of the Northern Hemisphere. In a 2009 Pew Foundation study, for instance, nine out of ten African Americans said they believe in God, 87 percent claimed religious affiliation, and 79 percent reported that religion is very important in their lives. "African Americans," the study concluded, "stand out as the most religiously committed racial or ethnic group in the nation."[50] And the statistics for Latin@s are not far behind: 92 percent say they believe in God, 83 percent claim some religious affiliation, and 68 percent say that religion is very important in their lives, with another 20 percent reporting that religion is somewhat important.[51]

Generally speaking, hip-hop artists share this spiritual background. While secularism erodes the religious foundations of the Global North, the Global South seems to be shoring up these same foundations. However one explains these religious divergences, God is still something real and meaningful to millions of people of color around the globe. God is not dead, as Robert Orsi has noted: "Practices of presence became—and to a great extent they remain—

the province of people of color, women, the poor and marginalized, children and childish or childlike adults, the eccentric, the romantic, the insane, and those unhinged by life experiences that overwhelm their reason."[52]

It's true, of course, that hip-hop is "not a church girl, she's secular," in the famous words of Common, but this study offers evidence for the surprising persistence of religion in hip-hop. Hip-hop may not be a "humble offering to God," as John Coltrane described *A Love Supreme*, it may not be as ecstatic as gospel music, it may not be as consistently ethereal and emancipatory as the spirituals, but it remains, in countless cases, haunted by God.[53] Chapter 1 clarifies the meaning of a "street theology," arguing for the value of hip-hop in contemporary theology, and, vice versa, the value of theology for hip-hop studies. Chapter 2, "A Brief Sonic History of Hip-Hop," sketches the sonic and aesthetic signatures of some of the major schools and subgenres of hip-hop, showing how the music interweaves mystical-aesthetic and prophetic-ethical moments of creativity. Chapter 3, "Prophets and Emcees: Righteous Rappers," looks at four major figures of hip-hop—one on each coast of North America—whom the culture has crowned as examples of a more awakened or conscious form of hip-hop, their music and lyricism explicitly tussling with the question of God. Chapter 4, "The Return of God in Hip-Hop: Kendrick Lamar's Street Theology," focuses on the trend-setting influence of Kendrick Lamar, one of the most brilliant and theologically significant rappers of the third millennium. Chapters 5 and 6 each consider hip-hop in the Global South, with a focus, in chapter 5, on reggaeton and urbano and, in chapter 6, on Mexican and Chican@ rappers on the West Coast.

My aim in the study, as these wide-ranging chapters suggest, is to sketch a broad arc across the landscape of hip-hop, showing how religious themes are apparent in the various eras and geographies of hip-hop, existent in almost every nook and cranny of the culture. Less a passing storm than a consistent weather pattern, religious sensibilities, myths, ideas, and narratives saturate the genre, soaking deep into the various substrata of the music.

This, at least, is the overall aim of the work, the view of the forest from above the trees. As we move to the ground level, though, exploring each distinct seed and sapling, my conviction is that the culture of hip-hop contains a kind of "street theology," and that it forms the deep root system that joins various hip-hop artists together. From this perspective, just below the surface, in the underground of American life, hip-hop artists wrestle with issues that are near and dear to us all: justice and beauty, hope and despair, spirituality and God. Rappers like to style themselves, in fact, as street professors, ghetto scholars, or hood prophets, and this frequently means that their skills and scholarship (independent of respectable institutions like the academy, church, and state) not only have as much value as scholastic and social scientific knowledge, but that they carry more experiential weight than knowledge that is confined to the ivory towers of the world. Drawing their wisdom from very real, tangible, and concrete experiences of poverty, deprivation, and unfairness, they can be, at times, lucid and revelatory witnesses to the successes and failures of justice in the American experiment. Should we want to understand such things, we might open our ears to their shouts and hollers, paying heed, as James Baldwin once advised in his *No Name in the Street* (1972), to the voice of the streets: "Ask any Mexican, any Puerto Rican, any black man, any poor person—ask the wretched how they fare in the halls of justice, and then you will know, not whether or not the country is just, but whether or not it has any love for justice, or any concept of it."[54] Baldwin's counsel here, a favoring of the judgments and feelings of the disempowered, not only converges with the spirit of hip-hop in my view, but it also echoes a key biblical mandate: to hearken to the potential wisdom rising up from the dungeons and alleyways of the world, the voices crying out, as in Proverbs, on behalf of justice: "Wisdom cries out in the streets/ in the open squares she raises her voice" (Proverbs 1:20).

As I see it, then, the trope of the "streets" can be a helpful adjective in theology, indicating an interest in the musical, cultural, and artistic achievements of groups often confined to the bottom of history and society, a theology for the hip-hop generation. When DMX boasted of speaking for the streets, as in the epigraph above, it was synonymous with solidarity, an identification with those to whom DMX referred as his "dogs," folks treated like animals, lepers, or castaways. An ethical and artistic credo more than a gangster trope, attending to the streets meant hearkening to the marginalized peoples of the world, hearing their struggles, gripes, and cries for recognition and equality. When this note carries through the genre, as it does in countless cases, the preoccupation with the streets in hip-hop has the potential to ground the starry mind of many intellectual discourses, imbuing the rarified air of academic life with the voices of "low-down folks."[55] At one point, the blues, salsa, or jazz may have done this for America, but that role has now passed to hip-hop.[56] The street-level reporting; the rummaging through old records in search of the right musical phrase; the making of rhymes and yarns out of the abrasive realities of the city; the montage of various body languages in breaking; the aerosol argot of tags, pieces, throw-ups, or murals; the choice of one's kicks, clothing, and fashion, all of it is an act of ingenuity at the heart of the genre, the making of art with the bits and scraps that others have discarded.

In some of these ways, as we've seen, hip-hop bears a close likeness to liberation theologies, especially when a strong prophetic voice resounds in the music, or when the artist expresses a clear option for the poor and disenfranchised. Since the manner of "liberation" in hip-hop is as much aesthetical as it is ethical-political, however, relying on the arts to loosen the ties of injustice, hip-hop's particular variety of liberation is primarily artistic and festive, a tribute to the emancipatory possibilities inherent in music, dance, and celebration. Any street theology riffing on hip-hop, therefore, and speaking to the artistic and spiritual experiences of marginalized youth today, will look to the power of music not only to electrify the airwaves and rouse the body but also as a force that can set the spirit free.

CHAPTER 1

A Street Theology

Between God and Hip-Hop

Before jumping into the wide world of hip-hop, I'd like to take a moment here to mention some of the theological tributaries that have fed and emptied into the notion of a street theology, most notably various liberation and cultural theologies. They were foundational influences on my mind and spirit, expanding my field of vision and giving me a unique perception of the world, an ability to spot things unseen, and to recognize traces of God in unexpected places, which is why I insist that a street theology is a new iteration of liberation and cultural theologies, a footnote to their pioneering achievements. It may borrow, sample, and recombine them with hip-hop in novel ways, but the result remains indebted to their innovations in the realm of theology. Even the specific engagement with popular culture and the arts, a defining feature of a street theology, is a trait that began to emerge in the later stages of liberation theology, for example. While its earliest phases may have been suspicious of popular religion and culture (treating it as purely escapist and ideologically conservative), and may have emphasized the urgent need for economic, political, and social analysis (attacking the structural roots of injustice, poverty, racism, colonialism, etc.), liberation theology quickly realized that it needed a spiritual, cultural, and artistic anchor in this work, lest it find itself unmoored and uprooted. (Gustavo Gutiérrez's *We Drink From Our Own Wells* [1984] is an important example.) It realized that folk culture is mixed and messy, containing diverse forms of liberation, both verbal and nonverbal, spiritual and carnal, cultural and political. And it realized that cries of justice, as pressing and necessary as they are, are more persuasive and appealing, less bitter, when they are sweetened with the stuff of celebration, myth, art, ritual, ceremony, dance, music, and so on.

In some ways, US Latin@ theology, an offspring of liberation theology, was born on the heels of this insight, picking up the prophetic mantle of its forebearers with a particular concern for the popular, sacramental, and aesthetic traditions of Christianity in the Americas, especially in light of ordinary, quotidian experiences—a theology, as they described it, rooted in *lo cotidiano*, the everyday. (Roberto Goizueta's *Caminemos Con Jesus* [1995] is a pioneering example.)[1] For many of us in this tradition, the narratives and images of the Virgin of Guadalupe, the Black Madonna of Cuba (Nuestra Señora de Regla), El Cristo Negro de Esquipulas in Guatemala, or any number of popular religiosities in the Americas held a particular fascination, proving that the experiences of poor, Indigenous, and African communities were liberating in a variety of ways, sometimes prophetic and political (inspiring radical social change), sometimes purely spiritual and therapeutic (offering joy, solace, catharsis, dignity), and often a combination of both.

In the legends of Guadalupe, for example, the experience of beauty in poetry, song, art, and the natural world—*flor y canto*, flower and song, as the Nahuatl phrase puts it—is inseparable from the story's larger purpose: to act with justice, to love mercy, and to stand with the oppressed.[2] Beauty and justice are one in the story: "For the Nahuas," writes Timothy Matovina in one of the finest studies on the subject, "God was not primarily known through rational discourse but through the poetic beauty of *flor y canto*. It was predominantly through poetry that the Nahua wise ones spoke of the mysteries of God and of life beyond our present earthly existence. Thus it is striking that the *Nican mopohua* [the most influential account of the Guadalupe apparition, a section of Luis Laso de la Vega's *Huei Tlamahuiçoltica*, 1649] begins with the beautiful music Juan Diego heard that attracted him to ascend the hill of Tepeyac and ends with Juan Diego gathering exquisite flowers and presenting them to Bishop Juan de Zumárraga" (my addition).[3] And it's striking, of course, that the Virgin Mother appeared to Juan Diego in the first place, a dispossessed Indian of the New World, and that she appeared, specifically, on Tepeyac, a barrio of Native residents on the periphery of the city. (Mary identifies herself, speaking to Juan Diego, as the "compassionate mother of you and all your people here in this land.")[4] With Guadalupe playing the part of Wisdom/Sophia in Proverbs, or Mother Rachel in Jeremiah, a voice crying in the streets, demanding justice, mourning the death of her people, the story is another illustration of the biblical conviction that revelation occurs in unexpected places, and that the poor, ordinary, and marginalized can be agents of a revolutionary sort of wisdom.[5]

And this presumption is as old as theology itself, owing its logic to the fact that "theology," in its earliest years, was a form of reflection on popular religion, yoked to the lives, labors, toils, and ordeals of common peoples. "The result of this hybrid phenomenon (popular religion and elite philosophical reflection)," writes David Tracy about the origins of the concept, "became a new form of philosophy by Christians named *theology*: a philosophical reflection on popular religion."[6] If theology has its origins in these humble circumstances, inspired by the lowly fishermen, slaves, shepherds, day laborers, farmers, and field workers of the early church, a street theology is less a new innovation than a retrieval and recovery, less a newly fashioned subject than a remix of what came before.

If I can be presumptuous in claiming that there is something new and fresh about it, nonetheless, I would say that a street theology considers a broader spectrum of voices than classic theology, lending its ear to a diverse chorus of project dwellers, beat-makers, self-taught poets, outsiders, misfits, hustlers, and unchurched folk for thinking about the arts, culture, and God. Because various liberation theologies, including US Latin@ theology, largely placed the spotlight on traditional religious expressions, they tended to leave many youth cultures in the dark, those for whom religion is represented in non-traditional ways, like a prisoner or gang member with a tattooed image of Guadalupe on his back, a deejay or b-boy devoted to the spirituality of beats, rhymes, and shuffles, or a young woman, like the heroine of Angie Thomas's *On the Come Up*, who finds her voice and purpose through the social satire, poetic swag, and supercharged beats of the rap game.[7] If unorthodox and unconventional, such lives and experiences can open up new doors of experience, shedding light on the dark sides of the world and making for a theology that is more streetwise and connected to the struggles of young Americans beyond the pale of church and academy, a theology for the ghetto and barrio youth of today's world.

To put it simply, many traditional theologies, including mine on the baroque in the Americas (*Wonder and Exile in the New World*, 2013), often concentrated on intellectual, proper, and traditional religious expressions.[8] While this has resulted in genuine insights and innovations, it hasn't been inclusive and comprehensive enough, tending to overlook, if not entirely ignore, the wild styles of the young and poor, a sin of omission when it comes to many of the outsiders of church and society, the lost souls. Could it be, however, that there is a distinct advantage in being an outsider, outcast, or exile? Can the view from beyond, or below, orthodox sites expand the horizons of theology with fresh outlooks, maybe jazz it up with verve, impudence, grace, swagger, instinct, intelligence, street savvy? Though shunned and denied a voice in many academic circles, these perspectives stand as a testament to the potential wisdom of society's outsiders, a testament to what Michael Eric Dyson has called a "thug's theology."[9]

But then again, even this affinity for misfits and lost souls has been seen before: nothing is new under the sun. A host of scholars in religious studies have long set their mind on such things, probing the everyday world for the sacred and sacramental, invoking a generous and all-inclusive understanding of grace, believing that God can be encountered by the fireside, stable, or streets as much as the churches, to paraphrase Meister Eckhart in the fourteenth century (a position, incidentally, that echoes his fellow Dominican Aquinas's analogical vision, where the supernatural shines through the natural and cultural worlds, throbbing in every atom of creation).[10] Instead of an approach to the study of religion that is dominated by textual studies alone, turning entirely on word-centered discourses, scholars in this school have broadened the prospects and horizons of religious studies, considering the potential manifestations of the sacred in visual, tangible, audible, and material forms, looking, in short, for the presence of God in all things, after the manner of St. Ignatius of Loyola, Eckhart, or Flannery O'Connor. From their perspective, seen through the eyes of saint or poet, creation is shot through with holiness, abounding in every fleck and filament of human experience, the ordinary as much as the exceptional. Nothing lies outside the purview of religion, a conviction that has prodded scholars in this mold to rummage for traces of the divine where others won't dare to look.[11]

Consistent with this intuition, Robert Orsi has spoken of a "theology of the streets" in some of these ways; instead of searching and prying among trees and rivers for signs of the numinous, however, he scouts the world of popular religion and culture, his eye trained on the manifestations of the sacred in the lives of ordinary folk.[12] Notice, for example, how he traces the materialization of Guadalupe in the lives of Latin@s, her image marking the bodies and lives of *cholos*, farmworkers, and others: "She appeared first in 1531 to the man named Cuauhtlatohuac—He Who Speaks Like an Eagle—but known since his baptism as Juan Diego on the hill of Tepeyac where the mother-goddess Tonantzin had been worshipped by her people, and she appears today on bolo ties, playing cards, tattooed on the skins of *cholos* in East LA or South Phoenix, on belts, pillows, towels, cigar boxes. . . . in the struggles of farmworkers, in the places of the sick and dying, carved in soup bones, and in ravines on the border between Mexico and the United States."[13] In this account, Guadalupe is shapeshifting, protean, and graceful, moving and migrating with her people, capable of appearing in myriad forms and customs. Unconfined to the hill of Tepeyac, she can turn any space, desert or hill or alleyway or urban barrio, into a sacred site.

The study of urban popular religion is concerned with such possibilities and revelations, the surprising appearances of the sacred in the messy phenomena of "parks, stoops, alleyways, hallways, fire escapes, storefronts, traffic, police, courtyards, street crime and street play, and so on."[14] Needless to say, these settings and circumstances are fundamental to hip-hop as well, shaping much of the ethics and aesthetics of the culture. And they are fundamental to what James Fischer has called a "street Catholicism," a rougher and edgier form of Catholicism, consisting of figures still clinging to the ship of the church, but perhaps from the side, in the water, or even from the doomed position of the plank, the eccentric, wild, and unmoored ones, like an F. Scott Fitzgerald, James Joyce, Federico García Lorca, Gabriela Mistral, Jack Kerouac, Andy Warhol, Jean-Michel Basquiat, Flannery O'Connor, Simone Weil, Federico Fellini, Martin Scorsese, Bruce Springsteen, Billie Holiday, Claude McKay, Toni Morrison, et al.[15] Whatever the faults—or virtues—that kept them on the margins of Catholic life, clinging to the edges if not marooned, their unconventional and peripheral positions seemed to act as a boon to their imaginations, putting them in the same dinghy-like boat as other outcasts, wanderers, sojourners, and exiles. Their solidarity with outsiders can be felt in their creations, the grain of the streets in their artworks. Addressing what he sees as major themes running through this variety of "street Catholicism," in a nice abridgment of the topic, Fischer highlights three major themes: first, a focus on family, neighborhood, and local region; second, an affection for poor, wayward, fugitive, disaffected, and lost souls; and third, a politically quietist, even fatalistic, outlook, with an emphasis on personal self-expression over sociopolitical and communal engagement.[16]

As we'll see, these features are as common in hip-hop as tattoos on a rapper's body, covering almost every visible dimension of the genre—though I will complicate and quibble with each aspect as we go along, particularly the mark of fatalism. While true in many cases—hip-hop was born, after all, in the aftermath of civil rights when a widespread feeling of disillusionment and cynicism set in—there remain many instances where the streets are not only sites of violence and doom-laden curses, but places of celebration, activism, protest, marches, and dreams of redemption.

As I see it, in any case, there are several advantages in considering hip-hop in light of "ultimate concerns," as Paul Tillich defined theology. If theology's temptation is elitism, hip-hop's temptation is anti-intellectualism, a danger that resembles the kind of populism, even demagoguery, that the extreme right has exploited in modern politics. ("There's still a taboo," Nipsey Hussle once remarked about the culture of hip-hop, "against speaking intelligent, representing intelligence.")[17] As a rigorous, questioning discipline, theology can add a sharp, intellectual edge to the conversation, just as much as hip-hop can chasten theology's highbrow tendencies. In the matter of ethics and aesthetics, theology has something important to say. As I suggested earlier in the introduction, there are mystical-aesthetical and prophetic-ethical trajectories that predate hip-hop by a couple of millennia, and that surface in the various genres and schools of hip-hop. Besides the obvious appeals and considerations of the divine in hip-hop, which abound in the genre, these mystical and prophetic dimensions—the former a transporting experience of transcendence, the latter an inspired voice of judgment and justice—constitute, in my opinion, the "religious" dimension of hip-hop. And both dimensions are noticeable in the Christian scriptures, including the particular accent of the "streets" that I'm stressing here, a certain shibboleth that identifies the trope of the streets with the disenfranchised sites and communities.

Think of the parable of the Great Banquet, for example, where Jesus recounts the life of a man planning a lavish feast, only to receive a series of excuses and snubs by the most privileged in town. Exasperated by their refusals, he finally directs his servant to summon the most deprived in their place: "Go out quickly into the streets and alleyways of the town and bring in here the poor and crippled, the blind and lame" (Luke 14:21). The parable amounts, in my reading, to a revolutionary shift in consciousness, a startling disruption of the traditional hierarchies and castes of society—the last shall come first, the first shall come last. No longer fixated by the epicenters of power in Rome or Jerusalem, Jesus, like the prophets before him, champions a decentered vision here, one that honors the individuals and groups on the peripheries of society. He bestows dignity upon their lives in the process, trusting that their perspectives, sometimes unruly and vulgar, sometimes fractious and rebellious, sometimes sinful and flawed, are worthy to be invited to the table of fellowship. The "streets," in this reading, are places and predicaments created by the exclusion, banishment, and impoverishment of certain groups, and Jesus made them the primary target of his message.

The Gathering of Fragments

Fast-forward two centuries later, and hip-hop emerges in the late twentieth century with a similar sensibility, passionate about redeeming lost and discarded materials (persons, places, and things). This principle, I'm suggesting, is a remix of the biblical imagination, privileging the periphery over the center, the streets and barrio over empire and temple, the poor over the rich. Hip-hop redirects our gaze to the margins and cracks of the world, forcing attention on the alleyways and underworlds of history, demanding recognition of the potential beauty that exists in other people's trash and junk. It came into the world, if Hua Hsu is right, roughly at the moment when these kinds of rummaging practices were in vogue in American culture, apparent in deejays, graffiti writers, poets, literary critics, and artists like Andy Warhol, Rammellzee, and Jean-Michel Basquiat: "The eighties produced a new type of person, accustomed to the trash and junk, whose life was calibrated to maximum resourcefulness, cutting stuff apart and putting it back together."[18] The ragpicker, sifting through the detritus of society for things that could be salvaged and refurbished, became a source of inspiration for many artists in this regard, none more than Basquiat, an artist, according to Keith Haring, who worked wonders with discarded materials, "transforming things found in the garbage into beautiful *objets d'art*."[19] No one, however, captured this spirit more clearly than Rammellzee, the great graffiti writer, and co-author, alongside K-Rob and Basquiat, of the classic "Beat Bop" (1983): so committed was he to rescuing waste materials, and foraging through other people's trash and junk, that he named himself the "garbage god."[20] It's a fitting designation not only for Rammellzee but for hip-hop in general: the music and culture was always something cobbled together out of recycled scraps and debris, less invented than discovered, less composed than assembled.

In my estimation, this principle is deeply Christian, really, a conviction that there can be grace and beauty in what is unclean, disreputable, despised, and low. For St. Paul, notably, Jesus was a garbage God of sorts, intent on saving what has been cast into the dustbins and garbage heaps of history, "the refuse of the world, the dross of all things" (1 Corinthians 4:13). On this fundamental point, the biblical tradition converges with hip-hop, both of them believing that history and society are redeemed by their least-respected members.

No wonder, then, that black folk in America were quick to claim Jesus as one of their own, a "nigger Christ, on the cross of the South," in Langston Hughes's unforgettable words.[21] No wonder that this Jesus, a God of the disinherited, as Howard Thurman famously suggested, has resonated with the experiences of marginalized and oppressed groups throughout the ages, including with various factions of hip-hop, as I hope to show in this study.[22]

And though theology has not always lived up to this ideal—too often it has betrayed, misconstrued, and distorted this daring insight—in its finest cases, it is a proof of the potential wisdom evident among the lowly and unlettered, of the grace found in experiences of deprivation and loss. Theology is fundamentally concerned with unearthing such possibilities, which is why the work of a theologian is comparable to an archaeologist or deejay, the former digging among rubble and ruins, the latter digging in the crates. Instead of a complete whole, as David Tracy has maintained, theology is a constellation of fragments, hints and glimpses of the Infinite. It is, as the metaphor of fragments suggests, partial, limited, and incomplete, a form of knowledge that is patched together like the remains of an ancient temple, the samples of a rap, or the dismembered relics of a saint. We never possess, in other words, the whole body of truth, only a partial shard, artifact, or relic—there are always pieces missing. "It seems impossible," Virginia Woolf writes in this elegiac spirit, "that we should ever compose from their fragments a perfect whole or read in the littered pieces the clear words of truth."[23]

Instead of bemoaning and mourning the loss of absolute knowledge and perfect wholes, however—from religious fundamentalism to the Eurocentrism/logocentrism of the Enlightenment—Tracy sees the splintering and deconstruction of these systems as an unexpected opportunity, the loss opening up new vistas and occasions to reconsider all of the cultural, artistic, and religious phenomena that Western modernity has excluded, discounted, and repressed. Like a crack that lets the sunlight in, such rifts and fragments—such as the spirituals, the blues, and hip-hop, or the disruptive voices of the mystics and prophets—are resources that have the potential to rupture established parameters of knowledge while letting in previously unheard voices and histories, previously untold tales of those defeated and deliberately forgotten.[24] More than resources to shore up against our ruin, as T. S. Eliot bleakly presumed, Tracy regards such fragments as explosive in promise and possibility, with a power to shake the dungeon, to remember the great spiritual, in order to break the chains of bondage.

Of course, the Bible itself has this potential, and it, too, is a pastiche and medley of such testimonies, composed—if "form" and "redaction" critics are right—out of fragments of oral tradition. Emerging in the early twentieth century, out of the ruins of World War I, form and redaction scholars argued that the Bible was a collection of diverse filaments—stories, sayings, legends, myths, formulas, rituals, songs—eventually stitched together by a masterful weaver of sorts.[25] They argued that the biblical writers were editors or redactors more than single authors, and that their particular form of inspiration occurred in the process of cutting, splicing, editing, and arranging their respective texts, a skill of borrowing more than inventing.[26] Instead of creating it out of thin air, or receiving it word for word as a form of dictation (as in the Quran), gospel authors composed their texts out of preexisting oral traditions and stories, joining them together in beautiful and graceful patterns, making a symphony out of eclectic parts and voices (e.g., apocalyptic texts, wisdom literature, Greco-Roman biographies, prophetic discourses, the Torah, rabbinic folklore, mystery cults, parables, proverbs, sayings, and so on). "It is quite apparent," Robert Alter explains about the constellation of fragments that is the Hebrew and Christian Bibles, "that a concept of composite artistry, of literary composition through a collage of textual materials, was generally assumed to be normal procedure in ancient Israelite culture."[27]

Hip-hop, if you can guess where I'm going, is a contemporary example of something similar: it, too, is an example of the kind of creativity that occurs primarily in the (improvisational) process of selection and assembly. Rather than art that is created out of nothing, like light out of the void, hip-hop reuses the existing sounds and colors of the world, making swirling and rainbow-like patterns out of the prevailing winds and customs. A drum loop from James Brown, a horn riff from John Coltrane, a bass line from Parliament, marching snares from Mardi Gras bands, a piano run from Nina Simone, a religious sample from gospel, classical strings, the cacophonous noises of the city, the raw diction of urban youth, hip-hop is nothing if not a collection of fragments, the music arranged and layered together by an expert deejay or producer so that it coheres in a mosaic-like pattern, standing as a revealing portrait—in both its brokenness and beauty—of ghetto and favela life.

Biblical and theological knowledge, in any case, can bring something valuable to the table of hip-hop studies, its ancient wisdom—a depth of centuries more than years—acting as an elder voice to the young genre. If the past is any indicator, the fashions of hip-hop, like all things human, will fluctuate and swing, ebb and flow, pivot and return; the central drift of this book is not dependent on what happens to be the rage at the moment. It may be true, as I suggested in my introduction, that we need prophets more than ever in our age, voices that can stir the embers of resistance until they rage and burn brightly. We need prophets and saints more urgently than a plagued town needs doctors, as Simone Weil put it in the mid-twentieth century. Can there be any doubt, however, that humanitarian crises are unrelenting in human history, and that Jesus, as Pascal said, "will be in agony until the end of the world"? The demand for ethical vigilance and responsibility, as much as the necessity of aesthetical principles, in other words, are timeless features of biblical and theological legacies, inherent to the very nature of theology, and inherent to the very nature of hip-hop. Both elements demand our attention.

But before continuing to paint in broad brushstrokes, we need to look much deeper, paying attention to individual lines, tinges, and nuances. Since we are dealing with a species of beauty in hip-hop, and not a category of journalism or sociology, it goes without saying that we must parse the musical vocabularies in order to fully understand their meaning and significance. Great deejays and producers, like all musicians, paint with great attention to detail and design, a groove here, a vamp or loop there, a guitar lick, repeating synthesizer stabs, and so on. In some instances, the composition can be a whirlpool of sonic and spiritual energy, drowning its listeners in its swirling, churning, scintillating grooves. In other cases, it can flip a switch and turn hushed, still, and quiet, a gentle trickle of a flow that is ideal for chilling and contemplating. In either instance, we need to listen carefully to the music and culture of hip-hop itself, attending to the sounds, sights, and voices of its best artists and practitioners. As obvious as this may sound, this approach is not always the norm in academic considerations of hip-hop, especially when references to scholarly discussions and theories are piled so high that they end up obscuring a clear-sighted view of the culture. In the worst cases, hip-hop is ventriloquized, made to say what some critics want it to say without considering that it has its own voice.

Besides this focus on hip-hop itself, finally, it should be clear by any casual glance at the table of contents that my preference in the study is for the most influential and successful figures in the genre, as opposed to artists in the genres of alternative or Christian rap. I'm drawn to mainstream artists—the tributaries of the culture—because, for one, their music is often better than a lot of gospel rappers; and, second, because their considerations of faith and society are frequently more subtle, nuanced, and critical than the latter. More an ongoing struggle rather than a completed fact, a painful ordeal and process rather than a carefree dogma, mainstream artists present us with examples of a complex, sophisticated, living faith, filled with moments of failure, doubt, uncertainty, and confusion. They arrive at a similar awareness as many existential or postmodern theologians—God seen through a glass dimly and darkly—but they take a different and more scenic route than conceptual analysis or formal reasoning.

Though my focus is on the musical, lyrical, and spiritual features of rap, the language and idioms of the body—in b-boying and other dance-centric forms of hip-hop—figure prominently throughout, but particularly in chapters 5 and 6. Attention to the kinetic and physical aesthetics of hip-hop, not to mention the pure musical signatures apart from the words, reminds us that hip-hop cannot be reduced to lyrics on a page, cannot be stripped of its bodily, emotional, and aesthetic properties.

"This Is America"

As a test case for the balancing of aesthetics and prophecy in hip-hop, and an example of beautifully assembled fragments, consider Childish Gambino's "This Is America" (2018): it's a remarkable work of art, and has touched a nerve like few others, generating a gushing stream of commentary and enthusiastic acclaim. By some estimations, the music video was streamed more than sixty-five million times in the first week (in the United States alone).

The song opens with South African choral melodies, cheery and untroubled, a perfect harmony of a cappella vocals. The musical accompaniment is bare and minimal at the start, a light pattern of metal jingles from a rain stick or Egyptian tambourine, a finger-picked acoustic guitar, and bright and breezy male voices crooning the lines "We just wanna party/ Party just for you/ We just want the money/ Money just for you." Childish Gambino now enters the picture, strolling and dancing his way to a shoeless black man strumming his guitar—a nostalgic image from the bucolic age of blues and folk music, perhaps. After striking a "Jump Jim Crow" pose (parodying minstrelsy and America's long history of distorting and plundering black culture), he proceeds to pull out a gun and fire a blast to the bluesman's head. The effect is shocking, brutal, grotesque, a sudden blow to the head, a disruption of the carefree and blithe opening. Like a surrealistic image from the films of Luis Buñuel, the scene, and what follows, is dreadful and traumatizing, a subversive satire of America's addictions to guns, racism, materialism, and social media.

And the music registers it all: as Childish Gambino commits the murder, wearing a hollow and callous grin, totally indifferent to the victim, the music abruptly shifts from lighthearted folk melodies to the sinister, menacing, and street-savvy sound of trap. What began as a cool breeze, a gentle strum of a folk guitar, suddenly leaps into another register, the winds now howling, the sky darkening, and the violently charged atmosphere producing rattling thunderclaps and lashing rain. The music has turned apocalyptic and nightmarish, marking a dark change in mood, as if we've taken a wrong turn and are heading straight for disaster. The low-end bass, a heavy monotone thud, sounds ill-omened; the high-pitched synthesizer is eerie and dreadful; the drum-machine claps are spine-chilling, like the sound of waves slapping the side of a sinking boat; and Childish Gambino delivers his lines in fragmented, gnomic, and lurching bits, sputtering through the song, as though he's simulating the jerky, jolting flow of a roller coaster. The song chronicles, in all, a world in exile from the heavenly realm, a world estranged from peace and justice. Just when the listener was lulled into contentment, happy to dance and frolic in the Eden-like garden of American life, horror interrupts the song and brings ruin to the scene. Instead of moving forward, leaving past bigotries and brutalities behind us, history drags us backward, as in a moonwalk. Time is out of joint.

Apocalyptic signs are pervasive in the video too: a hooded figure on a white horse, galloping in the background, evokes the horsemen of the apocalypse in Revelation; crowds of people, rioting or simply running in terror, are scattered throughout; police cars, with their lights flashing in warning, denote a state of emergency; there are burning cars, falling dead bodies, a brutally slain gospel choir and, at the end, Childish Gambino fleeing in absolute terror, his eyes bulging, muscles straining, and torso stretched forward as if he is lunging not only to escape the threats that hound him, but to escape from his body altogether. Much like the obscure and nightmarish imagery of Revelation—grotesque beasts that represent Roman aggression and persecution, warhorses as symbols of Death and Hades running roughshod over the innocent, corrupt merchants as symbols of economic injustice, allegories that correspond with exile and the sack of Jerusalem in 70 CE, omens of the end of the world (stars falling from the sky, the sun covered in sackcloth, the bloody moon, etc.)—the song is a jumbled collection of fragments, epitomizing our degraded and conflicted present, with America now replacing Rome in this modern apocalypse. If you recall that the book of Revelation—however bizarre and unearthly it seems—was written by a persecuted and oppressed group of people, under the bootstraps of Rome, the resonances with "This Is America" are even more clear, the two of them both giving voice to the casualties and victims of imperial might. Once wrested from the hands of biblical fundamentalists, in fact, the book of Revelation includes some of the most liberating verses and images in the New Testament.[28] For David Tracy, this last book of the Christian Bible, which ends with the desperate plea "Come, Lord Jesus," is a collection of some of the most threatening and demanding fragments in the Bible, their unruly and wild arrangement acting as a reminder of "the genuinely public, political, and historical character of all Christian self-understanding; a challenge to all the privileged to remember the privileged status of the oppressed, the poor, the suffering. . . . and a challenge to face the reality of the really new, the *novum*, and the future breaking in confronting every present, exploding every complacency."[29]

Each of these purposes surfaces in "This Is America," even though the song, unlike Revelation, lacks a secret revelatory content, a heavenly messenger, and, above all, the hope of redemption. (The Greek *apokálypsis* suggests an "uncovering" or "disclosure" of a heavenly truth and salvific knowledge.) As I see it, the eye-assaulting chaos and violence of the video, causing the viewer to recoil to the point of whiplash, blurs the lines between apocalypticism from the biblical tradition and tragedy from the ancient Greeks, the former convinced that there is a redemptive arc in history, the latter not so sure, seeing history as a wreckage and pile of debris, littered with countless wasted lives and irredeemable deaths.[30] Still, if the song lacks a definitive revelation, and avoids identifying a clear culprit for so much sin and suffering, there is surely a burning message here, and it comes out in the sonic signatures, graphic images, and disjointed verses. Just as the book of Revelation once urged resistance to the Roman Empire, it seems to urge resistance to the accommodating pressures of pop culture, as well as resistance to the horrors of racism in America. Immediately after the head-concussing change in music, for instance, both at the beginning and after the murder of the gospel choir (a reference to the murder of nine black church members in Charleston in 2015), Childish Gambino chants the lines "This is America/ Don't catch you slippin' up/ Look at how I'm livin' now/ Police be trippin' now/ Yeah, this is America/ Guns in my area/ I got the strap/ I gotta carry 'em." If the song mocks the frivolous addictions of America's youth—for social media, selfies, fashion trends, vain pleasures—it also assails America in general for its deadly addiction to guns, violence, and racism. Notice the reverence shown the gun in the video: it's swaddled in cloth and carried with great care as though it's a sacred object. Human lives, by contrast, are treated with relative indifference; gun rights matter more than human rights.[31]

The music, meanwhile, is banging. The short, sporadic, broken phrases of the rapping are consistent with the triplet pattern of Southern rap—Three 6 Mafia, Migos, Gucci Mane, et al.—just as the cluster of yelps, blurts, woos, and skrrts at the end of the bars by Young Thug, Quavo, Slim Jxmmi, and 21 Savage peppers the song with Southern flavor. And the trap beats, too, are deeply Southern, a sonic style indebted to Miami bass, New Orleans's gangster bounce, Houston's chopped and screwed, Chicago's house, Memphis's horrorcore, and Atlanta's crunk. In trap music, the feeling of urban confinement—like being caught in a snare, maze, or mousetrap, or else, in a criminal twist of the term, a stash house—is translated into the aural equivalent, the music capturing "the sound of a nation not under a groove but underwater, trying to hold on to the shores of light, but decidedly heading out into dangerous and uncharted depths."[32] There is, as Jesse McCarthy notes here, a gothic aura to the style, its pealing, cracking thunderclaps sounding like death knells, presaging an apocalyptic end to a society that can't seem to advance on matters of race and equality. Grimy, fatalistic, and chilling, a sound built on 808 kick drums, crisp snares, fluttering hi-hats, and dark-sounding synthesizers, trap serves "This Is America" well, commenting in sound as much as words on the claustrophobic pressures of the Trump era: the empty and titillating forms of pop culture, the moral numbness and nihilism, the racial anxieties and tensions, the festering wounds of despair and loneliness, and the age's casual acceptance of outrageous injustices and cruelties.

Seen in the longer arc of hip-hop, the beats of the song build on major key notes of rap music's booming, asphalt aesthetics. Think of these groundbreaking moments: Grandmaster Flash and the Furious Five's pioneering "The Message" introduced an unhurried, almost dejected rhythm to the genre, adding a "disturbing fatalism to the angry, dryly spoken rhymes," in the words of Geoffrey Himes of the *Washington Post*.[33] Run-DMC crafted beats that mirrored the bruising and gritty toughness of the streets, chipping away at all superfluous melodies, choruses, and arrangements in order to sculpt an austere and spartan sound. They made music that was hard-hitting, proud, and threatening, a sonic style divested of the fancy, racially neutered, and club-friendly vibes of disco. N.W.A. and Public Enemy, additionally, banged out rhythms and beats that represented the noises of urban life, all the cacophony and dissonance of the streets: screeching car tires, police sirens and helicopters, gunshots, harsh timbres, clashing rhythms, staccato attacks, and beats that assaulted the eardrum.[34]

"This Is America" maps similar histories, similar sounds of blackness. It chronicles the relentless loops of violence in America, the echoing reverb of racist legacies, and the pervasive traps, patrolled by "police who are trippin'," that ensnare and ambush black lives. Foreboding and portentous, the heavy bass and horror-like synth lines shatter any worldview built on nostalgia; it doesn't look backward as much as forward, warning of destruction like Jeremiah on the eve of the sack of Jerusalem. If Jeremiah pinpointed slavery as one reason for the Babylonian captivity, Childish Gambino points to America's perpetuation of cycles of racial violence, discrimination, and Jim Crow-like segregation as a cause of the current crisis. The chaotic atmosphere of the song and video captures the pulse of our times, the feeling that prophecy has failed and now gives way to the strange and frenzied images of the apocalyptic. In fact, as I write these words (May 31, 2020), there is rioting in the streets of America, provoked by the brutal killing of a black man, George Floyd, by a group of police officers. Like so much of hip-hop, "This Is America" is witness to such racial violence, screaming out loud for the world to take notice, prophesying doom upon a body politic that has eyes but does not see, ears but does not hear. If a riot is the language of the unheard, as Dr. King maintained, "This Is America" is a musical equivalent, a snapshot of the unrest and racial disturbances that plague contemporary American life. Sketching a world that is splintered in shards, dismembered in violence, drunk on frivolous and shallow diversions, the song moves your body, heart, and soul like a powerful requiem.

While so much madness plays out in the world, Childish Gambino, meanwhile, dances and preens with schoolchildren behind him, totally oblivious to the deaths and catastrophes around them. At least ten different dances, from the South African Gwara Gwara (popularized by DJ Bongz's song "Ofana Nawe") to the "Shoot" dance of BlocBoy JB, are paraded in the video, all captivating. Childish Gambino's movements are particularly revealing, as they embody the conflicting themes and emotions of the song, the dialectical clashes of joy and tragedy, music and murder, harmony and conflict, vanity and social awareness, sweet folk melodies and bitter street realities. Notice how Childish Gambino twists and contorts his shirtless body, how he swings between disjointed and agitated motions, on the one hand, and fluid and graceful ones, on the other. His facial expressions, too, shift from vacuity to agony, from self-absorbed posturing to grimaced, twisted ugliness. He captures in his body alone the warring, writhing rhythms of the song, as if the tortured minstrel history of the Jim Crow age—the "grotesque theatre of jigging and cake-walking," as Doreen St. Félix has noted—courses through his body.[35] Sinuous and spasmodic at the same time, his body captures the agony and elegance of black history in America.

I see a slight resemblance, as well, to the moves of the undead in Michael Jackson's "Thriller," a fitting likeness since "This Is America" portrays a culture that is beset by deadening and zombie-like forces. References to "straps" (guns), "bags" (money or drugs), designer brands (Gucci), whippin' (cooking up drugs, making money, or driving expensive cars), and rampant narcissism (I'm so cold, I'm so dope, I'm so pretty, I'm so fitted, etc.) are littered throughout the song, parodying America's addictions to pain-killing narcotics and toys—playthings that have the power to turn their users into zombies. With his carefree grins and self-absorbed postures, all delivered in a mocking tone, Childish Gambino turns the video into a burlesque, lampooning the vain nature of contemporary pop culture, not excluding varieties of trap music. (It's impossible to miss the reference to "I Get the Bag," by Gucci Mane, feat. Migos.) Homicides, racial violence, injustice, acts of terror, all these things happen while Childish Gambino and his backup dancers go on dancing as if nothing has happened, posing for selfies, checking their followers on social media, and worrying about getting money. So many amusements and distractions keep Americans blissfully ignorant and unfeeling; they keep Americans numb and indifferent to the suffering of others. This is America.

While it may be true, as T. S. Eliot has noted, that human beings cannot bear too much reality, and that we all seek shelter in fictions and fancies, "This Is America" questions the *kinds* of fictions and fancies in which Americans live. It contests the most shallow and self-indulgent fancies of American pop culture, the ones that wallow in banalities and that reduce the black experience in America to exotic and demeaning caricatures: grins and gunplay, dancing and partying, delinquency and drug use, hedonism and decadence. With apocalyptic urgency, the song mocks our fallen present. It is a scathing indictment of versions of art and entertainment that are opiate-like and escapist, numbing the mind, fogging the conscience, and making us callous in the face of violence and injustice, our souls unmoved by suffering. No wonder that Childish Gambino, when the song turns silent before the last refrain, pulls out a joint to get high; the act extends his prophetic parody, holding pop entertainment responsible for the kind of apathy that is anesthetizing to the soul like a blunt is to one's spirit. In this pessimistic account, American popular culture, including the American dream of wealth and success, is all id and ego, with no room for the soul or God. Vanity of vanities; all is vanity.

And yet, notwithstanding the bitter, tragic wisdom that the song delivers, how can one possibly miss the sheer beauty of the music, rapping, and dancing, the visual theater of it all? There is a dazzling array of artistic styles in the video, all elegantly arranged by Childish Gambino, Ludwig Göransson, and the Japanese American filmmaker Hiro Murai. The debris and detritus of these art forms, splintered by histories of violence and bigotry, are reassembled in the video into a mosaic of black life that does more than simply mirror our torn and tattered lives and cityscapes; it also puts on festive display the rich surplus of black arts in America, the accumulated genius of slaves and their descendants, the "styles upon styles upon styles" of African American traditions and cultures.[36] While the chilling soundscape pushes the song to the precipice, the colorful parade of beauty in the video charms and thrills the viewer, pulling us back from the edge. It makes the song bounce and swing with a profusion of grace, an abundance of joy; and it proves that aesthetic forms like the spoken word, dance, and the chords of music have long been resources against the tides of tragedy, against the storms of injustice and oppression. Above the dark, menacing beats of trap, then, there is a note of hope, resilience, and, since trap always aims to unseat the listener's body by way of dance, a mystical element, whereby the dancer's self is undone and dissolved in the thunderous blasts of the bass, like a tree transformed into smoldering smoke and ashes, incinerated in a blaze of sweaty bliss. Too often undervalued by conscious hip-hop, dance is celebrated, cherished, even revered in "This Is America," celebrated as though it was the purest form of beauty, a rhythm that captures transcendence in ways that require no words, no commentary.

Thus, "This Is America" revels in beauty while simultaneously facing up to the unseemly and ghastly in history, the crosses as much as the glories and raptures. It dramatizes, that is to say, a rough and fragmentary form of beauty, one that defies bourgeois, Hollywood ideals of prettiness, one that peels away artificial layers of beauty, one that absorbs the terror and suffering of history, a tragic or sublime beauty. While it echoes the prophets and

Marx in this satire—a criticism of the ideological superstructures (pop culture, music, film, technology, morality, politics, religion, etc.) that encourage accommodation with the powers that be—it ultimately remains a celebration of the potential of *art* to propose counter-narratives to the repressive aspects of American society and politics. Aesthetics coexists with prophecy, carnival with apocalypse, celebration with violence and terror.

Instructive for many reasons, Childish Gambino's composition will serve this study well in the pages that follow. Since we're dealing with the humanities and not mathematics, there is no perfect formula for our purposes. The history of hip-hop doesn't always neatly balance prophetic and aesthetic concerns; sometimes, the music is deeply endearing, deeply thrilling, and deeply problematic. I wrestle with this all the time. Perhaps, then, my tactic is more like a blueprint and draft than a hardened formula, a strategy that tries to avoid glaring traps. If we steer too close to one side or the other, with a Scylla or Charybdis looming, there are several risks involved: on the one hand, an uncritical embrace of the aesthetical inventions and pleasures in black and Latin histories—say, musical ingenuities, the virtuosities of dance, rhythmic and percussion-driven sonorities, festive and rapturous celebrations, spiritual and religious extravagance, sexually suggestive customs and arts, and so on—risks confirming the kind of primitive and base caricatures that "This Is America" is parodying ("we just wanna dance, we just wanna party"). To reject and disparage these things, though, carries its own liabilities, to which the prophets are especially prone. For all their iconoclastic genius, the prophets can be shortsighted, if not blind, on the matter of aesthetics, and this deficiency has the tendency of souring their words, turning them into the joyless, repressive, disembodied, and dour ethos that we associate with Puritanism ("the haunting fear," as H. L. Mencken defines it, "that someone, somewhere, may be happy"). Rarely advocates for the pleasures of dance, comedy, music, and art (with the notable exception of the band of prophets in 1 Samuel 10:5 where they are depicted as dancing in ecstasy with "lyres, tambourines, flutes and harps"), the prophets risk, as Nietzsche argued, turning everything that is joyful, noble, funny, and playful about the human experience into the stuff of sin and depravity. It is, no doubt, this heritage, along with plain old racism, that produced moral panic and mass hysteria at the first sight of the blues, jazz, rock 'n' roll, and hip-hop. So much twisting, gyrating, jerking, shouting, and moaning were all equated with wickedness; so much joy and exultation—a joy that "runs, bang, into ecstasy," as Langston Hughes put it—became emblematic of the devil's work.[37]

Hip-hop has always indulged itself in such ways, sometimes raging in anger and accusation, sometimes abandoning itself to Dionysian pleasures alone, and sometimes succumbing to bad choices and awful taste. And no outsider was ever needed to remind the music of its faults; each extreme has engendered criticism from within its ranks, as the Childish Gambino song makes clear. After hitting hip-hop hard for its many failings, and subjecting hip-hop to a purgative and parodying treatment, "This Is America" is instructive as both self-criticism and vindication of hip-hop's potential as art and prophecy. The violent interruption of African melodies, blues riffs, and gospel shouts in the song—beyond the obvious indictment of racial violence in America—is an argument on behalf of hip-hop's aptitude for messy, streetwise rhythms, its knack for capturing, even more than the ethereal voices of gospel or jazz or folk music, the gritty world of ghettos and barrios. The sudden sonic booms, 808 thunderclaps, and jagged, fragmented verses in "This Is America," so the song implies, are the best forms for naming and expressing the chaotic and broken circumstances of urban life in America and beyond. Life on the edges of the modern world is not only sweet and harmonious, we are reminded; it can be dissonant and strident, disjointed and brutal, and so we need musical and theological vocabularies that can capture both transcendence and earthiness, purity and sin, sublimity and the banging, cacophonous noise of the streets; we need hip-hop's low-end frequencies to anchor us in the dirt and grime of the world.

CHAPTER 2
A Brief Sonic History of Hip-Hop

You can feel the lyrics, the spirit coming in braille
Tubman of the underground, come and follow the trail.

Chance the Rapper, "Ultralight Beam"

Analyze life's ills, then I put it down type braille

Jay-Z, "Hard Knock Life"

When dissecting rap lyrics, it's easy to forget that we are dealing with something sublime in music, something that, for existing just beyond the horizon
of language, must be experienced. I am fond of Jay-Z and Chance the Rapper's
use of the braille metaphor in this regard, a reminder that music must be felt
and fingered, carefully touched, rubbed, and weighed before we presume to
explain it. In a rush to get to the meaning of the words on the page, quickly by-
passing the sonic qualities, critics risk tone-deafness, stuffing their ears with
wax out of fear that the song, like the pitch of the Sirens in Homer, may cause
them to lose their minds, or seduce and overwhelm their will.

It's an easy mistake to make, whether in music criticism or theology: the
impulse to systematize, classify, explain, and define is fundamental to each
genre, and when unchecked, it can lead to the domestication and taming of
what is wild in human experience, what startles and mystifies. It can lead to
an overinflated and overconfident form of criticism, heedless of limits and
heedless of transcendence. At the bottom of the temptation, as music critic
Simon Reynolds rightly notes, looms the "impulse to master what masters

43

you; containing music within a grid map of systematic knowledge is a form of protection against the loss of self that is music's greatest gift."[1] The impulse to "master what masters you" is, of course, a form of idolatry in theological terms, the desire to contain and control the otherness of God, the desire to possess as opposed to being possessed. It protects a person from letting go, from risking the kind of loss of ego that is a condition for the possibility of enlightenment or ecstasy. In music criticism, the equivalent is an exaggerated intellectualism, the tendency to rationalize what is irrational in music, to subject the indeterminate to precise and prosaic terms. The equivalent is the reduction of music's thrills and mysteries to mathematical reasoning, like interrupting a concert with a lecture on Pythagoras. (It was Pythagoras, incidentally, who first conceptualized music as a rational science of sounds, attempting to define and constrain it by the use of numbers and ratios.)[2] The stuff of theory, targeting the mind, may inform the audience, my point is, but it won't cause involuntary convulsions in the nerves and muscles, and it surely won't wreck the house. Whether hip-hop waxes poetic, turns philosophical, gets the party crunk, soars high and exalted, swings low and dirty, screams in half-intelligible phrases, or rolls off a litany of alliterative bars, it is, ultimately, like any other genre of music, a sensual and mystical force, capable of lifting a listener off their feet.

Once lingering with the music, though, losing ourselves in the sound, and bringing to my mind how little words suffice, the work of criticism—now more modest—can become valuable and instructive. Hip-hop does use words, after all. And it uses them, in fact, with great frequency and abundance, as when Jay-Z and Chance the Rapper, in the above bars, craft rhymes that not only swagger and boogie to the beat, but simultaneously claim to analyze life's ills, capture the pulse of the times, pinpoint the woes of society, and, finally, light the way through the underground landscapes of American life. Since America has long been blind to the struggles of the poor and disenfranchised, as the braille metaphor implies, hip-hop plays the role of the blind prophet in many instances, helping us to see and experience the world from a new perspective. It proves that blindness can be an asset, teaching us how to move and navigate through dark spaces like a bat in the night, the physical limitation flipped into a clairvoyant gift.

The braille metaphor of Chance and Jay-Z, then, contains both dimensions at the heart of this study, and at the heart of my understanding of "street theology": first, the assumption that music works at a frequency of feeling, touch, intuition, ineffability, and style (which is what I mean by its mystical-aesthetical features); and second, that music, in this case hip-hop, can jar awareness and awaken the conscience (its prophetic-ethical features).

In either case, the experience of the music is fundamental, which is why the lyrics of the artist, or the words of a critic, can never replace the savoring and taste of a song. The stuff of words and commentary, even in the most conscientious artist, will always come up short if the music can't spark a flame of enthusiasm and excitement. Words are like straw, to recall Aquinas's metaphor: they only hint at, or evoke, what cannot be seized by language. But before they can serve this purpose, we must learn how to listen, as the Shema demands ("Hear O Israel . . .").

Old School

The search for the perfect beat has always been the driving force of hip-hop. Deejays and producers have made beat-making their primary reason for being—digging in crates for forgotten breaks, excavating buried treasures of sound, looting old LPs, and looking around street corners for the right sonic boom, din, and clamor to characterize life in urban America.

Consider some of the seminal works of hip-hop, beginning with Grandmaster Flash and the Furious Five's "The Message" (1982): the song set a tone for later street-centric forms of hip-hop, shifting the listener's attention from the party—centered in the house, park, or disco—to the more perilous context of urban blocks. Apart from the masterful lyrics, the plodding beat and rhythm (the work of Ed Fletcher and Jiggs Chase, members of Sugar Hill's house band) gave the song a slower, colder, and more bluesy vibe than most early hip-hop. Jeff Chang called it "the grimmest, most downbeat rap ever heard" at the time; Adam Bradley and Andrew DuBois spoke of the song as reflecting the hard, unforgiving, metallic reality of city life; Loren Kajikawa described the rap's use of breaking glass, angry car horns, police sirens, screeching car tires, and subway trains as instilling an edgy and harassed sound appropriate for any beleaguered city setting.[3] While the lack of dance energy in the song was a deficiency if you were up in the club (which is why Grandmaster Flash initially did not want to make the song), the slow and seething tempo was an asset for the emcee, giving him the time and space to offer a detailed report on life in the hood.

The song may have sacrificed ebullient dance rhythms for a more brooding mood, but the decision would lend poetic gravity, social insight, and elegiac depth to the young genre of rap. Thanks to "The Message," the precedence of dance grooves in the hip-hop of the 1970s—a correlate of the deejay's precedence over the emcee—was giving way to the age of the emcee. The spotlight would begin to fall more heavily on the words let loose from the rapper's mouth, their speeches and stories now sounding more and more like social commentary. In this case, the rap dramatized two tragedies playing out: first, the life of a young black man caught in the traps of a New York ghetto, his fate subject to the indignities of poverty, prejudice, prison, and an untimely death; and second, now as the music video wound its way to the end, the plight of the Furious Five themselves, as the camera turned to the group and captured police officers rushing upon them in the streets, barking out threats, putting them in handcuffs. In either case, the song epitomized the constraints, burdens, and perils of being poor and black in America.

And things were just getting started with street-centric hip-hop. By the mid-1980s, the new style got another shot in the arm with Run-DMC, making it sound more swollen and street-tough than ever. With the rise of this trio from Hollis, Queens, the emcee started to sound more rugged, aggressive, and confrontational than ever, their words rushing out of their mouths like a drumroll in a battle march.[4] Collectively, the group was the source, the Adam's rib, from which all later ghetto-centric rappers would derive. By playing the role of a roughneck prophet, dressed in the urban jungle's equivalent of sackcloth, Run-DMC put an infinite distance between themselves and the fancy, slick styles of disco and funk. In lieu of disco glamour, or the Afrofuturistic style of Afrika Bambaataa and the Zulu Nation—a cross between tribal warrior-kings and pimps—Run-DMC copped the plain, austere, and rough style of an urban hustler and street cat. And their music followed suit: after scrapping their music of the ritzy, dreamy sounds of disco—"sixteenth-note hi-hats, ringing 9th and 6th chords, slick vocal inflections"—and making the drumbeat more pronounced, the rappers added even more percussion with their voices and cadences, complementing the banging beats with banging lyricism, a staccato volley of bars and rhymes.[5] Gary Jardim, appropriately, likened their sparse and stripped-down sound to a battering ram that police used to pummel and assault their way into a house in the ghetto, catching its residents by surprise.[6] Raps like "Sucker M.C.'s" (1983), a favorite of mine in childhood, used a bare four-measure loop with hand claps, bass kicks, snares, and a hi-hat at the end. Booming drums and shouted chants were mixed together to create a magic potion of sound that charmed and assaulted the ears at once. This was, as the Beastie Boys called it, the new style, a savage, defiant, electronically based hip-hop, a brazen repudiation of anything fancy and bourgeois.[7]

Aptly named, *Raising Hell*, their third album, added even more fuel to the anger that had been smoldering in the urban blocks for years. In idiom, syntax, and sound, it was a cocky and confident battery of noise, a punch to the gut: "Loud, raw, and sonically huge," writes Marcus Reeves, "nothing about its rhythm was constructed for crossover appeal—no disco-fied re-creations or pop melody overtures or dance-centric grooves."[8] Run-DMC proved that the combination of rhyme skills, hood bravado, and bare-bones beats could be as eloquent and gut-wrenching as anything more complex. After Run-DMC, in fact, too much ornament—samples, harmonies, melodies, instrumental arrangements, fancy language, and so on—now seemed inappropriate for a music that sought to capture life in the starved underbelly of American life; simple sounds and words, without superfluous trimmings, were truer, they implied, to ghetto life. This was the beginning of the Reagan era, after all, when the federal government began to drain social, welfare, and educational resources from many cities across the country, leading to depleted cityscapes and depleted opportunities, and Run-DMC became one of the most popular rap groups to translate these realities into a musical vocabulary. They may not have verbalized their disaffection in the manner of black nationalists, but their beats, rhythms, and swaggering rhymes articulated the fury felt by many kids in the margins of American life, the potency of the music only increasing as it was distilled down to its purest and rawest form. It may be hard to imagine in 2021, now that hip-hop is mainstream, but middle-class America, including the black middle classes, found the relentless beats of Run-DMC as unpalatable and "ghetto" (in the pejorative sense) as the Afro or the pants that sag far below the waistline. Russell Simmons, co-founder of Run-DMC and Def Jam, put it in these terms: "They don't understand it . . . They're bourgeois blacks. The guys remind them of the corner, it's street. It's too black for them."[9]

If anyone understood it, however, Eric B. and Rakim surely did. Their debut album, *Paid in Full* (1987; production by Marley Marl and Eric B.), was cut from the same grainy cloth as Run-DMC's work, but with a much heavier reliance on sampling, the music a patchwork of different threads and colors, all woven together by Rakim's delicate, deft touch on the mic. One of the first great emcees, Rakim had a deep and commanding voice, a laid-back flow, a tricky repertoire of rhymes, and tons of soul. He broke new ground in hip-hop for what a rapper could do with his or her words, complicating the syntax, using off-beat rhythms, stuffing bars with internal and multisyllable rhymes, and sometimes ending a phrase unexpectedly and then picking up where he left off in the following bar, a trick he learned by studying jazz greats, especially John Coltrane. In consequence, his syncopated rhymes redirected, like a boulder thrown into a stream, the conventional rhythms and flows of hip-hop.

In terms of concept and philosophy, though, the street sages known as the Five Percenters were stronger influences on Rakim than any jazz master, their instruction on the teachings of Islam a decisive influence: "Studying Islam," he notes, "made me more cerebral and more conscious of the underlying meanings of things. It showed me how to read in between the lines of what I saw around me and analyze everything a little deeper . . . Islam made me want to live up to the expectations of being thoughtful and righteous. Islam set me up to become the MC and independent man that I wanted to be."[10]

An offshoot of the Nation of Islam, and even more unorthodox than the
NOI, the Nation of Gods and Earths, or Five Percenters, was the brainchild
of Clarence 13X (1928–1969), a former member of the Nation of Islam who
sought to bring his version of Islam to the "hustlers, pimps, drug dealers, and
thieves on the street corners who needed it the most," to quote U-God of
the Wu-Tang Clan.[11] "The focal point," Rakim tells us about their impact,
"had shifted from the mosque to the hood, the street, the park, and the
stage—wherever MC's grabbled the mic."[12] Instead of proselytizing middle-
class black folk, the Five Percenters concentrated on the black underclasses,
helping poor and disadvantaged youth recognize and uncover, beneath the
humble outer layers, the truth about their divine origins, a message that was
explosive for presuming that God resided, like a pearl within a shelled mol-
lusk, within the souls of the most unwanted members of society. Composed
of a "supreme mathematics" and a "supreme alphabet," Five Percenter theology recalls ancient Pythagorean and Platonic principles—where knowledge
of geometry is knowledge of the divine, as Plato put it—as well as the mystical principles of letters, as in Kabbalist and Sufi traditions. Numbers and letters, in other words, contain secret meanings, their simple appearance, like a
rabbit's hole, hiding a mysterious and labyrinthine warren of significations,
principles, and beliefs. Never mind what a prosaic math teacher might say,
numbers and letters are infinitely mysterious in this view.[13] And, deciphered
correctly, they add up to a novel and revolutionary insight, one that under-
mines the usual accounts of black life in the United States: "The 120 Lessons," says U-God, "taught us to unlearn the lies that shackled us and replace that with genuine attempts to fill in history that was purposefully left out
of the history books. From birth, we're bombarded with a single idea: that we
were and are slaves. . . . Even at a young age, these degrees, these 120 Lessons,
gave me and my crew our first real knowledge of self."[14]

It's hard to say if Rakim would have been a masterful emcee without the
Lessons, but I think it's fair to say, at minimum, that the "supreme alphabet"
taught him to examine language, in his own words, "like a scientist examining
an atom, considering it from every angle, seeing what I could get out of it."[15]
Ordinary words, seen with his seer-like eyes, almost always had false bottoms
in this respect, giving way to a deep ocean of esoteric possibilities. And because the man was often trying to school his audience, neither the shouting
manner of Run-DMC nor the garbled, slurred enunciation of many Southern rappers worked for him. The words meant too much, the ideas were too
weighty; they couldn't be muddled, lest they risk confounding his listeners.
He used his words carefully and thoughtfully, hoping that he might make a
street-corner kid suddenly turn righteous.

Fitting for such lofty purposes, Rakim has become one of the first rappers to be venerated in the culture, his gift with words cherished the way that St. Anthony of Padua's tongue, jaw, and vocal cords were turned into relics in the Middle Ages. Like St. Anthony, patron saint of lost things, revered for his power as an orator and a preacher as well as for his undying love for the poor, Rakim used his tongue and vocal cords to rescue the lost and forgotten of the late twentieth century, and to share with them one of the most radical and rebellious ideas imaginable: that human beings are made up of divine material, the stuff of stars.

Defiant, Militant Hip-Hop

If Run-DMC and Rakim were too street for middle-class America (as Russell Simmons suggested), Public Enemy was too ominous. By the 1980s, as Reagan's war on drugs and war on crime dropped bombs on black, brown, and Indigenous communities (with policies, for instance, that equipped police departments with military-like arsenals to target, abuse, incarcerate, and sometimes kill ghetto residents), and as the emcee increasingly replaced the preacher of old as the voice of the black poor, Public Enemy arose from the ashes like dark, avenging angels, their voices an eruption of long-suppressed rage. While Run-DMC and Rakim blazed trails for ghetto-centric styles, Public Enemy broke new ground for militant hip-hop, sounding an alarm, echoing the commotion of the streets, and exhorting everyone to "fight the power." More riotous and frenetic than Run-DMC's music (thanks to advances in sampling and sequencing technology), they made use of a cacophonous mixture of noises—furious beats, squeals, sirens, scratches, loops from soul and funk—to assault the airwaves, stir up black pride, and denounce white supremacy. Phrases from Malcolm X were added to beats from R&B, soul, and funk; high-pitched squeals of the saxophone were joined with funky drumbeats; scratches and jarring noises coexisted with Chuck D's volcanic baritone; the grooves, grunts, and shouts of James Brown and his band the J.B.'s were boosted with computer-enhanced drum kicks; loops were added on top of loops. The result was a polyrhythmic and sonically dense sound that covered all 360 degrees of the black experience, a delirious collection of samples. It resembled a jam session, tossed together with the skill of a master conductor, which in this case was the production crew known as the Bomb Squad, a name that says it all. Aiming for a sense of urgency, the Bomb Squad increased the tempo of the music and called for Chuck D to race through the verses, his couplets attacking the mic with impunity. While the thunderous bass line and speaker-wrecking volume were constants—perfectly married to Chuck's D's deep-throated, roaring, stentorian voice—the Bomb Squad also added a barrage of trilling, strident, and dissonant sounds—the "devil's interval," or tritone—when they needed to unnerve their audience, adding a sinister and threatening flavor to the sound. Their song "Rebel Without a Pause," for instance, was acrimonious, shrill, dissenting, and unruly. "The song's harsh timbres and clashing rhythms," writes Loren Kajikawa, "gave rise to the sound of insistence that Pareles described as uncompromisingly confrontational and that the group itself referred to in song titles such as 'Bring the Noise,' 'Louder Than a Bomb,' and 'Countdown to Armageddon.'"[16]

In approximating the upheaval of Armageddon—earth-shattering bass, sonic tornadoes, lyrical hailstorms, solar eclipses, blustery mayhem, tumultuous crowd noises—Public Enemy converted the apocalyptic beliefs of the book of Revelation into audible revelations, proclaiming judgment against America for its sins and crimes. Like Malcolm X on his soapbox, Chuck D, the central voice of the group, used orotund rhetoric and rhymes, laced with grunts, shouts, and howls, to accost everyone within earshot. By turns menacing and theatrical, threatening and histrionic, dissonant and sonorous, tragic and comic, prophetic and jester-like, the group discharged lyrical and sonic riffs against all homogenized middle-class values. And, recall, Flavor Flav wore an oversized clock around his neck, signaling that time is up, and that one must act now on behalf of racial justice, at this moment! The clock implied not chronological or sequential time (*kronos*), mind you, but a disruptive and decisive moment of judgment (*kairos*), what Mexicans refer to as *la hora de la hora*, a moment of truth, a reckoning. It signified, in short, a prophetic and eschatological notion of time, with the angel of history blasting his horn in anticipation of the apocalypse.

This was far more than ghetto reportage; it was righteous belligerence, a riot in Dr. King's or Malcolm X's understanding of the term. Peter Shapiro sizes up their contributions in these words (specifically describing *It Takes a Nation of Millions to Hold Us Back*, 1988): "No punk or speed metal album has harnessed the power of chaos and rage as effectively; no folk album has been as articulate in its anger; no reggae or gospel album has been as righteous; no avant-garde album has been as experimental and as coherent."[17]

Reality/Gangster Rap

As timely as this tradition still seems to my ears in 2021, this sort of ethical-political criticism lost its sharp, cutting edge in the 1990s, got blunted by cheaper thrills. In lieu of black medallions, raised fists, and dreadlocks, in lieu of protest and agitprop, hip-hop started to dance to a different beat, a more raw and crude and truculent brand of sound. Forget the deep messages and thoughtful rhymes, rap music became drunk on guns, drugs, gangster fantasies, and macho aggression, the souls of the rappers seemingly escaping through their mouths. The reign of deft and tricky rhymes, deep spirituality, and knotty wordplay was over. The appeal to the angels of our better nature in civil rights and black power, the gods among the Five Percenters, or cultural ancestors and griots among spoken-word pioneers were replaced by the devils of our nature.

N.W.A. is the most famous case. In the world they helped create, the vocabulary of hip-hop underwent a sea change yet again, turning more grimy and muddy, rude and foul, like waters polluted by the sludge and muck of industrial life. What Toni Morrison has noted about the deterioration of language applies to N.W.A. and other gangster rappers: "Children have bitten their tongues off and use bullets instead to iterate the void of speechlessness, of disabled and disabling language, of language adults have abandoned altogether as a device for grappling with meaning, providing guidance, or expressing love."[18]

To be fair, though, N.W.A. produced music that mirrored the crack-infested streets of their blocks, music that typified the harsh and cruel realities of 1980s Compton. They suspended any and all scruples in their tales of the dark side of American life, offering gritty and graphic—gothic, even—descriptions of what happened to black youth in the infernos of American cities. They established themselves as diagnosticians of social ills, police brutality, and economic ruin in urban life, and they diagnosed these things without offering any answers or cures, without pretending to be preachers or prophets. They delivered street knowledge in unfiltered and undiluted forms, a kind of reportage—however exaggerated and sensational—from the foxholes of the ghetto. Because sheepish behavior didn't guarantee fair and just treatment by the white world, they depicted themselves as creepy, callous, and wolfish, predators, not prey. In this feral condition—a metamorphosis more like Ovid's Lycaon than the meek Gregor Samsa—they were finally unmuffled, now at liberty to bark and rage against the dystopian conditions of their city. If their raps were vulgar, grotesque, and shocking, Compton life was even uglier, they implied. Children were raised in drug-infested hoods, chased by crooked cops, dogged by racism and gangs, imperiled by poverty, subject to failing schools, circumscribed in opportunity, and doomed to life in prison or an early grave. These realities, accepted with casual indifference by the

American public, were far more appalling than the curse words that they used to hurl at the police.

Apart from the glaring failings in taste and judgment, anyhow, there were numerous moments of prophetic clarity on their groundbreaking album, *Straight Outta Compton* (1988). The music video for "F- the Police," for one, flips the script on the judicial system's abuse of black and brown folk and puts the police on trial, with Judge Dre presiding. It opens in a courtroom with each rapper offering testimony to abusive police violence. Ice Cube is first to raise his hand, promising to tell the truth, the whole truth, and nothing but the truth: "A young nigga got it bad 'cause I'm brown/ And not the other color so police think/ they have the authority to kill a minority. . . . Searchin' my car, lookin' for the product/ Thinkin' every nigga is sellin' narcotics." MC Ren and Eazy-E are next to testify, and they are equally scathing, their depositions like cups of wrath running over respectable behavior. The song, in essence, is a fantasy where the black man is large and in charge, where the last come first and the first come last, an apocalyptic subversion of the status quo. Anticipating the explosive anger of the LA riots of 1992, the Ferguson Uprising of 2014, or the protests and riots of 2020, it presents a case against generations of abuse by police and other authorities. Tired of acting like welcoming mats for such indignities, they rejected docile and gentle and reasonable manners, calling instead for the fire, the whirlwind, and the earthquake, a raging storm of rhetoric. They aimed their savage lyrics at a society that had been historically savage against black Americans, a society that had continued in the 1990s, long after the gains of civil rights legislation, to send young black males to prison at five times the rate of white males, a society where black males were twenty-one times more likely to be killed by the police than white counterparts.[19] With these things in mind, they shouted their lyrics, wrapping their voices around each word as though they were trying to wring the neck of a rooster.

And the music, dark as a coal mine, told the same story; before the lyrics said anything, we were presented with a world that is rough, conflicted, and unfairly prejudicial against black youth. For Jeff Chang, the song was an anthem "for the fatherless, brotherless, state-assaulted, heavily armed West Coast urban youth"; Greg Tate said it "put listeners within point blank range of LA gang mentality"; David Mills remarked that it was "about as easy to ignore as a stray bullet ripping through your living room window"; David Toop called it "a nightmarish record, its sound effects of police sirens, gunshots, and screeching tires depicting a generation virtually in the throes of war"; Loren Kajikawa noted how the rappers had to practically yell when rapping, "as if they must raise their voices to be heard over the cacophony."[20] And

Kiese Laymon, now speaking about the broader pattern of police abuse that it exposed, read the song as an epitaph of sorts: "The existence of the song is proof that even if we could not bring as much material suffering to white folk as they did to us, we could memorialize and channel the spirits of those beaten and killed by nasty-ass cheaters."[21]

In such ways, Dr. Dre, the mastermind of the group's organized noise, orchestrated the chaos of Compton life into an eloquent musical pattern, memorializing the abused and dead with raucous beats. Following the lead of Marley Marl and the Bomb Squad, Dr. Dre used funk samples, the TR-808 drum machine, horn drones, gunshots, screams, screeching tires, and his own musical instincts to craft combative and ruffian rhythms, raiding the eardrums with anarchic sound waves. The music careened through the track, as if it was swerving to avoid the police, grinding as a matter of survival, protesting in fits of outrage, macking for fun, and creeping like a thief in the night.

The album, and this is the crux of it, captured the fallen world of South Central Los Angeles, a world close in miles to "Lalaland," but infinitely distant in lifestyle and opportunity. In contrast to the sunny beaches, star-studded avenues, and wide-open spaces of California dreamscapes, N.W.A. drew scenarios of besieged and blockaded spaces, a world constricted by poverty, gangs, police forces, and "tough on crime" laws that led to the mass incarceration of black and brown young men. Their sketch of ghetto life echoed what anthropologists like João Costa Vargas wrote about the "widespread social forces galvanized against Black spatial mobility" in South Central Los Angeles.[22] It revealed the grim underbelly of SoCal, a world as confined and claustrophobic as the bottom of a well.

If the sexism, hedonism, and violence of the album belong in hip-hop's dump yard, as I surely believe, the album's indictment of social ruin—the effects of crack cocaine, economic disinvestment, police abuse, judicial prejudice, gun laws, and political apathy—remains disturbingly relevant in the new millennium. In this light alone, the album was a canary in a coal mine, an indicator of the racked and rent social fabric in parts of the United States, past and present.

Meanwhile, on the East Coast, the Wu-Tang Clan represented another variant of this legacy, a philosophy steeped in the mystical teachings of the Five Percenters, on the one hand, and the jarring and violent realities of New York ghettos in the 1980s and 1990s, on the other. With the release of *Enter the Wu-Tang (36 Chambers)* (1993), Wu-Tang took a stab at reclaiming East Coast supremacy in hip-hop, once a bedrock assumption. Making due with shoddy lo-fi equipment, raw chops, kung fu movie samples, streetwise spirituality, limited choruses, and haunting melodies, *Enter the Wu-Tang* captured the unnerving tension in the New York air, as if they were registering a coming danger like an animal sniffing the air for a predator's scent. If only to protect themselves from such threats—"Protect Ya Neck," they advised—their lyrics were rabid and foaming at the mouth, they growled and snarled.

"Bring da Ruckus," to take only one example, opens with a sample from the kung fu movie *Shaolin and Wu Tang*, and then gives way to Ghostface's verse, a collection of ten bars or so. As Ghostface enters the cipher, RZA mutes most of the music, creating a gap or "drop-out" in order to foreground the rapper's lines. The delayed rhythm adds suspense in the song, as we await the banging drumbeats to kick in. And when the beat does arrive, it arrives in full force, hell breaking loose, a raucous cacophony of various drum loops, spooky squeals, menacing pitches, minor piano keys, honking horn sounds, reverb, echo, and attacking vocals. Naturally, percussion is a major force in the song, but it's hardly uniform in timbre: cracking finger snaps, kick drum and snare hits, and a variety of other thumping drumbeats (with one loop that sounds close at hand, and another one that wallops and echoes from a distance, as if it was recorded in a dusty dungeon deep below the earth, ricocheting off chamber-like walls), all of them have their own texture. There's a volcanic energy through it all, a pounding force that sounds like the music is discharging and venting gases that have been trapped underground too long. It indicated, in my mind, a refusal to remain silent, a refusal to give prejudice or poverty or despair the final word. It indicated spiritual resilience, a toughness that came from the soul as much as the body.

The architect of the group, RZA, would make sure, in fact, that their wall of sound, big and esoteric like an Egyptian obelisk, would speak to the soul as much as the body. He took up music as some kind of spiritual exercise, honing his skills on the streets of Staten Island ("Shaolin," as they called it), as if he was some Peripatetic philosopher or Buddhist monk. Before founding Wu-Tang, it was his practice to walk the streets as a form of meditation: "Like most meditation," he writes, "those walks on Staten Island didn't create something; they revealed something—something that was already floating over the island, ready to take form."[23] A midwife of these truths more than a lone creator, RZA was able to deliver what he learned on these treks to the hip-hop world, rendering them in a musical vocabulary that was simultaneously ethereal and street. His walks, meandering and pensive, were exploratory exercises, surveys of outer and inner worlds. They opened up the doorways of his imagination, bringing him face to face not only with the street corners of his world, but also, as his book on the subject suggests, the Tao.[24] In this way, the search for the perfect beat, the perfect meter, and the perfect rhyme was always connected to the search for the Way for him, the music a reflection of the mysterious rhythms and flows that course through the universe.

N.W.A., by contrast, never learned such things, never, as far as I can tell, sought transcendence or the Tao. They were deaf to the street wisdom that Inspectah Deck expounds upon on "C.R.E.A.M.": "Ready to give up so I seek the Old Earth/ Who explained working hard will help you maintain/ to learn to overcome the heartaches and pain/ We got stick-up kids, corrupt cops, and crack rocks/ And stray shots, all on the block that stays hot/ Leave it up to me while I be livin' proof/ To kick the truth to the young black youth." N.W.A. may have kicked the truth about ghetto life in the United States, but they were rarely living proof of some higher truth, and even more rarely willing to listen to women's voices for wisdom and insight, as the Wu-Tang verse implies (the Old Earth is code or cipher for an older, wiser woman, and the song narrates the growth of this young man as he internalizes her advice). Wu-Tang, it's true, had some of the same flaws as N.W.A. (a fierceness that can be indistinguishable from violence and hostility), but the traces of mysticism and Eastern philosophy in their music — or Socrates's philosophies on "Triumph" — gave their music a deeper purpose, and prevented it, in my opinion, from going over the edge of the abyss. As Diotima was to Socrates in *The Symposium*—the mysterious priestess (possibly Egyptian) who taught the young Socrates about wisdom and love—the Old Earth was to Wu-Tang, only in the Wu-Tang's case the wisdom was raw and streetwise, and contained the revolutionary concept— inspired by the Bible—that these young black men, though descendants of slaves still living in segregated communities in the 1990s, had the potential to be divine, and the cream of planet earth, a lesson, as we've seen, that many rappers on the East Coast would absorb.

G-Funk/Hip-Hop Soul

While Wu-Tang was aspiring to the hermetic knowledge of the Nation of Gods and Earths, and Ice Cube was claiming the Lessons of the Nation of Islam, Dr. Dre marched to a completely different tune on *The Chronic* and *Doggystyle*. Known as G-funk, the music not only turned away from the spiritual and political themes of black power, it also turned away from the clamorous fury of N.W.A. It embraced slow and easy rhythms, perfect for laid-back gratifications. In contrast to the frenetic and violent world of N.W.A. or Wu-Tang, a world beset by countless hazards and terrors, Dre's "gangsta funk" concentrated attention less on the ghetto as a site of danger than as a site of pleasure and possibility.[25] In order to strike a cooler and more celebratory note, and to complement Snoop Dogg's breezy and sedate flow, Dr. Dre chose relaxed, smooth, and chilled rhythms for *The Chronic*, borrowing from the laid-back grooves of Donny Hathaway, Quincy Jones, and George Clinton. They furnished the soulful mood of the album, but the thematic content was unmistakably his own. His vision of "liberation"—personal, materialistic, neoliberal, hedonistic—explicitly disavowed the collective dreams of civil rights and black power (all key to the R&B and soul generations), and put the focus on self-determination and self-aggrandizement; getting paid, and by any means necessary, became synonymous with liberation. The pleasures of the body were extolled over the life of the mind, dance rhythms over meditative vibes, gangster cool over prophetic rage, aesthetics over ethics, sweet low-riders over sweet chariots. In his mind, the rage for social justice and righteousness was now spent and exhausted, faded and washed out. Enough already, Dre rapped on "Let Me Ride," with "medallions, dreadlocks, or black fists."

Dr. Dre, appropriately, turned to the symbol of weed, or chronic, to characterize the mellow, anaesthetizing, and ludic music that he was making. He turned away from all sociological or ethical-political concerns toward a stricter concern with songcraft, aiming for a sound that was cool and chilled out, a sound that put "hooks and beats on cruise control," as Marcus Reeves puts it.[26] This was music for leisure and recreation, for partying and cruising in the six-fo. Marx or Adorno would have called this brand of music an "opiate of the masses," and they would have been right in some ways; it was, indeed, escapist like cannabis or chronic, decadent like a Mardi Gras festival, and purely individualistic like a Reagan-era capitalist. For Dr. Dre, though, it was enough for this brand of hip-hop—with its droopy flows and signature "funky worm" synthesizer squeals (from the Ohio Players' song by that name)—to wring drops of joy and pleasure out of ghetto life.

Say what you will about it, *The Chronic* delivered some of the most influential, funky, and soulful grooves in hip-hop. With juicy riffs from funk, live rhythm guitars, whistling keyboard lines, cracking snares, soulful choruses, and the pleasing whine of the synthesizer, Dre composed music that would have youth around the world feeling the flow, bobbing their heads, and leaning like a gangster. R&B was the not-so-secret ingredient of the subgenre, the smooth rhythms and melodies much more pleasing to the ears than N.W.A.'s rancorous and clashing sounds. The music blends were mellifluous, honeyed, and sweet on the ear. They rolled over the listener in bouncing ripples, making you feel that you are riding on hydraulics and smoothly cruising the bumpy streets.

For the G-funk classic "Let Me Ride," for example, Dr. Dre sampled

"Mothership Connection" by Parliament-Funkadelic, a song that includes the supplicating bridge "Swing down, sweet chariot/ Stop and let me ride."[27] In Dre's refurbished version, however, the flossy low-rider replaced the heavenly chariot. One can point to the title of Dizzy Gillespie's "Swing Low, Sweet Cadillac" (1967) as a possible model, but it's clear that Dre's music is a product of the early 1990s, especially in its hedonistic revels and political cynicism. "Everybody was trying to do this black power and shit," Dr. Dre reported, "so I was like, let's give 'em an alternative."[28] This alternative had California "tatted" on its chest and would mirror the unhurried pace of life in SoCal, fixated on riding the waves of pleasure and fun. Released months after the 1992 LA riots, *The Chronic* would put on wax not the anger and frustration of Compton and other ghettos (he already did this with N.W.A.), but rather the brief elixirs of freedom and friendship made possible by the post-riot gang truces. *The Chronic* spoke to, writes Jeff Chang, "the ecstatic sense of freedom of being able to drive down the street without worrying about cops or enemies."[29] It communicated a wild and anarchic freedom, coasting through the streets of Los Angeles unmindful of getting ambushed or profiled. Because the real thing was lacking, it would broadcast the *fantasy* of freedom, the fantasy of mobility for those hemmed in the hood. Ironically, the illusions of freedom in the music were proof of the exact opposite: the dreams of lighting out for the open road were proof of how much communities of color felt confined, even interned, by the cellblocks of their city. At least in this way, *The Chronic* remained anchored by the painful realities of the streets, even if these things are now seen through the rearview mirror of the low-rider, fading into the background as the Impala rolls away.

The automobile, in other words, became a means of flight in the music, the equivalent of the train in the blues. Paul Gilroy's phrase "auto-autonomy" is perfectly applicable, the term encapsulating the pleasures of momentary escape on the road, a passage to somewhere else, anywhere else.[30] Attention lavished on cars in Los Angeles—rims that bling, paint that pops, lo-pro tires, bouncing hydraulics—was part of this quest for freedom, too. If beautifying one's derelict neighborhood was beyond your power, you might, at least, beautify your clothing, walk, talk, car, or all four. If your home was shabby, you might turn your ride into a chic mobile home of sorts, creating a moving piece of pomp and pageantry. Perhaps we should see Ezekiel's chariot in this way: pimped out with sapphire, crystals, and "wheels of topaz or beryl that gleam" (Ezekiel 1:16), it must have represented splendor, color, freedom, and above all, God's resplendent presence to the Israelites during a period of confinement, captivity, and exile. (Ezekiel lived and prophesied during the Babylonian Exile, 597–539 BCE.) It must have represented a chariot that could, as the African American spiritual puts it, swing low and carry them home, a vehicle of transcendence.[31]

Be that as it may, the differences between Ezekiel's chariot—notwithstanding the way it is blinged-out—and Dr. Dre's low-rider are more glaring, of course. Seen in the broader context of Ezekiel's oracles, or the Hebrew prophets as a whole, Ezekiel's chariot is a medium of communal redemption, as well as a vehicle of judgment against any vision that fails to speak on behalf of the poor and needy, that withholds bread from the hungry, and that exploits desperate individuals by usury and other acts of greed (Ezekiel 18:10ff). By contrast, the low-rider that appears in the chronicles of G-funk glides through the streets of Compton without any mindfulness or concern for others, asleep at the wheel. It lacks Ezekiel's wakefulness.

The vogue that G-funk established, at any rate, was not a lone voice in hip-hop; this trend, a marriage of hard-core rap and chilled rhythms, also surfaced on the East Coast with P. Diddy, Biggie, and Bad Boy Records, and later in the South with No Limit and Cash Money Records. I myself was never fond of P. Diddy—he always seemed to me that he was too blinded and mesmerized by the color of money, like Jay Gatsby—but there is no denying that he had a fine ear for musical talent; he was a pioneer, really, of R&B and hip-hop fusions on the East Coast, what came to be known as "hip-hop soul." If he didn't create "hip-hop soul" out of thin air—Kid Capri had been fusing together R&B vocals with hard rap beats on the East Coast, and G-funk's influence was felt everywhere—P. Diddy, to his credit, knew what flavors and tastes mainstream America craved, and he hustled like a shot caller to supply the product. And then, pure serendipity, he stumbled upon Biggie, the rotund rapper with a rich and resounding baritone, and a remarkable gift for storytelling, turns of phrase, and hypnotic rhymes piled on top of each other. From an ethical standpoint, this version of hip-hop replaced Dr. King's dream of equality and justice for all with dreams of private wealth and privilege and took a step backward; from an aesthetical perspective, thanks to Biggie's deft lyricism, hip-hop was as entertaining and skillful as ever.

I can't think of a better example of the changing spirit of the age—a step forward and backward at once—than Biggie's "Party and Bullshit": the song sampled the bongo-driven ballad by the Last Poets, "Niggers Are Scared of Revolution," a song that roasted and ridiculed black folk who preferred partying over the serious business of social action. The Last Poets complain that black men love to "talk about pimping," and love to mess around with pool, craps, and other amusements, and, ultimately, only want to "party and bullshit." Biggie, like a young student bored by a staid lecture, not only disregards the message, but turns the anthem into a party song, flipping the Last Poets' satire and parody on its head! And he does it with so much rhythm and flow that it sucks the listener into the song's powerful jet stream of sound. Call it shallow if you wish, but if you read between the lines, Biggie has a point to make with the dance-happy song: namely, that for all the activist rhetoric of the 1960s and 1970s—with the likes of the Last Poets, Public Enemy, Brand Nubian, et al.—nothing has changed. If anything, with the onset of the crack epidemic, it's gotten worse.[32]

In terms of style, in any event, Biggie quickly found his voice with the help of P. Diddy, now adjusting and calibrating his flows to run slower and smoother, making them match the easy ripples of the Isley Brothers, DeBarge, Grover Washington, Mtume, and so on. Others might have slipped or fallen before the challenge of a new simmered-down rhythm, but Biggie was a rare mic controller, capable of switching flows, voices, and perspectives at a moment's notice, capable of deft wordplay. While he could be menacing and nihilistic—say, with "Gimme the Loot," "Unbelievable," "Warning," "Suicidal Thoughts," "Somebody's Gotta Die," or "Kick in the Door"—he also flourished with lighter and breezier joints like "Big Poppa," "One More Chance," "Hypnotize," "I Got a Story to Tell," "Mo Money Mo Problems," "Going Back to Cali," and "Juicy." With the velvety and tantalizing R&B that P. Diddy brought to the table, Biggie's mouth watered with delight, the rapper now chewing on his words a bit slower and less aggressively than when he first spit rhymes on Brooklyn street corners. This new rap persona didn't attack the mic in the manner of Chuck D or Wu-Tang; he caressed and charmed it instead, dropping one suave line after another, and usually on top of nicely chosen samples, like Mtume's addictive "Juicy Fruit." The rhymes trickled out of his mouth smoothly and leisurely, hanging in the air long enough to let the words sink into his listeners. And though Biggie could add shades of thematic depth to his verses—as in the powerful description of stress and desperation that comes with being poor and black in America on "Everyday Struggle" or "Things Done Changed"—he usually worked within the confining parameters of P. Diddy's ghetto chic. But even in these cases, he could be magical with trivial subject matters, converting shallow and base themes into something golden. Some of the rhymes may have been simple and straightforward, but Biggie added all sorts of metrical and rhythmic variations—enjambment, counter-stresses, prosodic innovations—to sweeten and enhance the lyricism. For this reason, his rhymes, agile and swift and unpredictable, are impossible to evaluate when only seen on the page, the sonority of the words so much more mesmerizing when heard. When he interpolates, to take only one example, the extremely corny line from Shawn Brown's "Rappin' Duke" (1984) on his classic "Juicy"—"duh-ha, duh-ha"—he magically transforms the phrase into something cool and melodic, a sound that is guttural and honeyed at the same time, part moan, part grunt, part warble, all soul. Biggie's bars and flows were almost always stimulating in this way, his words vibrating and surging through your veins, recharging the drained cells of your body.

But as far as myths go, or theologies go, the "culture of bling" that P. Diddy and Dr. Dre helped create was awfully small. From a theological perspective, the sin was not only ethical in nature ("what does it profit a man if he gains the whole world and loses his soul?"); the sin was also aesthetical, a glaring lack of taste. Will Ashon puts his finger on the right pressure point: "The criticism of Puffy shouldn't have been for a lack of realism, but for embracing the wrong alternative to 'realism,' a wet dream of cut-price oligarch chic. To replace reality with such a weak and sickly myth, with such a lack of imagination, that was the sin."[33] And though Biggie Smalls redeemed some of P. Diddy's sins, it remains true that he was constrained by a limited repertoire of topics and themes, a vision awash in the venal, covetous, and self-absorbed dreams of consumer capitalism. If he had lived beyond his twenty-four years, we may have witnessed the young man leave the familiar shores of Bad Boy Records and begin to navigate deeper and more uncharted waters. Truth is, this had already started to happen in the year before his untimely murder. In the wake of Tupac's death, and after he was hospitalized in a car accident in 1996, Biggie underwent an existential crisis that jolted and altered his soul. He started talking to God: "God was like," in his own words, "you moving too fast, Bam! Slow down. Lay in this bed for the next two months and think about what you're going to do."[34] He also had a new tattoo etched on his forearm, Psalm 27: "The Lord is my light and my salvation, whom shall I fear?" Staring death in the face, literally laid out on his back, had a way of jarring the young man, forcing him to turn his focus to fatherhood and more eternal matters. Like so many blues pioneers in later years, I imagine that Biggie would have gradually emerged from the darkness, walking, talking, rapping, and blinking into the light.

Alternative Rappers

In spite of the popularity of gangster chic in the late twentieth century, hip-hop produced various alternatives in the 1990s and early 2000s that resisted the affiliation with gangster rap, many of them emerging from the shadows to offer competing versions of "street knowledge." Sometimes dubbed "conscious," "knowledge," "alternative," "underground," or "bohemian" rap, these artists offered more nuanced studies of street life, expanding the concepts of rap beyond the conventional yarns of crime, drug use, material excess, and sexual conquest. In the process, they blazed a path for the post-gangster, post-bling era of hip-hop.

For groups like Freestyle Fellowship, the Hieroglyphics, the Pharcyde, De La Soul, A Tribe Called Quest, the Fugees, the Roots, Mos Def, Talib Kweli, Immortal Technique, Lauryn Hill, Common, Bahamadia, Black Sheep, Digable Planets, Brand Nubian, Jurassic 5, Organized Konfusion, et al., hip-hop was more complex and sophisticated than gangster rap had ever imagined, its soul deeper and more byzantine. To prove this point, many of the beat-makers of these groups sought to redraw the boundaries of the hip-hop nation, expanding into uncharted terrain, exploring new, exotic sounds. The influence of jazz surfaced in many instances, its presence indicating, as jazz often does, profundity, sophistication, and creativity. For the track "Inner City Boundaries," by Freestyle Fellowship, for example, bebop aesthetics were front and central. Emerging from the underground hip-hop scene of Los Angeles (affiliated with the Good Life Café scene), the group found inspiration in all manner of music: live jazz bands at Leimert Park, Billy Joel's piano licks, the J.B.'s juicy bass lines, and riffs of the jazz guitarist Grant Green. For "Inner City Boundaries," the group employed live jazz instruments—upright bass, saxophone, bongos, xylophone, drum set—and delivered their lyrics in a similar jazzy fashion: improvisational, spontaneous, choppy, and with scat vocals that sounded like they were speaking in tongues. Peculiar and eccentric, their rapping had a stream-of-consciousness vibe to it—and what they said mattered to them as much as how they said it. The sung chorus of "Inner City Boundaries" says it all: "I've gotta be righteous, I've gotta be me/ I've gotta be conscious, I've gotta be free."

The collaborate Native Tongues crew—a collection of the Jungle Brothers, A Tribe Called Quest, and De La Soul—worked in this vein as well. They had a pied piper influence on the school of "alternative" or "bohemian" rap, setting the tone for more colorful and catholic sounds in hip-hop, a near "cubist array," in Joseph Patel's words.[35] They created a new blueprint for the house of hip-hop, somewhere beyond the cookie-cutter designs, where alternative sounds and themes would be valued and prized. The Jungle Brothers' joint *Straight Out the Jungle*, to take one example, opens with African acoustics, drawing from Mandrill and Manu Dibango in addition to the godfather of funk, James Brown. Doing their part to revive Afrocentrism, their music and message combined aesthetics of the global African diaspora with the syntax and slang of African Americans. And then there was the incomparable group De La Soul: the production of Prince Paul on *3 Feet High and Rising* took beat-digging to a more virtuosic and erudite level. He cribbed all sorts of sound,

from pop and lounge rock to the requisite P-Funk, adding pastels and fuch-
sias and upbeat yellows to the stock black-and-white palettes of mainstream
hip-hop. The psychedelic depth of his arrangements, matching the cryptic
nature of the verses, conveyed the impression of mystery and esotericism in
the music, the sound itself suggestive of complexity and obscurity. Even if
one couldn't fully decipher the rhymes (they were as enigmatic as the writing
on the wall in the book of Daniel), everyone who heard them was certain that
they were deep, as if they came from the mouth of a sage or sibyl who knew
more than anyone else.

Many of these things, minus the cryptic language, could be said about
A Tribe Called Quest's work, too; Ali Shaheed and Q-Tip would scavenge
for forgotten licks and beats among a variety of genres: the Beatles, Lou
Reed, psychedelic soul, and, of course, jazz. Their albums, *The Low End Theory* (1991) and *Midnight Marauders* (1993), are true classics, tight and measured, smooth and silky, groovy and funky, soft and hard. Tribe proved that
mellow cadences and cool flows could have the force of a thousand ham-
mers, like cascading waters carving into a granite coastline. They didn't
need to boast about cookin' up bricks, moving kilos of weight, or bustin'
caps in order to communicate vigor; their deft lyricism, sonic pastiches, and
abstract wordplay were weighty enough. Their power was spiritual more
than muscular, an unseen force like gravity or God. And while others messed
around with jazz, biting here and there, A Tribe Called Quest inhaled deep
lungfuls of it, breathing it in like fresh air in a stale, musty room.

Their soundscapes were awash in samples, as I've said: there were sitar
riffs from Rotary Connection, light piano grooves from Eugene Daniels, funky
guitars from RAMP, and, of course, percussive loops from all sorts of soul,
funk, and jazz masters, like Lou Reed, Luther Ingram, Rufus Thomas, Jimi
Hendrix, Grover Washington, Sly Stone, Minnie Riperton, the Ohio Players,
et al. Q-Tip, the gifted producer and rapper of the group, left no doubt that
he was a sophisticated crate-digger, capable of quoting obscure musical licks
like a gray-haired archivist. But at the same time, he wasn't a curator only interested in the old, nor an Afrofuturist only fixed on the future; Q-Tip thrived
in the here and now, offering new and original interpretations of past sounds.
It's tempting to compare Q-Tip's wide-ranging sampling to the sonic palette
of the Bomb Squad, but there are fundamental differences: they were both
"using samples as their primary weapons," notes Hanif Abdurraqib, "it's just
that Q-Tip was using the sample as a razor, and the Bomb Squad was using
samples as a machine gun. What Q-Tip's ethos was—trimming the useful
edges of a sample and blending multiple elements in the same song to create
a type of harmony—was almost antithetical to what the Bomb Squad aimed

for. While Q-Tip looked for connective tissue to create a single sound, the Bomb Squad was invested in piling noise on top of noise to create discord instead of harmony."[36]

They both spoke on behalf of the downtrodden, moreover, but while one sounded hot and raging, the other was cool and harmonious; one style was rife with dissonant noises and hit you over the head with a bass-wielding club, the other charmed and hypnotized with a magical wand, waving it over you until they got you to believe that Afrocentrism was the shit. In concept and thematic scope, too, the rhymes were often magical in their ability to alchemize the stuff of mundane life. It might be easy, upon a glance at the lyrics alone, to overlook this gift, but once you hear it performed, it becomes something infinitely richer and more mysterious than what exists on the page, like listening to a Quranic recitation in lieu of a plain reading. Q-Tip, aka Abstract, and Phife Dawg, aka the Five-Foot Assassin, were a complementary pair, a Don Quixote and Sancho Panza, respectively; Q-Tip employed his falsetto voice in a philosophical and seductive manner, while Phife was guttural, earthy, and pragmatic. They blended together beautifully, crafting introspective, thoughtful, playful, and spiritual concepts on the bedrock of jazz horns, funky bass, drum machines, African chants, blues licks, soft rock, and anything else that pleased their ears. Call them modernists, magical realists, postmoderns, or whatever is in vogue, they were true artists.[37]

At the end of the day, this "alternative" school was simultaneously iconoclastic and deeply orthodox: deconstructive of the many idols of the rap game (money, guns, drugs, etc.), on the one hand, and yet deferential toward the principles of hip-hop laid down by Afrika Bambaataa and the Zulu Nation. More than entertainment alone, they practiced hip-hop as an art of self-fashioning, not unlike the way a sculptor molds a block of clay, chiseling here and there, cutting and hammering, blasting and polishing, hoping that the inner beauty of the genre, and of their own souls, would be released in the end. If each of the arts of hip-hop was cherished and cultivated in these circles, the element of "supreme knowledge"—part of hip-hop's periodic table—received particular attention, its power as explosive as the discovery of atomic energy. And it was a discovery that they could hardly contain within themselves, bubbling up in buoyant and idealistic chords, a sharp divergence from the menacing minor keys of gangster rap. They expanded the sonic canvas of hip-hop in these ways because they couldn't see themselves in many of the customary sketches of gangster or mainstream rap. They sought out avant-garde sounds and themes—jazz licks, bouncing piano riffs, scat syllables, psychedelic vibes, and spiritual keys—to better represent the wild diversity of the black experience in America.

The Dirty South

If the alternative scene satisfied a taste for sophisticated, suave, and conscious motifs, the hip-hop exploding out of the Dirty South in the mid-1990s and early 2000s, like a pent-up volcano, let loose earthier and coarser rhythms— low-down, sensual, funky, guttural, greasy, down-to-earth, a firestorm of hot passions. Intentionally slighting profundity, and embracing compulsive dance rhythms, big fat beats, and a slurred lyricism that was just shy of gibber- ish, they made music that was exuberant and rambunctious, better suited for house-wrecking, club-bouncing, and rolling in the whip than anything more profound. Never mind the acclaim of mainstream media, or middle-class au- diences, they sought, above all, the love of the streets, desiring the esteem of Calliope, Melpomene, Magnolia, East Point, Decatur, and so on, the proj- ects and regions in which they were born and bred. And while some critics would line up to denigrate the Dirty South—blaming it for the death of "real" hip-hop—hardly anyone could deny that the music was charged with seismic power, the beats and rhythms shaking the tectonic plates of hip-hop and al- lowing places like New Orleans, Miami, Houston, Memphis, and Atlanta to suddenly come into view for the first time. Previously overlooked and under- appreciated, by the late 1990s Southern rap had begun to emerge from the briar patch of hip-hop like the legendary Br'er Rabbit.

Because politics had done little to help in this process of extrication, po- litical change having little or no impact on the daily lives of the underclasses in the late twentieth century, Southern rap turned to the stuff of music and celebration as their preferred means of liberation, even if it was just a small taste of it, a bite or nibble. Music, dance, and festivity, they declared in no uncertain terms, could relax the burdens and yokes of black life in imme- diate and physical ways, the sounds and bodily thrills stirring up the kind of life-affirming joy that we associate with the original spirit of hip-hop. The pioneering emcees in the South Bronx were, after all, "masters of the cere- monies," masters at hyping and enlivening the crowd, masters of the party. Since the focus was on the deejay in the early years, the emcee's formula for rap usually consisted of brief rhymes and simple catchphrases, nothing too complicated. Instead of speaking to the head, and cramming the mind with information, early hip-hop spoke to the heart and hips, making them skip and race with excitement. And Southern rappers picked up on this. They used James Brown–like grunts, shouts, and catchphrases, as well as the bass-heavy grooves of funk, to work the audience into a sweaty, rowdy mess. What Hua Hsu has written about P-Funk is also true of the Dirty South: "In a lot of music, bass is an ethereal presence, enforcing a song's spine in a way that you feel but rarely listen for. Yet Parliament built entire songs around the bassist Bootsy Collins's squiggly lines, sensual growls, and mighty thumps. The backbone, after all, is connected to the rear."[38]

Southern hip-hop built its music around these things, shoring up the scaffolding of the song with fat beats, brassy synthesizers, live instruments, and soul-crooning lyrics. They baptized their listeners in a long legacy of Southern aesthetics: food and fashion, preaching and signifyin', the spirituals and the devil's music. If coastal rappers have been more thoughtful and soulful in their lyrics, seeing rap as an occasion to instruct and inspire, one might argue that Southern rappers are more soulful in style and sonority. By embodying an unrefined and raw form of music, they brought hip-hop back to the roots in Stax soul, down-home blues, sweet gospel, and pure, uncut funk.[39] Or even back to the first stirrings of rock 'n' roll—what Nik Cohn says about classic rock music applies perfectly to Southern rap: "The lyrics were mostly non-existent, simple slogans one step away from gibberish. This wasn't just stupidity, simple inability to write anything better. It was a king of teen code, almost a sign language, that would make rock entirely incomprehensible to adults."[40]

Speaking of Southern lyricism, we would do well, as we wander through the corridors and mazes of hip-hop, to keep in mind Adam Bradley's helpful equation for evaluating pop music. He suggests that there is a continuum concerning the role of lyrics: on one end, the lyrics are virtually insignificant and servants of the music; at the other end, lyrics are king.[41] In the former case, the propulsive energy of the song is below the waist, in the groove and the bass, in the booty and feet, in the visceral delights of the form and style. Borrowing from A Tribe Called Quest's classic album, he calls this the "low end theory."[42] As we move to the other end of the continuum, however, the importance of the lyrics grows in importance, and demands greater attention to what is being said. The words are now freighted with meaning and purpose; they aim at the mind and spirit, hoping to school, provoke, and elevate the listener. The message matters more than the party.

Bearing this in mind, it might be said that much of the music of the Dirty South belongs, and *proudly*, at the low end of Bradley's continuum. But even this judgment, fair as it is, risks overlooking the richness and complexity of Southern rap, its sense of pomp and pageantry, its gospel fits of emotion, its signifying wit, its Afrofuturistic imaginings, its rich folklore and musical legacies, its old-time religion.

In the New Orleans scene, for instance, carnival's bubbly customs were undeniable influences: the call-and-response patterns of Mardi Gras Indians, raucous and up-tempo rhythms, bottom-heavy percussion, fast and sinuous flows, brass accents, clanging cowbells, chanted phrases, marching-band whistles, xylophones, masquerading and theatrical prodigality, riotous snares and the energetic dancing of second-line revelers ("buck jump time"), all of these things contributed to the region's raucous joys. "Bounce music," as it was called in New Orleans, would bottle these various ingredients, and then jazz them up with the streetwise sounds of hip-hop, particularly Miami bass, the Triggerman beat (from the song "Drag Rap" by the Showboys), slurred Bayou accents, and shout-outs to local projects like Calliope, Melpomene, and Magnolia.[43] The music struck a spirited, rousing, and, well, bouncing energy that lived and breathed for dancing, music with fizz and full-bodied flavor, music that bubbled, popped, and gushed like a shaken bottle of champagne.

New Orleans wasn't the only team in the game of Southern rap, however. If we shift our attention to other cities of the South—Memphis and Houston, for instance—the music changes tempos, flows, and cadences, dropping into a lower gear to mirror the crawling traffic in Memphis and Houston, the swampy, slurred eloquence of the Delta blues, the laggard rhythms of a West Texas drawl, or a warped music tape left out in the summer heat. While Miami bass and New Orleans bounce tended to be up-tempo, electric, and feverish, "prompting spastic dance-floor gyrations," the music that developed in Memphis and Houston was frequently languid and droopy, a cooling out of the hot, bouncing, clashing atoms of Miami and NOLA clubs.[44] The beats, druggy and dreamlike, were slowed and lengthened in order to extend their duration, making for good cruising music, swangin' and bangin' style. The bass oozed and crawled out of the speakers, causing everything in the car to quake, tremble, and throb. Houston's DJ Screw, a pioneer of the style, would decelerate the rhythms of rap, making his 45 records spin at 33⅓ revolutions to best approximate life in the Houston ghettos, languorous and distorted. Writing for the *New York Times*, Neil Strauss sized up the sound this way: "The results of DJ Screw's labors often sound like rap records played underwater on an old cassette deck that's running out of batteries and needs its tape heads cleaned. It is not music to dance to but music to lose yourself in, as if it is the last sound echoing in your head as you drift off to sleep."[45] Matching these drunken, rolling rhythms (heard on DJ Screw's mixtape *3 'n the Mornin'*, for instance), the pronunciation of words was likewise slowed and stretched to the breaking point, making the speech sound as if it had to travel through thick, humidified air, lagging and dawdling as it traveled to the ears.[46] The syllables, even before their release, seemed to be crammed together in the rapper's grill-packed mouth, competing for room in this congested space. As in the classic blues, scat singing, or in the low-pitched chants of Tibetan monks, there was a slurred and garbled eloquence about it.

Using local diction, inventive slang, and raggedy vocals, the strength of this form of rap was in the musical textures at the surface.[47] If violence was done to the rapped syllables, for instance—bending, twisting, pressing them into submission—it was to squeeze a new tone and cadence out of them, making them sound fresh even when the content was predictable. And, no doubt, the content was predictable, mainly revolving around dope-slanging, tippin' on fo-fos wrapped in Vogues, ridin' slab, sippin' on lean, flaunting one's candy-painted ride, and puffin' on swishas and sweets. The music was tight, the flows cool, and the concepts no deeper than a mirage in the desert sun— low end theory *par excellence*.

But just when we presumed to size up the Dirty South as the dregs of hip-hop, the Dungeon Family, from Atlanta, came into play and complicated the picture, adding touches of metaphysics and Afrofuturism, Southern cuisine and folklore, church music and funk to the genre. Goodie Mob's *Soul Food* was foundational in this respect, an album that combined the sacred and profane legacies of the South in one poignant dish. Ray Murray put it this way: "So when Goodie Mob came with *Soul Food*, it was like we were talking to your soul. We're giving nourishment for your spirit, that was the vibe."[48] Unlike more menacing and violent portraits of the "Dirty South" (say, in Master P, the Geto Boys, or Three 6 Mafia), or the disorderly spasms of "crunk" (say, in Lil Jon or the Ying Yang Twins), they rapped about the stuff of the soul, adding a spirit of righteousness to hard-core street parables; and, unlike cleaner and more sublime portraits of the South (say, in Arrested Development), they captured the coarse and sullied facts of ghetto life. In the end, *Soul Food* was "conscious" enough to satisfy the purists and prophets of hip-hop, and raw and grimy enough to satisfy profane tastes. The right balance of these things enabled Goodie Mob to strike a righteous note on the album without coming across as preachy or pedantic.

On the album, they took their listeners to overcrowded prisons ("Live at the O.M.N.I.," "One Million Niggas Inside"), toxic projects ("Cell Therapy"), internal mazes of the soul ("Thought Process"), and, of course, to the haunted landscapes of the Old South, "where you was bought, you was sold" ("Dirty South"). The rap "Dirty South" patented the term that would become all the rage, but unlike later renderings, the memory of slavery remains a part of the phrase's accent with Goodie Mob: "Life's a bitch, then you figure out/ Why you really got dropped in the Dirty South/ See in the third grade this is what you were told/ You was bought, you was sold." Some songs throb with anger for having to live in these circumstances ("I Didn't Ask to Come"); others are canticles of praise for the mothers of the group ("Guess Who"), or psalms of desolation that strike a bluesy pining tone, relinquishing rapping for a sung gospel refrain ("Free"). On the latter, CeeLo's voice quivers and soars into ethereal heights, striking mournful and aching notes: "'Cause I wanna be free, completely free/ Lord won't you please come and save me/ I wanna be free, totally free/ I'm not gon' let this world worry me." The sighing world-weariness of the verse is the key to CeeLo's otherworldliness in the song, his discontentment prodding him to look beyond the promises of the world. Man does not live by bread alone, CeeLo indicates in uncorked, gospel-like emotions.

My favorite song on the album is the delicious "Soul Food," a song that captures the past and present of the black South.[49] A pronounced Southern twang and drawl resounds in each rapper's delivery (gliding vowels, dropped syllables, swinging phonemes, laminal consonants), with enough vocal idiosyncrasies—T-Mo has a conversational, tenor flow; Big Gipp's verses are grainy, full-toned, and booming; Khujo sounds rough, huffy, and riled up; and CeeLo's falsetto tone is honeyed and dulcet—to supply the song with rich variety.

While the Southern dialect, garbled deliveries, and low-slung drawls are evocative of the blues in the song, the chorus gives us a clear taste of gospel fare, too, the voices coming together in serene and lilting harmonies, "curlicues, flowers, and frills." This is not the shouting, sweat-drenched catharsis of gospel, however, not naked shows of passion and heart-bursting joy, not the paroxysms of emotion that we associate with church revivals and such. Closer to the quiet and cool mood after a church has already gone up in smoke, when prayer follows the rapture of the Holy Ghost, the chorus on "Soul Food" is the peace after the storm. It's gospel music, for sure, but composed and tranquil. It invites everyone, especially the poor, the marginalized, and homeless, to the bounteous table of music, distributing beats and rhymes like the bread of communion.

If Goodie Mob captured the spiritual intensity of the black South, OutKast spotlighted life in the streets, clubs and, farther away, in the starry skies above. Sometimes street scholars, sometimes metaphysicians, sometimes players and jesters, always Southern in slang and style, OutKast has been among the most gifted groups in all of hip-hop. In record after record, André 3000 and Big Boi came to embody the image that they projected on *ATLiens*: that they were aliens from another galaxy of hip-hop, somewhere beyond the familiar stratosphere of hip-hop, rare stars in a constellation of ordinary planets. With traces of P-Funk's Afrofuturism, Sun Ra's *Space Is the Place*, Afrika Bambaataa's *Planet Rock*, or De La Soul's *3 Feet High and Rising* (all obsessed with outer-space motifs), songs like "ATLiens," "Elevators (Me & You)," "E.T. (Extraterrestrial)," or even "Two Dope Boyz (in a Cadillac)," all from *ATLiens*, took listeners on a far-flung journey, galactic and celestial, while remaining rooted in the hoods of East Point, Decatur, and so on.[50] Transcendence and earthiness were shared sites of revelation. If the funky bass lines, drum claps, and absorbing melodic hooks kept the listener grounded on the earth, the peculiar sounds on the album—alien ripples and burbles, distant echoing clangs, eerie synthesizer tones, uncanny coos and sloshes—transported the listener to another world. (Some samples were taken from Attilio Mineo, *Man in Space with Sounds*.) "Elevators," in particular, has a spacious and languid ambiance, with echoing rim shots, weird rings, and one of the coolest hooks on the album: "Me and you, your momma and your cousin, too/ Rollin' down the strip on Vogues/ Comin' up slammin' Cadillac doors." Though the lyrics on the page don't do it justice—its pleasure is sonic, not semantic—the conceit in the song is otherwise clear: OutKast has "elevated" the entire genre of hip-hop, reaching mountaintops where few have tread.

For a study of street theology, though, the song "Liberation," on *Aquemini*, is particularly valuable, going further than any other song to reach for higher states of consciousness. It comes on the heels of "Nathaniel," an a cappella rap that considers the prison-industrial complex as a contemporary extension of slavery in America.[51] Before carrying the listener into the starry skies, I take the placement of "Nathaniel" to suggest, we must consider all the social and racial circumstances that preclude freedom, the earthly realities that seek to ground black lives. Only at this point, after wading into the muck of the American judicial system, does OutKast try to expand the listener's mind, using almost every genre of black music in the South—jazz, blues, gospel, and spoken-word poetry—to indicate the power of beauty to set the soul free.[52] As sophisticated and chic as any song in the annals of R&B, soul, and hip-hop, "Liberation" opens with a grand piano arpeggio that immediately gives the song an elegant classical feel. As soon as the flurry of percussion, Afro-Latin congas, and soulful vocal harmonies kicks in, though, we know that this epic comes from somewhere outside the classical, European world. The song is a parable of "liberation," a deep dive into the meaning of freedom for the Dungeon Family (including CeeLo, Big Rube, and Erykah Badu). Each member is given a verse to parse the meaning of the term.

André begins his testimony with a self-reliant message: Don't conform to the expectations and blueprints of others, rise above the herd, be yourself. Big Boi tells us that his mama always told him the same thing, "you have a choice to be who you want to be." CeeLo, the most theological of the group, sings of his journey through the desert of life, and of his desperate longing for God, like the biblical Psalmist: "Oh, Lord, I'm so tired, I'm so tired/ My feet feel like I walked most of the road on my own." Before succumbing to any self-pity, though, CeeLo turns his thoughts to others: "There's not a minute that goes by that

I don't/ believe we could fly . . . People, keep your head to the sky." And then there's Erykah Badu's beatific vocals on the song: Her voice is so beautiful—a mezzo-soprano that is ethereal and ululating, with a dash of blue notes—that she could utter foolish things and it would sound profound. Packed with feeling, her singing points past the words toward something deeper and more ineffable. Her subject concerns the pressures and burdens that others—record companies, friends, the public—place on an artist. Her advice, sung like some angel of Harlem, is to "shake that load off and sing your song/ Liberate the minds, then you go home." Finally, Big Rube closes the song with a spoken-word recital, the only verse that refrains from rapping or singing. His thoughts roam widely, from a consideration of the violent threats in a black man's life ("Glock rounds, lockdowns, and burials") to the wasted language of thoughtless rappers, spreading words recklessly and unmindfully. He decries the misuse of words and imagery in hip-hop, a betrayal, he suggests, of black royalty.

The Afrofuturistic themes of *ATLiens* and *Aquemini*—be yourself, sing your song, navigate your life by the stars and heavens—may sound like platitudes, but OutKast had a way of transforming simple messages into the stuff of weighty knowledge, schooling their listeners on the many varieties of emancipation, spiritual, aesthetic, and social alike. With galloping unpunctuated rhyme patterns, deeply soulful vocals, and otherworldly themes, the group was nothing if not daring and original, "equal parts red clay, thick buttery grits, and Mars," to quote Kiese Laymon.[53] In the case of OutKast, in the end, much like Parliament-Funkadelic, there was never a contradiction between tearing the roof off this sucker, on the one hand, and black uplift and spiritual transcendence, on the other. They were allied projects, like hands clasped together in moments of prayer, partying, and fist-extended protest.

Hip-Hop Post-2000

Since the early aughts, with the Dirty South taking over hip-hop, and the "alternative" scene's wide-ranging palette of sound becoming the norm, the borders between different regions and styles in hip-hop have become more and more porous. Less like a tree putting down roots in one place than the ever-shifting and migrating winds, hip-hop today has been increasingly variable and free, unbound by regional and national borders. Thanks to beat-making software and the internet's facilitation of exchange and communication, hip-hop has traveled faster and farther than ever before. The new millennium has brought greater liberty for producers and deejays, their minds and choices less restricted, their remixes more varied, their inspirations as broad as the globe. If hip-hop went local in the 1990s and early aughts, the trend lately has veered national and international. No longer constrained by any one region or style, hip-hop has become a cornucopia of flavors, a splash of G-funk's melodic qualities, Public Enemy's political purposes, N.W.A.'s ghetto reportage, Southern trap beats, Jamaican dancehall, African kwaito, gospel and blues, salsa, boogaloo, bachata, et al.

In the early days of hip-hop, to recall for a moment, the lines were quickly and firmly drawn between musical genres, especially when it came to the borders between rap and rock music, the two of them, or so we assumed, opposing and clashing rhythms, a wall of sound as impassable as Trump's big steel wall. Communities of color lived on one side, white kids on the other. Obviously, there were countless border crossings, to and fro, but the widespread impression, reinforced by MTV's milky-white representation of rock in the 1980s, was that hip-hop was made by and for black and brown America, on the one hand, and rock music by and for white America.[54] Yes, the assumption was simplistic and crude, but if there is anything that I can remember with clarity about middle school, it is that hip-hop culture was seen as a colored thing, and that communion with it part of our baptism in the muddy waters of race and class in America. The music and culture made me feel, viscerally more than anything else, related to blackness in some spiritual way, made me feel a bond with the outsiders of American life. When you're brown, I suppose that one can try to go white, as some assimilationist-minded Latin@s are wont to do; but hip-hop, and my love of basketball, made me want to go in the other direction, identify with the deeper shades of brown. Associating with hip-hop immersed me in a world of black sounds and styles that I would later, especially in the wake of liberation theology's hold on me, want to explore, study, and honor.

In retrospect, looking back to the 1980s, I would say that the tall and rigid walls between rap and rock music served a valuable purpose in some ways: there was no mistaking hip-hop—a hermetically sealed subculture at the time—for anything but the voice of underserved, underground, and underappreciated communities. As hip-hop gradually became more and more mainstream, oozing up from the underground, this sentiment got lost in translation, losing a clarity of purpose for what it gained in popularity. And yet, before I succumb to nostalgia, the gains in hip-hop from the 2000s forward have been very real. Contrary to the assumptions of purists and romantics—for whom the history of rap is not progressive but regressive, degenerating, Hesiod-like, from the Age of Gold to the Age of Iron—the state of hip-hop in the new millennium, notwithstanding all the realities of commodification and the like, is not synonymous with decay or decline. As it has snowballed in popularity, in fact, hip-hop has increasingly picked up all sorts of bits and pieces, from cultures near and far, growing bigger and more universal, and smashing through the barriers that once divided various cultures and ethnic groups. The music video for Run-DMC's "Walk This Way" (1986) was a crucial turning point in this regard, the rappers literally acting out the fall of these barriers as they kicked down the walls that separated them from Aerosmith. The song united rock and rap, marrying metallic guitar riffs to rapped vocals, record scratches, and drum machines, thus conveying a unity of sounds and aesthetics that the lyrics of the song never captured. The words, come to think of it, are frivolous drivel—though rich with alliteration and assonance—compared to the collaborative fusions of the sound. The track, in the end, proved prophetic, creating bridges in a world fractured by rifts and gaping ravines.

There are other walls that have been falling in hip-hop, post-2000, however: I think, for example, of the divide, once insurmountable, between rapping and singing. If the arc of hip-hop has been bending in any one direction in the new millennium, it is toward R&B's honeyed, melodic lyricism, a feature that is so widespread in contemporary rap that it's rare to find an artist who doesn't have broad vocal range, who doesn't swing between spitting and singing. It's now hard for a pure lyricist to thrive; we want our rappers to croon as much as rap, hum and warble as much as sling darts.[55] In some ways, this vogue is an extension of G-funk and Southern rap—or even some of the earliest forms of rap, à la Busy Bee Starski or Slick Rick—but without many of the gangster vaunts. Hip-hop has discovered what gospel and R&B has taken for granted—or most forms of music, really—namely, that aching syllables, melismatic vowels, melodic curlicues, rapturous shouts, and bluesy stretched-out drawls can convey some of the soul's deepest emotions without relying on words alone. It has learned that singing verses can express a wider spectrum of emotions than classic clipped, machine-gun raps, that the right twist of the tongue, throaty rasp, or drawn-out syllable can season even the most plain and banal word with rich and addictive flavor.

The turning point in contemporary hip-hop was Drake's mixtape *So Far Gone* (2009). Before his presence on the scene, rappers regularly collaborated with singers—with the former providing the bars, the latter the pining emotions and soothing melodies—but very few rappers sang the verses themselves; they left the melodic hooks and flavorful refrains to others to spice up the rap. "Drake exploded the notion that those component parts had to be delivered by two different people, and also deconstructed what was expected from each of them," writes Jon Caramanica. "It is a startling turn, representing the almost complete reconstituting of the genre's DNA."[56] Though Caramanica overstates the case—various female emcees in the 1990s, say Missy Elliott, Mary J. Blige, Erykah Badu, and Lauryn Hill, had already brilliantly blurred the distinctions between rapping and singing, as did Organized Noize–produced rappers like TLC and CeeLo Green—but if we're speaking about the influence on the contemporary generation, he's probably right. "The game needed life," Drake raps on "The Resistance," "I put my heart in it." Which is to say that Drake put melody in the game of hip-hop like a shot of adrenaline, reviving it with stronger jolts of emotion. With his cascading flood of melodies—bending and expanding his vowels like an accordion, zigzag-ging between rapping and singing—Drake smashed the dams that separated speech and song.[57] The new throng of rappers—say, Future, Young Thug, Rae Sremmurd, Fetty Wap, Travis Scott, Post Malone, A Boogie wit da Hoodie, Juice WRLD, Lil Baby, et al.—are all devotees of his legacy, trying to make their own mark with similar swings between rapping and singing.

Another advantage of the melodic trend is psychological: rappers now turn to singing as an exercise in soul-searching. What was almost unthinkable in the late 1980s and 1990s—a brand of hip-hop that peels away our protective layers to reveal a vulnerable and sensitive core—has become commonplace. Emotional and soulful confessions—portraits of loneliness, anxiety, depres-sion, drug abuse, jealousy, guilt, fears of death, threats of nihilism—now fill the pages of rap narratives. "A preoccupation," writes Jesse McCarthy, "with depression, mental health, a confused and terrible desire for dissociation: this is a fundamental sensibility shared by a generation."[58] In the 1990s and early aughts, there were trickles of this (noticeable in Scarface, Tupac, DMX, and Kanye's *808s and Heartbreak* [2008], for instance), but the trickles have turned into gushing, broken faucets of emotional content in today's world, a crescendo of howls and cries. Revelry in the genre has now found quiet places for rumination. Kid Cudi, Lil Wayne, Drake, Kendrick Lamar, J. Cole, Future, Logic, Wale, Juice WRLD, XXXTentacion, Lil Uzi Vert, Lil Peep, Lil Xan, Mac Miller, Isaiah Rashad, Frank Ocean, YoungBoy Never Broke Again, all have sought out spaces of the kind, niches and corridors from which to pour out their feelings and bare their souls. They can be surprisingly intimate and sensitive in their songs, whispering and crooning into the mic the way a per-son leans into another to make an intimate confession. If Jay-Z is right that "You can't heal what you never reveal," this generation seems intent on using hip-hop as an agent of healing and therapy, intent on replacing rap's familiar hearts of stone with hearts of flesh.

There are numerous individuals, groups, and schools of hip-hop that I've left out in the above sketch—particularly the more righteous, religious trends of hip-hop, as well as Latin genres, all subjects of subsequent chapters—but I only wanted to paint in broad brushstrokes at this point, leaving a more care-ful analysis of individual cases for later study. It's only a beginning, a laying of tracks and routes that we will expand upon throughout this study. It should be enough to recognize that hip-hop, even when incisive on social struggles, is not simply a form of sociology. The crafting of lyrics, the execution and flow of a verse, the colorful dialect or slang, the tagging and bombing of street spaces, the making of beats, the twisting and gyrating of dance, the spinning of a tale, cultural crusading, social agitating, spiritual probing, the dream of a better future: all are foundational in the culture of hip-hop, and examples of its ideological power. They represent the various ways that youth have tried to reinvent themselves with the help of hip-hop.

C H A P T E R   3

Prophets and Emcees

Righteous Rappers

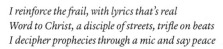

I reinforce the frail, with lyrics that's real
Word to Christ, a disciple of streets, trifle on beats
I decipher prophecies through a mic and say peace

Nas, "Memory Lane"

If sonic and aesthetic qualities are fundamental to hip-hop, adding color and flavor like stained-glass windows in a temple, prophetic sensibilities are something like the sunlight from above in my judgment, the source of the culture's most incandescent visions. Whether in the meaning of the words, or in the sound and style alone, hip-hop stands out from the crowd of pop music by its colorful and blistering way of speaking the truth, approximating in many instances the iconoclastic, visionary, and defiant traits of the biblical prophets.

At the same time, not every figure in hip-hop fits the mold of a prophet; if we stretch the category too thin, trying to squeeze everyone into it, the mold will burst and serve no purpose. A criticism of religious and moral failings is, after all, a fundamental part of prophetic oracles, the driving force behind their social and political criticism. For this reason, I suggest that we narrow our focus to examples that ring true to the biblical prophetic tradition, ones that echo the spiritual, ethical, and theological principles of the Bible. Such figures, the righteous rappers, bear the closest resemblances to the biblical prophets, their souls conduits of divine and spiritual truths, their voices mouthpieces of the poor and mistreated, their songs not only beguiling and entertaining, but also reminiscent of the exhortations, diatribes, jeremiads, laments, and howls that resound throughout biblical texts.

Biblical Prophecy

In the biblical tradition, to clarify the term, prophecy is an inspired and lyrical mode of speech, a divine revelation that wells up in the recipient—a fire in the bones, as Jeremiah described it, or the roar of a lion in Amos's terms—until it proves uncontainable, bursting forth in scorching accusation, rebuke, and warnings of impending disaster. The Hebrew prophet, writes Paula Fredriksen, was both seer (*ro'e*) and spokesperson (*nav'i*), a visionary who invoked the future as a warning, threat, and promise.[1] God came to them, in their telling, with overwhelming force, interrupting their lives, displacing their egos, and causing convulsions of emotion that were some combination of joy, love, wrath, and awe. In such a state, beside themselves, they cried out against all the wrongs and injustices that they observed, especially when it came to the sins of the rich and powerful; those, says Amos, "who crush the poor into the dust of the earth," and "who sell the destitute for silver, the needy for a pair of sandals" (Amos 2).

As apoplectic as the prophets got, however, they never lost their way with words; on the contrary, they managed to fashion their words—or lyrics, really—with great artistry, imbuing them with rhythm, assonance, sound play, and musicality. Hoping their pronouncements would not fall flat, the prophets resorted to poetry in order to leaven their speech, adding gravitas to what they said, and charging it with sonority and emotion. Poetic language, they presumed, was not only more fitting for the (majestic) nature of divine language; it was also a more fitting vehicle for emotional nuance and pathos, giving the writer the tools to plumb the personal and intimate depths of the human soul, including their very own.[2]

Because the classic prophets of the Hebrew Bible were also largely autonomous from the royal courts and temple—autonomous from politics and religion—they spoke from the vantage point of the streets. What was largely a public setting, and where the prophet came face to face with the most vulnerable of residents, became a platform and pulpit for the prophet, a site on the tattered edges of society from which they would release their words like a swarm of hornets attacking the negligent consciences of the rich and powerful. And when words were not enough, the prophets turned to theater, even histrionics, to dramatize their message, resorting to role-playing to bring attention to the ways in which the people had betrayed the covenant, failing in their love of God and love of neighbor. Lacking the class privilege of priests, scribes, or kings, then, the prophets used the only resources they possessed: pathos and eloquence, gesture and spectacle, charisma and gut-wrenching lyricism.[3]

Though rap has touches of each of these features, it seems to me that it is most clearly prophetic, in the biblical sense, when used as a weapon of the powerless against the strong, David's slingshot against the behemoth Goliath. It is most clearly prophetic when it wears the mantle of the orator, declaimer, and storyteller to express kinship with the downtrodden and un-sung groups of history. And it is most clearly prophetic when it turns places that are routinely ghettoized and demeaned—the ghetto, hood, streets, slum, barrio—into objects of pride, transforming a disgraced and unsightly condi-tion into something beautiful, the way the evening sky can turn a city's pollu-tion into a spectacular sunset.[4] Traces of each of these things can be observed throughout the culture of hip-hop, and among each regional style, as we can observe on the East Coast, beginning with a figure like Lauryn Hill.

East Coast: Lauryn Hill's Womanist Hip-Hop

I've already noted earlier some of the righteous inclinations in East Coast hip-hop, the way many pioneering rappers, even the most hard-core, scattered jewels of wisdom in their verses. By the mid- and late 1990s, however, rap seemed more interested in actual jewels and rocks than jewels of wisdom or knowledge, the mood of the period turning more materialistic and indulgent than ever. Silver and gold, contra Proverbs or Bob Marley, was judged better than wisdom, more valuable than the things of the spirit.

Lauryn Hill was an exception to the rule, an artist who turned the clock backward and forward at the same time, recovering bits and pieces of black history while pushing hip-hop into the new millennium.[5] She danced to her own tune, refusing to succumb to the pressure of peers or the mentality of mobs. Standing tall as a female emcee in a testosterone-dominated genre was enough to admire about Hill, but it was not her only asset. I always appre-ciated, for one, the way she affiliated herself with a form of diasporic black-ness, her imagination transcending North American borders and stretching like a long umbilical cord from Newark and Brooklyn to the Caribbean and Africa. It seemed to me the kind of vintage "blackness," far-reaching in its solidarity, that was at the heart of Dr. King and Malcolm X's visions of jus-tice. But most of all, she captivated me with her brand of hip-hop, a learned, deft, and otherworldly brand that had little in common with the "shiny suit" era, awash as it was in glitter and gold. Lyrically and aesthetically, Lauryn Hill took a scalpel to these forms of hip-hop, operating like a surgeon to cut, slice, and peel away the superficial layers of the age that seemed to cover up, like cheap makeup, the unchecked consumerism of the time. Perhaps, in an age that saw so much death and dying, some degree of escapism was necessary in the 1990s, even cathartic. But at some point, the banal celebrations of ghetto fab—the flaunting of cars, riches, jewels, designer fashions—start to sound monotonous, a constant drone of bees without the ability to pollinate one's soul; at some point, you need a biting dose of reality.

L Boogie's *The Miseducation of Lauryn Hill* (1998) was this dose, a sting and a shot in the arm at once. Her conscious lyricism, exalted gospel vocals, and fashion sense arrived at the right astrological moment, heralding, like the star of Bethlehem, the birth of a new, prophetic voice in hip-hop. Even her fashion choices inspired and unnerved; they were extensions of her sharp, intelligent, biting tongue. Like Samson's hair, or Stagolee's finely cut suit and wide-brimmed Stetson hat, her manner and style were part of her superpowers, hip in an unruly and defiant way, not to be messed with. She sported dreadlocks in a regal and natural manner like a lioness, sometimes flowing in an Afro, sometimes twisted and coiled in cornrows, always slick. And her clothes—militant leather jackets, retro tops and jeans, African and Jamaican colors and textures—made her look chic, rebellious, and beautiful without being reduced to a sex object. She had touches of Jamaican reggae in her, splashes of 1970s funk and soul, traces of Public Enemy's militancy, and the flair and emotion of gospel. In representation alone, forget the music for a moment, these choices identified her with the struggle of black folk around the globe, connected her with refugees and agitators, and defined her as a countercultural icon. Of course, the color of her skin spoke volumes too: in music videos and magazine covers, she displayed her blackness with pride, refusing the temptation to minimize or lighten it. If anything, she deepened the darker hues, welcoming and highlighting blackness the way that Frida Kahlo highlighted her Mexicanidad.

Frida Kahlo's clothing and accessories, to stay with this comparison for a second, revealed some of her most cherished values and convictions: her solidarity with Indigenous cultures and marginalized groups, her connection with the earth, her New World identity. As much as her paintings, her body became a canvas for her imagination, a blank slate that she turned into something striking and picturesque. She braided her dark hair over her head in the traditional style of La Malinche; put on Indian *huaraches*, or else leather boots worn by female soldiers in the Mexican Revolution (*soldaderas*); dec-

orated herself with long, flat Indigenous *rebozos*, pre-Columbian jade necklaces, fabrics with piñata-like frills, hair garlands and flowers, baroque rings,
clattering earrings, and so on. All of these things, a feast for the senses, linked
her with the peasants of Mexico, Tehuantepec women in particular: "The
costume she favored was that of the women from the isthmus of Tehuantepec," Hayden Herrera writes, "and the legends surrounding them doubtless
informed her choice: Tehuantepec women are famous for being stately, beautiful, sensuous, intelligent, brave, and strong. Folklore has it that theirs is a
matriarchal society where women run the markets, handle fiscal matters, and
dominate the men."[6] No wonder that André Breton, the famous surrealist,
referred to her as a ribbon wrapped around a bomb.

If Lauryn Hill wasn't a bomb, she was at least a bullet or storm aimed at
hip-hop's hot-air balloons in the 1990s. With her fresh gusts of energy and
purpose, she would bring down her rivals and critics, bursting their bubbles,
scattering them into a heap of broken pieces. And she could do it in a variety of ways, alternating between sweet soul music and hard-core hip-hop,
R&B seductiveness and rap's verbal assaults. She could blow softly in one's
ear with warm gospel vocals, at one moment, and then, on the next track,
blow rival rappers away like chaff. "With a singsong playfulness," writes Joan
Morgan, "she could engage her silky alto and disarm anyone who made the
mistake of taking her too lightly, then spit a death blow with the percussive-
ness of machine-gun rounds or metronomic machete swings, depending on
her mood."[7]

Remarkably, she did much of the writing, arranging, and producing for
Miseducation herself (with help from the New Ark production team), and
went on to earn a Grammy for Album of the Year in 1999, the first hip-hop
album to win the award. (To date, the album has sold more than nineteen
million copies.) Live instruments and layered harmonies evoked the music of
the 1970s, dancehall reggae and patois-inflected raps evoked the Caribbean,
and, of course, the spiritual content evoked communal and religious notes
from an older past, going back to the age of the spirituals and gospel, if not
biblical times. "Gospel music is music inspired by the gospels," Lauryn Hill
remarked about the inspiration for *Miseducation*. "In a huge respect, a lot of
this music turned out to be just that. During this album, I turned to the Bible
and wrote songs that I drew comfort from."[8] Hill is too modest here. She didn't
only draw from the deep well of the Bible, drinking and absorbing its spirits;
she also distilled it down to its most powerful and concentrated forms, turning the innocuous Bible of middle-class American Christians into radical and
subversive street scriptures, water into wine. What was a conservative book
in the hands of some, shoring up the status quo and even lending its authority

to racial discrimination, became a dangerous manifesto in her hands, good news for the poor and oppressed. In some ways, the act was fresh and innovative, but in other ways it simply recovered what was already startling about the gospels themselves: "The New Testament," as the Rev. Jesse Jackson has seen with clarity, "is the most revolutionary manifesto in history. . . . When you start dealing in terms like forgiveness and redemption and treating the least of these like they were you yourself, that's saying something that goes way beyond left-wing or right-wing. Homeboy, that's *witnessing*."[9]

A witness of this sort, Lauryn Hill's opus was rebellious and edgy, a defiance of the status quo. She stood in the legacy of black music—a Nina Simone, Aretha Franklin, Sam Cooke, or Al Green—that was trained in soul-shaking, body-quaking, house-wrecking religion, and all of it shows on the album. She cherished this older carpet of spirituality, and so rather than tearing it up altogether, she layered it with street-corner poetics and her own personal experiences, and the result was sensational, sometimes tender and sensitive, sometimes bluesy and wistful, sometimes sanctifying and prayerful, and sometimes, in the spirit of hip-hop, rugged, fibrous, confrontational, competitive.[10]

In the latter spirit, take "Lost Ones," for instance, one of the most hammering displays of lyricism on the album, a percussive flow that complements the hard-core hip-hop beats and record scratches on the track. (The hook samples Sister Nancy's dancehall hit "Bam Bam" [1982].) It begins with a declaration of personal emancipation and then turns into a dis: "My emancipation don't fit your equation/ I was on the humble/ You on every station/ Some wanna play young Lauryn like she's dumb/ But remember not a game new under the sun." In the late 1990s, rap's equation—a formula of material vaunts, drug hype, and supersized masculinity—had a hard time calculating a female rapper like Lauryn Hill. Similar to Missy Elliott, another brilliant female emcee who burst onto the scene in 1997 with *Supa Dupa Fly*, she didn't fit the mainstream equation for what counts as hip-hop. The decade of the 1990s, as I've said before, had a pall over it, and seemed to respond with shallow displays of fun and diversion, anything to keep one's mind off the spikes in homicide, bulging prisons, cycles of poverty, and forms of gnawing, unyielding nihilism. Older generations, facing such problems, did what they could to confront and challenge the Pharaoh; hip-hop of the late 1990s was doing everything it could, on the contrary, to be the Pharaoh. Lauryn Hill, needless to say, found the dream empty, full of dazzle and floss but devoid of soul: "Now, now how come your talk turn cold/ Gained the whole world for the price of your soul. . . . Now you're all floss/ What a sight to behold/ Wisdom is better than silver and gold/ I was hopeless now I'm on hope road/ Every man wants to act like he's exempt/ When he needs to get down on his knees and repent/ Can't slick talk on the day of judgment."

"Final Hour," another one of Hill's fast-moving, staccato, and declamatory raps, continues in this same vein, a warning about the high price of fame and fortune if neglectful of the values of the soul. Like the prophets Moses and Aaron—whom she invokes in the verses with inflections of a Jamaican patois, reading their legacy through reggae and the modern black diaspora—Hill decries idolatrous attachments to worldly treasures—"watch out what you cling to"—and envisions a revolutionary upheaval, the kind that would fix attention on the poor instead of the rich, outcasts and slaves instead of the princes of the world. Echoing the central tenet of liberation theology, she calls for a soul-altering change, a conversion that would prioritize the needs of the poor above all else: "I'm about to change the focus from the richest to the brokest/ I wrote this opus to reverse the hypnosis." Haranguing and cajoling at once, her raps on *Miseducation* are intended to re-educate her listeners, breaking the spell that holds people enthralled, their eyes flashing like dollar signs, to the sparkle and shine of American capitalism—they're counter-spells.

Many of the other songs on the album are more syncretistic, crossing boundaries between R&B and rap, soul, and reggae—she opens up her lungs on these occasions. "I Used to Love Him," with a sample from Raekwon's infectious "Ice Cream" (featuring Mary J. Blige), is a lovely feminist ballad about the pain and scars of love. "Father, you saved me and you showed me that life/ Was much more than being some foolish man's wife." "Ex-Factor" is a silky, doleful hymn as well, a portrait of a failed relationship. Hill sounds dejected and disappointed more than angry, her verses washing over the listener like a gentle ocean mist. The duet with D'Angelo, "Nothing Even Matters," is even more beautiful, pure shimmering soul. The music is minimal: some background organs, gentle beats, and finger snaps that sound as if they're responding in applause to the ethereal, sighing vocals of Hill and D'Angelo. The narrative is about the euphoria and all-consuming nature of romantic love, how it can fill your soul with so much joy that it leaves room for nothing else. (The song is rumored to be about Hill's love for Rohan Marley, the son of Bob Marley.) When D'Angelo sings, "See, I don't need no alcohol/ Your love makes me feel ten feet tall," we know that we're in a similar scenario as the biblical Song of Songs, where love is more intoxicating than wine, and more fragrant than the sweetest of perfumes. "Every Ghetto, Every City," now switching moods, is a nostalgic and lighthearted tribute to her younger days, when hip-hop was still young and fresh—the age, she notes, of Doug E. Fresh, Slick Rick, and BDP. And "Can't Take My Eyes Off of You" is a gorgeous rendition of the classic song by Frankie Valli (1967). With her beautiful melismatic gospel vocals on the song, Lauryn Hill did what Aretha Franklin did to Otis Redding's "Respect": she stole it and made it her own, unrivaled by others.

It was rare, as I mentioned in chapter 2, for a rapper in the 1990s to handle both rapping and singing. The unspoken assumption was that a clipped style of rapping, deep-throated and hard, was a better approximation of the nature of the streets than melody-rich lyricism. G-funk, Southern rap, and many female artists—Queen Latifah, Mary J. Blige, TLC, Missy Elliott, et al.—chipped away at this assumption, no doubt, but *Miseducation* demolished it. Nicki Minaj, for one, acknowledges the way *Miseducation* cleared the way for the rapping-slash-singing style: "She was a big part of the reason why I started wanting to incorporate singing into my music. I felt confident that if Lauryn could write her own material, rap and sing, and hold her own with the boys, then so could I."[11]

One of the most popular hits on the album, "To Zion," was Hill's powerful hymn to her newborn son, whom she named Zion. The name, of course, derives from the Bible: Zion is another designation for Jerusalem, and Hill rhapsodizes in the song in ways that recall Jeremiah's giddy anticipation of a day when the people "shall gather and sing aloud on the heights of Zion . . . Then shall young women rejoice in the dance/ and the young men and the old shall be merry" (Jeremiah 31:12–13).

Verse 1 begins with a measured and cool melody until her swelling joy, growing and kicking like the child in her womb, proves too much to contain in rapped verse, now spilling over into exalted harmonies: "The joy of my world is in Zion," she croons with joy and delight. Advised to think about her career and end the life within her, the song is about her refusal to follow the advice, choosing to see her child as a miraculous blessing in her life, a gift, not a curse.[12] Suffused with the wonder of childbirth, then, the entire song is framed by the dream of Jeremiah, as well as by the story of the Annunciation, where the angel Gabriel appears to Mary, a terrified and unwed young woman, and tells her that she will conceive and bear a son who will bring good news to the world. "But then an angel came one day," Hill sings. "Told me to kneel down and pray/ For unto me a man-child would be born." Notice the formal, elevated speech of the King James Bible: street slang is common throughout the album, but here she utilizes a consecrated and stately diction, redolent of the archaic, dignified language of the Bible. It suggests that something miraculous is happening to her, something out of the ordinary, and she waxes ecstatic about it, awaiting this blessing like a desert cicada anticipating the rain.

"I wanted it to be a revolutionary song about a spiritual movement," Lauryn Hill remarked in an interview about "To Zion," "and also about my spiritual change, going from one place to another because of my son." Her comment speaks volumes about the song and album as a whole, a record that chronicles Hill's spiritual development, and that theologizes in terms of feeling and experience as opposed to doctrine alone, as Ann Powers put it.[13] One can even trace a spiritual development in the track list of *Miseducation*: it travels from a more heated and cross condition, in the opening rap of "Lost Ones," to serenity in the subsequent songs, her spirit now finding a more enlightened attitude. The album ends, for instance, with the sublime "Tell Him," a song that is pure prayer and one of the most gorgeous songs on *Miseducation*. Since the song interpolates St. Paul's famous panegyric on love in 1 Corinthians 13, quoting it word for word, there's nothing inventive in the lyrics. The entire strength of the song is in Lauryn Hill's gorgeous execution, the notes bending, stretching, sighing, and pining throughout the track. She caresses the verses with so much sensitivity and nuance that they suddenly seem, no matter how many times they've been repeated and exhausted, completely new and fresh, the familiar words startling and moving once again, as if you're hearing them for the very first time. Her sermon begins with "Let me be patient, let me be kind, make me unselfish without being blind," and then continues, as she meanders through the biblical verses, to breathe new life into every phrase of Paul's text. Her vocal cords, quivering and shaking with emotion, eventually join the female background choir in beautiful undulating waves of oohs and aahs and keening moans. It's amazing how many subtle and complex emotions—and generations of black music and hardship and spirituality—she compresses into each bar, as though she's lived a hundred years in the song. Part exhortation, part persuasion, part praise, and all prayer, the song recalls in my mind Aretha Franklin's definition of gospel music: "Gospel is a higher calling; gospel is about beautiful and glorious voices and spirit-filled performances, people who are anointed."[14]

By suggesting that Lauryn Hill, or Aretha Franklin or Mahalia Jackson, theologized through feeling and experience, I mean something along these lines, an ability to charge language with fire and spirit, an ability to turn ordinary words into the stuff of revelation.[15] It's this dimension of music—the mystical—that one must experience in order to understand, taste in order to fully comprehend. And it's this dimension of *Miseducation*—all the God-talk, all the deep, uncanny emotions beyond the scope of reason alone—that seemed to grate on the ears of some secular liberals in the late 1990s. As if it was too wild, too surprising, too threatening, the album would have been better, they intimated, if she had only cropped out everything that conjured the transcendent and sublime in the album. I'm not sure what would have been left—something more rational, anemic, mundane, and vanilla white,

I imagine—but this attitude, scornful and condescending to believers, finds devotees not only in hip-hop studies but also in the modern study of religion.

Miseducation, at any rate, belongs to the numinous sphere of sound and experience. It soars into sublime heights without losing its bearing here on earth, without overlooking the struggle for racial, gender, and class equality at the heart of black history and black music. In this respect, the album riffs on Carter Woodson's classic work *The Miseducation of the Negro* (1933). If the purpose of Woodson's book was to revolutionize the education of black students—awakening racial consciousness, advancing moral and spiritual development, engaging social and political matters, wrestling with ontological and philosophical questions—Hill's *Miseducation* shares a similar purpose, a similar genetic makeup. Envisioning a record that would set straight the crooked nature of American education (demanding that we must first unlearn distorted histories and beliefs), *Miseducation* was concerned with a holistic pedagogy, a pedagogy of the oppressed, a pedagogy of gender, a pedagogy of the soul. Aiming so high in hip-hop can be tricky, of course, for it runs the risk of appearing haughty or inauthentic. For a black woman in the 1990s, expected to play handmaiden or stay out of the way, it was even trickier. She had to sound smart without being didactic, spiritual without being preachy, political without being propagandistic. Other conscious rappers flirted with similar dangers, but a black woman was scrutinized more ruthlessly. If she didn't skate carefully on the edges, she might fall—or get pushed—into the abyss. It's a tribute to her aesthetic, ethical, and spiritual balance on the album that she managed this and much more, not only staying on her feet but gliding into the air.

Chicago: Chance the Rapper's Street Scriptures

As original as Lauryn Hill was in the 1990s, she didn't stand alone on the Mt. Sinai of hip-hop. Other voices across the country could be heard drumming up enthusiasm for a more righteous stream of hip-hop, including figures like Common and Kanye West in Chicago. A few years before *Miseducation*, in fact, Common delivered a thoughtful run of high-quality albums, beginning with *Resurrection* (1994), followed by *One Day It'll All Make Sense* (1997) and *Like Water for Chocolate* (2000). As a Chicagoan, situated somewhere in the middle of the country, Common had the luxury of picking and choosing which affiliation to claim, the more thoughtful lyricism of the East Coast, or the rougher and more disreputable street legacy of the West Coast. Though he settled on a combination of both, the stronger impulse was his tongue-twisting rhymes and enlightened lyrics, a product of his college education

(Florida A&M University), on the one hand, and the spiritual proclivities implied in the album's title, *Resurrection*, on the other. On any one of these albums, Common's lyricism prances swiftly and playfully over the beats, displaying the introspective maturity of an old head and the exuberance and giddiness of a young cat coming of age. Speaking about such virtues, Common received no greater compliment than when Jay-Z, in a rare moment of modesty on "Moment of Clarity," paid him homage for his rhyming skills ("Truthfully, I want to rhyme like Common Sense").

As far as Kanye West is concerned, the matter is much more difficult, making any abbreviated account of his music tricky. The problem is that he has all the makings of a riddle: as a producer, songwriter, and lyricist, a triple threat, he is almost unmatched in the genre, a man of uncommon musical gifts; as a religious thinker, though, he can sound naïve, simplistic, egotistical, uninformed. While responsible more than anyone else for the inclusion of black gospel rhythms and feelings in contemporary hip-hop, for instance, he is also responsible for smuggling in, through the same door, both the prosperity gospel and a conservative, even reactionary, shoot of white evangelical theology, making him the darling of right-winged evangelicals in America (from pastors Rich Wilkerson and Adam Tyson to Donald Trump). His music is big and bold and luscious, his theology small and blinkered, lacking in the liberating tropes of the black church, as though he preserves the husk of black sacred music but discards the kernel. Read almost any account of African American Christianity, for instance, and you'll discover that this kernel was invariably theologically daring, a voice from the whirlwind of crisis and hardship, proclaiming the God of the disinherited, not the God of capitalism, the God of the beggar, Lazarus, not the God of the rich man, the unsettling and liberating God of Moses, not the God of Pharaoh. "The basic fact," wrote Howard Thurman on this exact note, "is that Christianity as it was born in the mind of this Jewish teacher and thinker appears as a technique of survival for the oppressed."[16] West's version of Christianity seems to me deficient on this point, belonging more to the temples (and malls) of American civil religion than to the makeshift churches of slaves and their descendants.

And yet, with this said, when it comes to Kanye's music—which is after all the crux of the matter—something more complex and brilliant surfaces, something that surpasses his personal judgments about life, politics, and religion, as though he becomes a medium of the Other when he is at work. Incongruities of this sort are not, after all, unusual in art and life: "The producers of great art," and I'm quoting Adorno here, "are no demigods but fallible human beings, often with neurotic and damaged personalities."[17] Kanye's life and art proves the point. From the very beginning of his solo career, with the sparkling debut *The College Dropout* (2004), there were immediate signs of this, the production and lyricism jumping out of the gate with the strength and grace of a Triple Crown winner. He immediately set a tone and style that outpaced rivals in hip-hop, running circles around others while avoiding the commonplace gangster boasts and threats of the day, selling himself, instead, as a searching, soulful, and imaginative artist, a scion of the spiritual lineage of hip-hop. Compared to this farsightedness, other rappers would seem benighted, like mill horses forced to blindly make endless circles. Not surprisingly, he tells us that he had Lauryn Hill's *Miseducation* playing on constant loop while making *The College Dropout*, for the influence shows in the soul samples, the righteous anger, the social commentary, and the thoughtful substance, especially on cuts like "All Falls Down" (which contains an interpolation of Hill's "Mystery of Iniquity"), "Through the Wire" (an autobiographical account of West's 2002 car accident), "Get 'Em High" (featuring the conscious rappers Talib Kweli and Common), "Slow Jamz" (a tribute to smooth soul music, featuring Twista and Jamie Foxx), and "Jesus Walks" (a dazzling affair, with gospel vocals, a children's choir, martial beats, chain-gang chants, orchestral breaks, and incisive lyrics about sin, racism, Christianity, and the current state of rap).

And he was only getting started with *The College Dropout*: subsequent albums had a supernova effect on hip-hop, radiating their influence on countless artists, including Lupe Fiasco, Kid Cudi, Childish Gambino, J. Cole, and another Chicago-born artist, Chance the Rapper. Kanye West lit the path for all of them.

Signs of his influence are all over the figure of Chance the Rapper in particular, one of Kanye's most interesting pupils, and one of the most hopeful and cheerful figures in hip-hop. There is no doubt that Chance walks in Kanye's shoes in terms of religious themes, but he also forges his own way when it comes to theology, his views closer to the black church—and to a street theology—than the work of his mentor. He brings rhythmic, topical, and spiritual range to hip-hop, coloring outside the traditional lines of the genre, and rendering the city of Chicago in bright and buoyant colors, the beats and rhymes as serene as watercolors.

Hanif Abdurraqib likens him, convincingly, to Gwendolyn Brooks: "She was a poet for the ordinary black Chicagoan, writing of their triumphs and failures, and understanding that a whole and complete life sat at the intersection of both. . . . Though we don't see the comparison often, Chance fits directly in the lineage of Brooks, more an archivist and community griot than the highwire gospel act that sells tickets and makes him fit comfortably on suburban playlists."[18] As community griot for the city, and mouthpiece for the struggles and joys of the black working classes, Chance also fits the mold, in my judgment, of another great Chicago native, the Cabrini-Green-bred prodigy Curtis Mayfield. Well known for his civil rights anthems, and for the soundtrack of the movie *Super Fly* (the pioneering soundtrack of blaxploitation along with Isaac Hayes's *Shaft*), Mayfield was the key figure of Chicago's "gospel soul," a music that tapped the burning emotions of gospel, combined it with the street funk of James Brown, Jimi Hendrix, Sly and the Family Stone, and George Clinton, and then added the conscience and activism of Dr. King and Malcolm X.[19] In consequence, he remained tethered to gospel values, even as he ventured into the grimy underworld of hustlers, gangsters, pimps, and prisoners. Notwithstanding the ghetto sensationalism of *Super Fly*, for example—an infomercial for cocaine and hyper-masculinity, in Mayfield's own judgment—Mayfield's soundtrack emphasized the ruinous consequences of drugs and violence, speaking for the victims of ghetto life more than the hustlers and macks who thrived at the cost of others. In Mayfield's gifted writing, buoyed by gut-bucket grooves and funky wah-wah guitars, the characters in "Freddie's Dead," "Little Child Runnin' Wild," or "Pusherman" come across as less heroes than foes or tragic victims of ghetto communities.[20] There was, in this regard, a rift between the screenplay of *Super Fly* and Mayfield's conscious and righteous music.

I would say that Chance the Rapper's music, now jumping forward a generation or two, strikes a similar dissonance—but now in relation to some of the more sensationalistic figures in hip-hop. He swerves away from the aggressive hostility of Chicago's drill rap, for instance, where the streets are so violent and heartless that they seem to swallow their own children like the god Kronos. In the drill scene, a bleak subgenre of trap, fraternity, fratricide, and fatalism are combined in dangerous and explosive potions of sound, the concepts so hard and dark that it's difficult to see tomorrow through the thick fog of violence.[21] But for Chance, Chicago is more complicated and layered and promising than drill presumes; not everyone is cliqued up or running around hustling sacks, not everyone is shedding blood to survive: "The interior of the land is always layered," writes Abdurraqib again. "Yes, sometimes with blood, but sometimes with bodies marching, with bodies moving, with bodies flooded into the streets chanting or dancing at the roller rink."[22]

"Sunday Candy," one of his early hits, says it all in the title. The song is sweet and spiritual, a bubbly tribute to Chance the Rapper's grandmother. Chance brings the feel of his grandmother's congregation to the track, plugging into the sanctified outlets of the black church, echoing the hosannas and amens of a spirited flock of worshippers. It opens with a jaunty and lighthearted piano riff, soft horns, organ chords, and percussive hand claps that sound like you're in church and Chance is testifying, his flow going back and forth between a rapping dialect and pure melody. Even the horns give the impression that they're intoning soft hallelujahs in a call-and-response pattern: "I got a future so I'm singing for my grandma/ You singing, too, but your grandma ain't my grandma/ Mine's is handmade, pan-fried, sun-dried/ Southside, and beat the devil by a landslide." Chance is playful and witty like that, full of sunshine and the lightness of being. He can pile together internal and external rhymes, dole out original metaphors, and deliver bars in a pleasing falsetto singsong, but the real sweetness of his music is in the homage he pays to people, places, and things that rarely surface in other narratives of hip-hop, the hidden parts of Chicago where black folk still go to church, care for their elders, love their children, and create music, community, and joy.

"I come to church for the candy, your/ peppermints is the truth," he raps to his grandmother, implying that she spoils him with a love that is sweet and edifying. If the Sunday candy of the song represents gospel truths here—faith, hope, and love—it appears that Chance is extolling his grandmother as a flesh-and-blood embodiment of gospel teachings, her life a testament to Christian values. She's the good shepherd for the rapper, the woman, through her sacrifices and devotion, who feeds him the bread and wine of communion, hence the refrain "You gotta move it slowly/ Taking in my body like it's holy." Though bubblegum songs in this vein often risk sentimentality and silliness, Chance is too close to Chicago's streets to suffer this fate. If he stresses the sweetness of life, it's not unlike the biblical story of Samson, looking for the honey in the carcasses of life. He knows both elements, in other words, the sweet and comedic, and the bitter and tragic, making his music wide-ranging, a journey that soars into the heavens and then plunges into purgatorial and infernal depths.[23]

Stolen innocence is the theme of Chance the Rapper's "Summer Friends," for instance, a song about the rising homicide rates in Chicago during the summer. Chance is slightly more somber than usual on "Summer Friends," recounting as he does the blight of violence in Chicago, but the song remains uplifting, swept along by gospel currents. It begins with a cappella choral voices, melismatic and soothing, until Chance the Rapper enters with sweet hums, purrs, and moans. The gospel vocals, combined with Chance's sung verses, conjure up an older Chicago, the Chicago of gospel greats and church-driven celebrations. Though his vocals are youthful and pretty here, there is enough rasp and sand in his voice to give it shades of the street, the rougher timbre paving the way for his consideration of street violence. Proof of Chance's deft lyricism, the verses draw the listener into the world in which he was born and raised, Seventy-Ninth Street in Chicago, giving us a snapshot of how his blocks have declined in the last few decades. Once a place of fun, play, and discovery, almost prelapsarian in their innocence, the song chronicles the deterioration of his streets as drugs and guns began to flood the neighborhoods, spelling disaster for things like day camps at the parks and other simple childhood adventures.

Chance's "Paranoia," from *Acid Rap* (2013), continues in this same spirit: "Everybody dies in the summer," he sings at the end of the song, expressing a wish for a longer springtime and fearing the monsoons of violence that seem to come with the heat. In order to keep the focus on Chance's commentary, the music is bare and mellow, nothing too elaborate. He begins by singing the refrain ("paranoia on my mind, got my mind on the fritz/ But a lot of niggas dyin', so my 9 with the shits"), but then pivots to rapping in verse 1, now speaking of his dreams and hopes of saving Chicago: "Pray for a safer hood when my paper good/ watch Captain Save-a-Hood, hood savior, baby boy," he chants in a composed, placid rhythm. As he addresses more directly the murder of young kids in the hood in verse 2, however, he picks up the tempo and pulse, as though his heart is beating faster and his blood pressure is rising. He doesn't exactly rage as much as he sounds frustrated, unable to tolerate the seeming desertion of the inner city by the powers that be: "They murking kids, they murder kids here/ Why you think they don't talk about it/ They deserted us here/ Where the fuck is Matt Lauer at?/ Somebody get Katie Couric in here/ Probably scared of all the refugees/ Look like we had a fuckin' hurricane here." Leaving aside his more affable persona for a minute, Chance hurls his syllables in verse 2, sounding exasperated and scornful, and diagnosing the problems of his city—as Jill Leovy does in her insightful book *Ghettoside*—as symptoms of public desertion, abandonment, and lack of political and economic will.[24]

"Paranoia" is coupled with another song on *Acid Rap*, "Pusha Man," dealing with some of the same issues as Curtis Mayfield's "Pusherman" from *Super Fly*. It's not as infectious as Mayfield's version—there are no bongo grooves, blues guitar, live drums, or Mayfield's cool, soulful, half-whispering crooning—but the songs come together in their assessment of the ghetto figure of the hustler. Both songs walk a narrow edge between sympathy and satire. Hew too closely to the glamorized version of the hustler, full of hedonism and hyper-masculinity, and you end up with a destructive fantasy; hew too closely to the reprobate version, full of sanctimonious fury, and you end up with an attitude that not only misses the social, political, cultural, and economic sins that created the conditions for the rise of urban criminals but also one that is blind to the sins within one's own soul. Mayfield himself puts it this way, speaking of the soundtrack for *Super Fly*: "It allowed me to get past the glitter of the drug scenes and go to the depth of it—allowing a little bit of the sparkle and the highlights lyrically, but always with a moral."[25]

Chance's version shares the ambiguity regarding the pusher or hoodlum: the boasting hook—"Pimp slappin,' toe taggin'/ I'm just tryin' to fight the man/ I'm yo pusha man"—is sarcastic, critical, and empathetic all at once. It locates the drug dealer in a broader social and economic context, as is clear in one of the best lines of the rap: "I'll take you to the land where the lake made of sand/ And the milk don't pour and the honey don't dance." A witty line, Chance gives us a portrait here of parts of Chicago that are more desert than lake, more wasteland than land of milk and honey, a world far from any Eden-like promised land. Seen in this context, the "pusha man," or "nitty" in Chicago slang, is a man with few resources and even fewer prospects, doing what he can to squeeze milk and honey out of the hard, dry streets. Chance sympathizes with the man's predicament in this regard, but without approving of or admiring his ways.

If "Pusha Man" is about the dry and desolate conditions of urban Chicago, and poor folk trying to wring water out of hard rock, "Acid Rain" is about turning wastelands into rivers. The song is one of the most philosophical and introspective tracks on the album (a favorite of Barack Obama). It meanders through the verses in a curious and probing manner, employing a stream-of-consciousness delivery with bars piled together haphazardly like cars in a junkyard. A rap of this sort reveals Chance's wide-ranging inspirations—he has listed Kanye, OutKast, Lil Wayne, Freestyle Fellowship, and Hieroglyphics as key influences—and also gives the rapper an opportunity to plumb the depths of his own soul. Traces of Eminem's rapping flow are apparent here, too, but Chance channels it in a more spiritual direction than anything from the mouth of Eminem, a chatty and relaxed sort of musing over a cool boom-bap beat and orchestral tinges. At one moment, he's confessing his sins, reminiscing about high school, expressing his fear of death, commenting on pop culture's preference for lies over truth, and paying homage to a deceased friend whom he witnessed get killed: "My big homie died young, just turned older than him/ I seen it happen, I seen it happen, I see it always/ He still be screaming, I see his demons in empty hallways." He's all over the place, playing with words, experimenting with ideas, repping his hood, swerving and tripping (literally) through the verses. And oh, not least, he's also grappling with God: the final bars describe him, in the manner of Moses or any number of mystics, as longing to see God's face: "And I still be asking God to show his face/ And I still be asking God to show his face." At this point, as though his rapped words won't suffice to capture an experience of the divine, he crescendos into a serene melodic voice, joyfully celebrating a new life, a man touched by God: "I am a new man, I am sanctified/ Oh I am holy, I have been baptized, I have been born again." The singing, at this point, thick with yearning, is commensurate with the religious emotions that swirl and surge within him, the spoken words giving way to a musical idiom of pure feeling.

Typical that Chance, even when feverish with anguish, quickly moves to a higher register, as though his fevers always break without too much trouble and he's back to being his normal, healthy, happy self. He simply doesn't have the tormented psychology of an existentialist, Delta bluesman, or emo rapper. (The term "emo," by the way, comes from the punk subgenre known as emo-core, or emotional hardcore.) He's almost nothing like, say, Bessie Smith's character in "Empty Bed Blues"—a person with the blues all around her bed and up inside her head—or Robert Johnson's protagonist in "Preachin' Blues," a man who feels the blues like a "low-down shakin' chill."[26] He's too bright and breezy for all that, a Pelagian more than an Augustinian. The Christian understanding of the Fall, with the wages of sin and sorrow, is very real to him, and very real to his corner of Chicago, but the Fall is more like a trip than a ruinous fall (incidentally, the terms "fall" and "trip" appear frequently throughout *Acid Rap*). Chance is the type of figure, in other words, who wants to believe that the world is now redeemed, and he acts accordingly, reaching out to help a fallen world back to its feet, hence the "captain-save-a-hood" ep- ithet on "Paranoia" (a rejoinder to E-40's "Captain Save a Hoe"). The world is not forsaken; broken, yes, but it remains full of grace, and worthy of praise. This conviction is even more obvious on his following album, the exuberant *Coloring Book*: the album is a vibrant, colorful work, combining affection for gospel music and church ties ("I'm still at my old church") with a brand of social activism (#SaveChicago) that motivates him to "clean up the streets so my daughter can have somewhere to play."

And the music on *Coloring Book*—cherubic, euphoric, and jubilant, with just enough profane touches to give it an earthy, urban quality—resounds with this hopeful spirit. Reminiscent of Steve Cropper's description of Stax Records—"a below the Bible-belt sound, righteous and nasty"—*Coloring Book* can move into the grimy low end of hip-hop with songs like the irresistible "No Problem," feat. Lil Wayne and 2 Chainz, "Mixtape," feat. Young Thug and Lil Yachty, or "Smoke Break," feat. Future (all collaborations with rappers from the Dirty South), and then suddenly ascend into the sanctified high end with "Angels," "Finish Line/Drown," "Blessings," and "How Great."[27] And even when on the former tip, the mood is vivacious, flamboyant, playful, and, well, colorful, as any album with the name *Coloring Book* must be. Gospel choirs and organs, exalted harmonies, Auto-Tune crooning, exuberant electro-funk, and singing verses figure throughout the recording, giving it a soaring and spirited feel as well as obvious touches of transcendence.

"I got my city doing front flips," Chance boasts in the opening bar of "Angels," as the video captures the rapper flying across the Chicago sky like a superhero, ghetto angel, or one of those vibrant floating images of Marc Chagall. The song is rollicking and beaming, a splash of light and warmth in a city famous for cold, dark winters. He skips and romps, soars and swoops through the verses, as if his spastic energy must find a release in rapping or else risk exploding. While he retains the sport and spring of youth that he exuded on *Acid Rap*, Chance's vocals are more settled and aged on *Coloring Book*, rooted in the mellow church melodies that silhouette the entire album. (Happily, there are fewer bleats and yelps, too.) As usual, his verses are clever and witty, as in this perfect metaphor of his style: "Got the industry in disbelief, they be asking for beef/ This is what it sound like when God split an atom with me." His flow and sound, he boasts, is so explosive that it's like a nuclear fission, a sudden explosion and release of neutrons, a chain reaction of unstable syllables, a surging and radiating energy. The music is lively and flamboyant as well—pealing horns, cheery keyboards, gospel vocals, drum machines and kettledrums, synth-pop frills—and his vocal exhibition even better: his flow is sharp and turns on a dime when the meter calls for it, moving slow and then fast, dropping into song, shriek, or singsong cadences that lack semantic meaning ("woo woo this woo wap da bam"). Too positive and upbeat to be dragged down into beefs with other rappers (he mentions Chicago's Chief Keef, in particular), he dismisses the inclination to beat the drums of war; instead, he turns sword-like lyricism into ploughshares, his spears into pruning hooks. The dream of the song, and the album as a whole, is to get Chicago neighborhoods, as the prophet Isaiah once put it, to no longer learn war (Isaiah 2:4). Through it all, Chance the Rapper wears his White Sox hat like an angelic halo: "Wear your halo like a hat, that's like the latest fashion/ I got angels all around me, they keep me surrounded." Surrounded by his guardian angels, speaking and flowing through him, Chance represents the kind of street theology at the heart of this study, a holiness that is fully immersed in the world but not of the world, incarnate in the messiness, violence, and injustice of the world but simultaneously looking to higher things.

These themes run throughout the entire album: "Blessings" is built on the foundation of church vibes and emotions, with a live drum set, gospel choir, and ethereal horns that cause the walls of Jericho, he sings, to fall like water. "I don't make songs for free, I make 'em for freedom/ Don't believe in kings, believe in the Kingdom," Chance raps while tossing in references to Black Lives Matter and recounting the many blessings in his life. And then, as if his many blessings were too bountiful for one song, he offers a reprise on the same theme, "Blessings (Reprise)." This time the music is sparse and spare: thin strums of the guitar, melodic hums, hand claps, and gospel harmonies. And he delivers his rhymes in a conversational, a capella, and spoken-word fashion, one word after the other like toppled dominoes. He's richly poetic and theological at once: "I speak of promised lands/ Soil as soft as mama's hands/ Running water, standing still/ Endless fields of daffodils and chamomile." He is not only counting his blessings in the song, but also dreaming of a world that shares its blessings with others, a world that gives out its resources freely and lavishly.

"How Great," finally, is a hip-hop rendition of Chris Tomlin's "How Great Is Our God," with Chance turning the rap into an impassioned sermon, his words now sounding inspired and sacrosanct. As we saw with Lauryn Hill, his diction turns formal and stately when ruminating on spiritual matters, the syntax and plain order of the words inverted to strike a sacred tone: "Hear, for I will speak noble things as entrusted me/ Only righteous, I might just shrug at the skullduggery," he raps, interpolating a couplet from Proverbs 8:6, "Hear, for I will speak of excellent things, and the opening of my lips shall be right things."[28]

In the end, *Coloring Book* is a fresh and clean splash of water in an industry that can quickly turn clichéd and stagnant, pooling like days-old water. Keep in mind, after all, that 2016, the year of its release, saw a drastic surge in gun violence in Chicago, with homicides increasing by 58 percent from 2015, returning to some of the levels previously seen in the 1990s. It was a tragic turn of events, as bleak and drab as some of the most menacing refrains heard in gangster rap. In the violent and heavy air of this kind of pollution, and corresponding hopelessness, *Coloring Book* appeared like a breath of fresh air, filling the soul with badly needed faith and hope. It might be counterintuitive to juxtapose the history of violence and injustice in America with hopeful, spiritual music, but Chance wants badly to be a dissenting voice in the chorus of war cries, materialism, and greed in American life, bringing truths and revelations to the world of hip-hop, shining his light on the dark spots of the world like a sudden flash of lightning. He is the latest incarnation of the redemptive gospel vision, adding his voice to older works like Mahalia Jackson's "Move on Up a Little Higher," Curtis Mayfield and the Impressions' "Keep on

Pushing," Aretha Franklin's "Respect," Bob Marley's "Redemption Song," or Stevie Wonder's "Higher Ground," all of them marching step by step with the unfinished dream of civil rights.

He adds a higher note to hip-hop in this regard. While some rappers appear to be in league with the Furies, intent on plucking out an eye for an eye, a figure like Chance the Rapper is clearly on the side of the Muses, his angels rushing through his bloodstream and turning poisonous impulses into antidotes for gloom and despair.[29] For embracing redemptive and religious aspirations, he's often compared to Kendrick Lamar, the subject of our next chapter, but the differences in sensibility are more striking to me. Lamar agonizes much more over the state of his soul than does Chance, a trait that puts Lamar in the company of some of the more tortured bluesy artists of old. Aretha Franklin's characterization of soul music applies perfectly to a man like Kendrick Lamar: "Soul music," she wrote, "is music coming out of the black spirit. A lot of it is based on suffering and sorrow, and I don't know anyone in this country who has had more of those two devils than the Negro."[30] Chance knows these devils as well, but the stronger specter in his life is clearly the celestial angel, a romping, strutting, and soaring figure, dancing on the head of a pin.

The Third Coast: Jay Electronica

If there are plenty of righteous figures in East Coast and Midwest hip-hop, the cases are harder to come by on the Third Coast. Looking for righteous rappers in the regions of the Dirty South, long associated with the most profane and hedonistic tendencies in hip-hop, may seem like a hopeless task, like the man searching for God in Nietzsche's famous parable. We know, nonetheless, that the type exists, as my discussion of Goodie Mob and OutKast in the previous chapter tried to show. Jay Electronica, a Muslim rapper from the Magnolia Projects in New Orleans (the same hood that gave birth to Soulja Slim, Juvenile, and Cash Money Records), is further evidence of things normally unseen in the South; he's a gem of the region.

Much like Killer Mike, another Southern rapper, Jay Elec mixes together tropes of the Dirty South with conscious motifs, the two elements rubbing together to create an original style. Killer Mike's self-characterization applies perfectly to Jay: "The passion of Pac, the depth of Nas, circa nine three/ Mix the mind of Brad Jordan and Chuck D and find me/ I spit with the diction of Malcolm or say a Bun B/ Prevail through Hell, so Satan get thee behind me." For rappers in this mold, drawn by the crescent moon of Islam, the true jihad is less a battle with an external enemy—a rival rapper, gang member, tribal foe—than a battle over one's soul, with Satan trying to claim it, and God trying to save it. They identify with the streets and underworlds of American life with the same intensity as other rappers of the South, but they are more inclined to fret over their spiritual condition than wallow in the pleasures of the flesh, more inclined to lock horns with the devil than with any street foe. "Though I tarry through the valley of death, my Lord give me pasture," Jay spits on "The Neverending Story." "If you want to be a master in life, you must submit to a master/ I was born to lock horns with the devil at the brink of the hereafter."

Though his album *A Written Testimony* (2020) is short on autobiographical details—and more personal journaling, à la Kendrick Lamar's *Good Kid, M.A.A.D City*, would have made it a stronger work—it's well known that Jay Electronica became a Muslim in his early twenties. References to the Nation of Islam, the Five Percenters, and even the Noble Drew Ali of the Moorish Science Temple abound in his work. His music is thus a testimony to the house-wrecking makeover that Islam wrought in his interesting life.

Early works, like "Exhibit C" and "Exhibit A," produced by Just Blaze, first put this rapper on the map. A sample of Billy Stewart's "Cross My Heart," "Exhibit C" (2009) includes some of the most poignant verses in the annals of hip-hop, a sharp and cutting swordplay of words, a rap attack that slices through the clamor of the music to get to the heart of the matter. There are no processed vocals here like so much of rap in the early aughts, no melodic hooks, no fancy crooning, just plain old rap lyricism, shooting straight from the hip. Opening the song with a heartfelt account of his homeless days in New York, and eventually his salvation at the hands of Five Percenters, the song grabs your attention and never lets go.

> *When I was sleepin' on the train*
> *Sleepin' on Meserole Ave out in the rain*
> *Without even a single slice of pizza to my name*
> *Too proud to beg for change, mastering the pain*
> *When New York niggas were calling southern rappers lame*
> *But then jacking our slang . . .*
>
> *Fightin,' shootin' dice, smokin' weed on the corners*
> *Tryna find the meaning of life in a corona*
> *Till the Five Percenters rolled up on a nigga and informed him*
> *You either build or destroy, where you come from?*
> *The Magnolia projects in the 3rd Ward slum*

Deft lyricism and deep narrative, Jay Elec puts it all together here. Seen in the history of New Orleans gangster bounce, such verses come across as rather startling, really, a shock of the fresh and new. He may have shared Third Ward origins with No Limit or Cash Money rappers, but he seems to have dropped out of the sky from New York circa 1990, when Five Percenters roamed the streets of Mecca, Medina, and Shaolin. Mainstream rappers seem unimaginative by comparison, their words smoke without fire, lacking his blazing, dragon-like energy, "spittin' out flames, eatin' wack rappers alive." And they lack, of course, his spiritual purpose, stated in no uncertain terms as a "revelation which has called me to guide millions of people/ towards their righteous destiny" ("Exhibit A").

From the very outset, Jay Elec belied all stereotypes of Southern rap. If the Dirty South has been synonymous with street ballers—style over substance— Jay brought fundamentals back to the game, moving with the skill of someone who was well versed in the basics of emceeing. He demonstrated an ability to combine complex rhyming patterns with a deep metaphysical substance that cut straight to the hoop. After dropping "Exhibit C" and "Exhibit A," however, he went dark, as if on injury reserve. We didn't hear from him for nearly a decade. It may be, as he's acknowledged, that it was tough living up to the hype. Or it could be that he's the type of artist who sweats and stresses every word, brooding over his rhymes carefully and meditatively: "When I lay down in my bed, it's like my head in the vice/ When I look inside the mirror all I see is flaws/ When I look inside the mirror, all I see is Mars/ In the wee hours of the night, tryna squeeze out bars/ Bismillah, just so y'all could pick me apart?" Before he puts his words on paper, as this passage from "The Blinding" suggests, he scrupulously ponders every bar, fretting every word, and suffering anxiety over the final product—perspiration is as much a factor as inspiration.

And both factors are evident in Jay Elec's *A Written Testimony* (production by Swizz Beats, AraabMuzik, Hit-Boy, Khruangbin, No I.D., the Alchemist, and Jay-Z). If you appreciate psychedelic vibes with minimal drumbeats and contemplative lyricism, this album will please your tastes. It's not as stirring as other works in Southern hip-hop, but if the purpose of hip-hop is to drop knowledge on a listener, then the album succeeds nicely, a classic study in the kind of hip-hop that aims straight for the head. There's a bristling energy on the album, in other words, but the fission occurs primarily in the nuclei of the mind and spirit, not the body. "I came to bang with the scholars," Jay writes on "Ghost of Soulja Slim," one of the strongest raps in this mode. The song references the famed Magnolia rapper—also known as Magnolia Slim— but moves in an avant-garde direction unfamiliar to Soulja Slim. Of course, OutKast paved the way in this regard, but the soundscape of "Ghost" is even more experimental, its peculiar accordions, strange vocal trills, jubilant children's voices, and eerie keyboard riffs setting it apart from mainstream hip-hop. While the song is militant and rebellious at its core, channeling the combative spirit of the Nation of Islam and King T'Challa from *Black Panther*, the music is eccentric and starry, as if it was sprinkled with angel dust.

"If it come from me and Hov, consider it Quran," Jay Elec quips. "If it come from any of those, consider it Haram." Haram is something forbidden by Islamic law and "Quran" means "recitation," the implication being that these rappers, reminiscent of a muezzin, will recite and chant their verses in the interest of the truth, displaying their eloquence to move and enflame their listeners, the way the angel Gabriel consumed the prophet Muhammad. Keeping in mind that the Quran was always delivered orally, sung more than spoken, the parallel that Jay Elec draws between Quranic recitation and rap is instructive. "From the very beginning," writes Karen Armstrong, "the Prophet drew on the Eastern tradition of sacred sound and the Quran records the extraordinary effect it had on the first audiences. Quranic recitation is the major art form in the Islamic world. It evokes a state known as *huzn* . . ." *Huzn*, she continues, tugs at the emotions as well as the mind, and is tantamount to humility, awe, sorrow, and a passion for justice. "This awareness, and the emotion it stirs on the part of the reciter, is communicated through the reciter's voice and artistry, heightening the listeners' sensitivity and moving them to tears."[31]

While neither Jay Elec nor Jay-Z move us to tears, and the sentiment of humility is generally missing in Jay-Z ("Hova," after all, is an abbreviation of Jehovah), both rappers locate themselves in this ancient lineage, expressing themselves by way of rhythm, melody, emotion, and vocal ornamentation—and, through it all, striving to be mediums of the divine. In this regard, Jay-Z has some smooth bars in the song, as when he claims not only to be the ghost of Soulja Slim—"I'm a soulja in that mode"—but also the ghost of Rumi, the medieval Sufi poet who made his words dance to music like a rapper. Jay Elec, in turn, expresses gratitude to Jay-Z for giving him the opportunity and platform—the minaret, he remarks—to call everyone to prayer with his adhan-like raps. (The adhan is the Islamic call to prayer, recited by a muezzin.) By claiming the legacies of both Southern rap and Islamic mysticism, the rappers combine the role of urban griot and sacred muezzin in the song, wantonly crossing the borders of the sacred and profane.

Other songs on the album are even stranger in sound: "The Blinding" has some deep thoughts—Jay Elec's introspective musing, parables of captivity and exile, apocalyptic references to the return of the Mahdi—but the music (a fuzzy bass line, metallic swishes, high-pitched whistles, periodic yelps) lacks a compelling rhythm, lacks a strong backbone. "The Neverending Story," with a tight and gentle groove from the Alchemist, is much more successful.

It's eccentric too, with far-out and spacey synths, cool guitar riffs, ghostly background vocals, the sound of gentle rainfall, and so on, but it interlocks nicely with the rapped soliloquies in the song, the music and verses coming together in a concert of pensive vibes. Above all, the music withdraws enough to allow the rappers to do their thing—Jay Elec's voice and diction, eloquent and crystal clear, low and baritone, doesn't have to compete with the music. His vocals stand out clearly and forcefully, their deep and rich tones perfect for the serious and weighty discourse of the rap. Verse 1 opens with the tale of his life, a story of learning and redemption, salvation stolen from the squalor of the projects. This is the kind of personal excavation that fans of "Exhibit C" had hoped for. He reminiscences about his early years, when he was a lost prodigal son, or, in another bar, a sleeping giant pulled "out of the ditch/ And I ain't even have to wiggle my nose like Bewitched/ I just up-shift to six, convert the V4 to a broomstick/ Though I tarry through the valley of death, my Lord give me pasture/ If you want to be a master in life, you must submit to a master." Instead of magic, the song implies, it was spiritual discipline and religious guidance that shepherded the young man through the valley of death—a variety of mysticism more than magic: "The prodigal son who went from his own vomit/ to the top of the mountain with Five Pillars and a sonnet."

Jay Elec's foundation here, rooted in Islamic ritual, ethical discipline, and submission to God, is what separates his brand of religion from Jay-Z's New Age spirituality. Jay-Z is fond of citing different religions—Santería, Islam, and ancient Egyptian mysteries in this instance—but one gets the impression that his understanding of each religion is rather thin and shallow, lacking in the depths of each particular religion, a mirage more than a deep sea of beliefs, practices, and experiences. Compared to Jay Elec, in other words, Jay-Z seems more frivolous on the theme of religion, as though references to Islam, the Orishas, or ancient Egypt make for some cool verses, but little else. There is no life-shattering revelation in Jay-Z, no wrenching conversion, no momentous decision, no existential compulsion that would unsettle and transform him, cause him to substitute his veneration of Mammon for the veneration of God.[32] As long as he believes that being a billionaire puts him in the firmament of the gods, why would he feel any such compulsion?[33]

"Ezekiel's Wheel" continues with a meditative, hallucinatory vibe, exploring far-out myths and ideas, intergalactic in nature. Devoid of a drumbeat, the music is minimal and very peaceful, composed of clattering sticks, a rippling keyboard riff, and cascading, soulful chords for the chorus. It's serene and calming. The title of the rap invokes the famous chariot vision of the prophet Ezekiel, his strange mystical vision of flying wheels and brilliant metallic throne, upon which God sits in splendor, hidden by a fiery, dazzling light. The historical context of the vision is important to keep in mind: Israel is in exile, taken captive by the Babylonians in the sixth century BCE, and Ezekiel, one of the deportees, is visited by God and summoned to address the nation. Given Israel's uprooted condition, and the ensuing destruction of the Temple, the image of the mobile chariot is historically sensible: it indicates God's willingness to accompany Israel into the darkness of exile, an ambulatory image for a people who can no longer worship on Mount Zion—Zion must come to them. Years later, of course, the spirituals would translate this vision of the divine chariot into a symbol of freedom, the chariot becoming an underground railroad, freedom bus, or car that might help one steal away to Jesus.[34]

In Jay Elec's case, however, the biblical tale of Ezekiel's chariot vision is refracted through the lens of the Nation of Islam and, no less, through the prismatic and gem-like refractions of P-Funk mythology. In the NOI's theology, Ezekiel's chariot was rendered as a Mother Plane, descending to earth to rescue black folk from the unremitting history of racial oppression. The Honorable Elijah Muhammad would pilot this Mothership, directing it to exact retribution on the wicked of the earth, much like the Son of Man in the book of Revelation. Whereas John's ire was aimed at the Great Beast of the Roman Empire, however, Elijah Muhammad directed his wrath at the white race, holding it responsible for draining the lifeblood of people of color like a vulture or vampire.

Now Parliament-Funkadelic, building on the mythology, gave these notions their own interesting twist: the Mothership became a party vessel. "Reimagining the death-dealing Mother Plane as an intergalactic party machine," writes Loren Kajikawa, "P-Funk mythology offered listeners a vision of dance-floor transcendence with racialized religious overtones."[35] George Clinton, aka Dr. Funkenstein, in essence, took the place of Elijah Muhammad, and instead of retribution he offered the remission of sin through music and dance. Suddenly, the weather went from dark and foreboding to colorful and psychedelic with P-Funk, as if the clouds parted and a rainbow appeared to wreath the skies. And all of this was dramatized at a P-Funk concert; a giant spaceship would descend from the sky above with Dr. Funkenstein piloting the way and the audience chanting, "Swing down sweet chariot, stop, and let me ride." George Clinton and P-Funk, in short, swept up their listeners in a flood of sound and celebration, welcoming everyone aboard their Mothership. Not only intergalactic, the Funk was also transcultural and universal in this vision, something everyone could get in on, a communion of different cultures, an interstellar utopia. It united black power and pride—this remained crucial to its fecund mythos—with a broader cosmic vision, reconciling the particular with the universal in a coincidence of opposites.

Jay Elec's music belongs to this same universe—God has commissioned him just as God once commissioned Ezekiel: "Son of Man, I am sending you to the Israelites" (Ezekiel 2:3). In the case of Jay Elec, though, the "Israelites" include all black lives scattered around the globe, especially his people in New Orleans. He is sent to rescue the lost tribes of Israel. This theme is scattered throughout *A Written Testimony*, but in the case of "Ezekiel's Wheel," in particular, mythological elements from the NOI and P-Funk are superimposed onto the biblical vision of Ezekiel. Just before the rappers begin their verses, for instance, a news report interrupts the song to report the appearance of a spaceship hovering over the city—Ezekiel's wheel is a space shuttle here, one that has a redemptive purpose, as in the religion of Islam, and a celebratory spirit, as in P-Funk. Jay Elec gets most of the verses in the rap, and he picks and chooses his themes randomly, with an ear for consonance and internal rhymes more than narrative. In verse 2, the rhymes come fast and frequent, the rapper cleverly piling together a host of multisyllable words that resonate with each other sonically. He's a bit more introspective in verse 1, however, specifically addressing the reason for his absence from the game of hip-hop: "Some ask me, 'Jay, man, how come for so many years you been exempt?'/ 'Cause familiarity don't breed gratitude, just contempt . . . Sometimes I was held down by the gravity of my pen/ Sometimes I was held down by the gravity of my sin." Any conscientious writer should be able to relate.

It seems to me, in the end, that Jay Elec's absence created an aura of mystery about the man and his work, teasing and tantalizing us by his withdrawal, a pregnant silence. Whether intentional or not, the disappearance, like a cloaked spaceship, matches perfectly the substance of his raps, as though his silence was an extension of his cryptic theology.

Whatever the case, *A Written Testimony* has a compelling redemptive core, the kind of vision described by R&B and soul music critic Craig Werner as a "gospel vision." In contrast with the "blues vision"—"an autobiographical chronicle of personal catastrophe expressed lyrically"—Werner describes the gospel vision as fundamentally communal and emancipatory in purpose. "The gospel vision," he writes, "is elastic enough to accept those who called the power Jah, Allah, Yemaya, or—like funkmaster George Clinton—the Mothership. At its best the gospel vision helps people experience themselves in *relation to others* rather than *on their own*. Where the blues offers reaffirmation, gospel offers redemption."[36]

Even though I prefer the term "redemptive vision" to "gospel vision" (especially in reference to non-Christian traditions), the distinction is helpful. It draws an illuminating boundary line, if blurry in many cases, between more private, self-reliant, and bluesy renditions of hip-hop, as in David Banner's mournful rapping on *Mississippi: The Album* (2003) or Future's anguished, guttural lyricism on *Dirty Sprite 2* (2015) and *HNDRXX* (2017), and a version of hip-hop that turns outward, looking to articulate the struggles and joys of an entire community. For all their differences, Lauryn Hill, Chance the Rapper, and Jay Electronica belong in the latter category, their music sharing many of the same aches, longings, and hopes for a common and collective salvation.[37]

West Coast: Tupac's Hood Theology

For all the explanatory value of these categories, redemptive or blues oriented, communal or personal, they come apart at the seams when trying to squeeze some of the more complicated artists inside, as in the case of Tupac. He is much more complicated and messy than anyone discussed thus far, an artist who drifted across every border, offended every norm, violated most conventions, making it almost impossible to confine him to any one category. Sometimes gangster, sometimes righteous, sometimes violent and nihilistic, sometimes tender and spiritual, sometimes sexist, sometimes a voice for black women, sometimes conscious, then hedonistic, the man was a paradox in human form, conflicted and divided against himself. Had he lived more than twenty-five years on the earth, he may have had the opportunity to untangle these contradictions, but it wasn't meant to be: he would suffer the kind of untimely death that he constantly rapped about, a fate that put him in the same company as thousands of young black males whose lives have been cut tragically short.

Considering Tupac, in any event, puts us in the thick of West Coast gangster rap, his legacy, for better or worse, tied to this style and era. Though the roots of gangster rap can be traced to the East Coast (Schoolly D, Boogie Down Productions, Kool G Rap, Ice-T), the genre really flourished, like a plant or weed, depending on your judgment, in the sun-drenched landscapes of the West Coast. In the sprawling context of Southern California, and its archipelago of urban hoods, all governed by certain gangs, the genre offered the public a shocking and lurid view of ghetto life, capturing much of the discontent, frustration, fears, and widespread outrage felt by many urban black and brown youth in the 1980s and 1990s. While usually skirting social and political advocacy, driving around them rather than hitting them head-on, many of gangster rap's plots and hard-boiled tales transported the listener to the deepest levels of the ghetto, sketching the ills that plagued their blocks—mass incarceration, white supremacy, segregated neighborhoods, failing schools, rival gangs, crack-infested streets, and, above all, crooked cops. At least in this sense, to discuss gangster rap, as a writer for the Source put it, "is to discuss the fundamental problems, conflicts, and opportunities of our society."[38]

The critics weren't wrong, nonetheless, when they accused gangster rappers of being misogynists, ruthless capitalists, hedonists and, spiritually speaking, nihilists. Many of them fit the profile, epitomizing maybe one or two or all of these types rolled into one. Ice-T's classic "6 in the Mornin'" was a case in point, the song registering the harrowing and hostile circumstances of urban black life in the late 1980s and early 1990s: "The batteram's rolling, rocks are the thing," Ice-T rapped in a sluggish and relaxed flow, characteristic of a smooth criminal. "Life has no meaning, and money is king." Cynical to the bone, this attitude, like Dante entering the gates of the Inferno, seemed to abandon all hope, turning against the dreamy aspirations of civil rights, faith in political and legal reform, and the comforts and fancies of middle-class religion. "They presented the world," writes Ta-Nehisi Coates, "in all its brutality and beauty, not in hopes of changing it but in the mean and selfish desire to not be enrolled in its lie, to not be coopted by the television's dreams, to not ignore all the great crimes around us."[39] On this point, at least, they had a perceptive eye for hypocrisy, spotting sins and crimes like a detective, warning of ruin like a prophet of doom.

Tupac's debut work, 2Pacalypse Now (1991), was written in this vein, bearing in the very title the threats and traumas of the day. The album, written just before the LA riots, borrowed from disparate sources, copping N.W.A.'s wicked reportage, Public Enemy's social commentary, and even Rakim's righteous purpose. He painted dark pictures of urban life, sketching walls around his subjects that seemed to be closing in on them. In the rap "Trapped," for instance, Tupac complained and howled about various injustices: quagmires of poverty, cops sweating and harassing black men, judges doling out long sentences that would haunt, if not totally ruin, a young man's future; "Soulja's Story" continued the social commentary, but now with a focus on interior landscapes, exploring the troubled psyche of an urban criminal, his family tree uprooted by crack, and his young brother following in his criminal footsteps; "Brenda's Got a Baby," another meaningful tale, spotlighted the predicament of single black mothers in urban life, casting a compassionate light on the struggles and violence they face on a daily basis. In such instances, Tupac navigated both social and psychological dimensions of urban life, taking his listeners into spaces that were often hidden behind iron curtains of indifference. Unlike N.W.A.'s wild flurry of blows, ruthlessly aimed in almost every direction, Tupac struck with sensitive touches in these songs, using thoughtful portraits of ghetto dwellers to get to the naked truth of American life. He operated with skill, intelligence, passion, and sympathy.

By Tupac's second and third albums, however, the legends of gangsters and thugs started to take on a stronger presence in his music, gradually overpowering the ethical-political commentary, the music increasingly smacking of bitter vinegar mixed with gall. The heroes of his music are now gangsters, pimps, and hustlers more than prophets; the liberationist thread of 2*Pacalypse Now* started to fray, as if he was slowly moving in the opposite direction of the Exodus, returning to the fleshpots of Egypt. By his fourth album, *All Eyez on Me* (1996), when Tupac had signed with Death Row Records, this change in direction seemed irreversible, the music adopting a more nefarious cast: "Gone were the messages of resistance and painful urban blues," Marcus Reeves writes, "replaced by a post-prison hedonism, materialism (thanks to the bundle of money provided by his label), and an egotistical drive to commercially crush his rap competition."[40] Raps like "Can't C Me," "Heartz of Men," "All Eyez on Me," and "Hit 'Em Up" were examples of this sort, his moral instincts now drowned out by venomous and vengeful impulses, an anger that was out of control, a death instinct bent on self-destruction. According to Shock G of Digital Underground, the young man that he once knew was gone, his new persona almost unrecognizable.[41] And Biggie, after staring into Tupac's seething, blood-red eyes at the time, said a similar thing: Tupac was bugging out.[42]

Many have explained the arc of his life, bending here toward an early death, in terms of the damage done to him in prison, the detrimental influence of Suge Knight (co-founder of Death Row Records), or else in terms of the excessive and explosive temperament of Tupac himself, a man, like a Jay Gatsby or a Greek hero, prone to seek glory in excess, transgression, and the lust for power. Whether he was ruined by his search for the American dream, Gatsby-like, or by an uncontrollable rage, Achilles-like, Tupac's life seemed to follow the course of a falling star, burning bright, intense, and far too brief.

But even as his life seemed to follow this declining and fatal course, with dark shadows menacing his every move, the music presents contradictory evidence. Contrary to a simple narrative of decline, in fact, his music moves in tangled and torturous patterns, at turns forward and backward, racing and fading, upward and downward. Sometimes spite and malice gained the upper hand, and then, suddenly, the rancor gave way to clarity, tenderness, and insight. In the latter vein, I think of the beautiful "Keep Ya Head Up" on his second album, a song dedicated not only to Latasha Harlins (the African American fifteen-year-old killed by a convenience-store owner in 1991) but, as he says in the first verse, "to my sisters on welfare," and to all young women in abusive relationships. "Please don't cry," Tupac raps in a delicate tone, "dry your eyes, never let up/ Forgive, but don't forget, girl, keep ya head up." Later, in verse 2, the song shifts to reflections on black pride ("I remember Marvin Gaye used to sing to me/ He had me feeling like black was the thing to be"), and then to social and political commentary ("They got money for wars, but can't feed the poor"). And the examples of genuine prophecy kept coming, album after album: on *Me Against the World* (1995), Tupac swerved back and forth between sharp, pensive observations of urban anxieties and traumas ("Me Against the World," "So Many Tears," "Dear Mama") and a nihilistic (and gnostic) repudiation of the world ("Fuck the World"), between thoughtful soul-searching and a despairing fury. Though unrelenting in his criticism of abusive cops and prejudicial laws ("Can you picture my prophecy," he raps on "Me Against the World," "stress in the city, the cops hot for me/ The projects is full of bullets, the bodies droppin'"), the ultimate villain in these songs is the eerie specter of death, a presence that haunts almost every song on the album, lurking and prowling in the corners, stalking every word and phrase. There is no doubt that he puts up a fight against it on *Me Against the World*, employing his music as an amulet against harm, but the listener gets the feeling that he is only a small boat fighting an immense tidal wave or a behemoth whale, his soul flailing and thrashing against the abyss.

Given all the peculiarities and contradictions of Tupac's life, no one adjective or description seems to size up the young man. I've always had the impression, though, that Tupac was something of what William James called a "sick soul," a person tormented by the weight of the world's sorrow, their psyche dogged by demons of doubt, confusion, despair, and melancholy. Though "sick soul" has an entirely negative connotation in English, James numbered some of the greatest geniuses of history among the type: an Augustine, Kierkegaard, Pascal, Tolstoy, or Dostoyevsky. Such figures seem to sense, with raw and painful acuity, the emptiness and weariness of life, the horror of innocent suffering, the futility of fame and fortune, the awful fleetingness of human life. Contrary to the healthy-minded and carefree souls for whom life is easy and trouble-free, these figures move through life as if they are going through the various stations of the cross, passing from one misfortune to another, a constant state of crisis. No matter their successes, they remain dissatisfied and restless, a state of being that can be, and here's the irony, both destructive and extraordinarily creative.[43] Unwilling to accept the world as they find it, they are more likely to seek out, whether here on earth or elsewhere, alternatives to the status quo, which explains both their convention-shattering creativity and their desperate longing for transcendent and otherworldly possibilities. Hanif Abdurraqib, speaking about Sun Ra, captures nicely the logic: "I've run out of language to express the avalanche of anguish I feel when faced with this world, and so if I can't make sense of this planet, I'm better off imagining another."[44]

This, if nothing else, surely explains Tupac's yearning for God, a major mark of his life and music. Like one of the rebellious and alienated characters in Dostoyevsky's novels, Tupac was haunted by God as much as by sin, anxiety, and dread. He turned to religion out of a sense of desperation, as though he was drowning and God was the only thing that kept his head above water.[45] In a sense, he sinned his way to God, plunging himself into the muck and mess of sin until he grew more and more disillusioned. Because these things, from greed and violence to drugs and sex without feeling or care, gave him neither satisfaction nor peace, he would throw himself at the mercy of God, finding more moments of repose here than anywhere else. Part lifeline, part protective armor, part salve for his wounds, religion seemed to offer him what nothing else could: deliverance, atonement, purpose, a thread of hope. Religious sentiments, simply put, flooded his mind, suffusing even his most profane raps with the smell of incense. On "Lord Knows," Tupac approximates the biblical Psalmist, for instance, his soul reaching out to God while his enemies surround him, wishing to do him harm. He sounds as if he is struggling to breathe as his stresses and burdens pull him under like a dropped anchor: "I'm losin' hope, they got me stressin', can the Lord/ forgive me, Got the spirit of a thug in me . . . My memories bring me misery, and life is hard/ in the ghetto, it's insanity, I can't breathe." On "So Many Tears," Tupac confesses to being lost and weary; when he asks, "God can you feel me/ Take me away from all the pressure and pain," it strikes me as both a desperate plea and a Job-like complaint at one and the same time, part beseeching, part query, part challenge. His situation is grave, and he turns to God as he is falling on his knees: "I'm fallin' to the floor beggin' for the Lord to let me in/ To heaven's door—Shed so many tears."

And these themes are unrelenting; even as he starts to lose his moral compass in later albums, as I suggested, he clings to a religious bearing. "Life Goes On," from *All Eyez on Me*, has the mournful flavor of a ghetto dirge, the words commemorating young black men who fall "victim to the streets"; "Only God Can Judge Me" registers a dark and fatalistic mood, with the rapper gripped by paranoia and despair, and the synthesizer striking the high-pitched sound of a flatline on a heart monitor. The representation of the "streets" here is ominous and malevolent ("the streets got our babies"), as though these hardscapes are fiends and demons more than physical spaces. In some ways, this perspective recalls the portrait of urban landscapes in the literature of the "lost generation"—the claustrophobic, oppressive, and violent nature of city life—but the sense of exile or estrangement in Tupac is so much more than a literary or philosophical vogue: one can feel his stress in the sounds and cadences, the welts and bumps of his life bleeding through the words like braille on the page. As he struggles to stay alive, in any case, Tupac lunges for God: "Oh my Lord tell me what I'm livin' for/ Everybody's droppin' got me knockin' on heaven's door." "I Ain't Mad at Cha," likewise, is a brooding and contemplative rap, an island of repose in an album that is stormy, violent, and turbulent, a still point in the surrounding tempest. Tupac sounds tranquil and penitent on the track, his words morphing into prayer: "Father forgive us for livin', while all my homies stuck in prison/ Barely breathin' believin' that the world is a prison/ It's like a ghetto we can never leave/ A broken rose givin' bloom through the cracks of the concrete." In spite of the constraining and bleak images (the ghetto as prison), a sliver of light appears in the song like a miracle, the rose blooming through the cracks, the sun parting the clouds, and God suddenly appearing beyond the horizon, bringing rest to the weary.

These religious themes also surface on Tupac's final album, *The Don Killuminati* (1996), but at this point he seems to be writhing and kicking more than ever, the tide submerging his soul. He is increasingly agitated and restless, ebbing and flowing, churning and tossing about and, ultimately, crashing against the rocks, a ship run aground. And yet even as he seems to be tangled in seaweed, the deep pulling him down, drowning in despair and rage, he throws up prayers to God like a last-ditch effort at salvation: "I'm a ghost in these killing fields/ Hail Mary catch me if I go." And later, as he wages a war between the impulse for God and a hankering for the stupor of alcohol, he tosses out these conflicted pleas: "Catch me Father please, 'cause I'm falling, in the liquor store/ That's the Hennessey, I hear ya calling, can I get some more?"

His legacy, all of this is to say, is a mixed bag, containing good and bad alike—the gifts of Prometheus and the ills of Pandora at once. Yes, he was flawed and tortured and sinful and damaged, but perhaps in spite of these things—or, maybe, *because* of them—he understood something about Christianity that is often missed by many of its most pious disciples: namely that God's appearance in human history assumed the flesh of an outcast and delinquent, a life associated with sinners and pariahs. The Christian God was a hidden God, writes Michael Eric Dyson, "disguised in the clothing of society's most despised members," hidden, says David Tracy, "both in the revolting physical sufferings of Jesus, as well as in the devastating spiritual *anfechtungen* undergone by Jesus in his desperate prayer for release at Gethsemane, his humiliating public trial, his abandonment by his friends, his brutal scourging, the mocking of onlookers, and his cruel death—a death by crucifixion, an extremely painful and humiliating public death reserved for the worst criminals."[46]

Tupac understood this feature of Christianity better than most churchgoers, his tortured soul pulling him closer to it. Suffering his own variety of *anfechtungen*—a feeling of anguish that bound him to the tortured history of black life in America—he recognized something powerful and revelatory about the symbol of the cross. "There's something liberating about the message of the cross," writes the Reverend Jonathan Walton on this point, "to those who are unjustly persecuted, those forced to suffer at the hands of an evil empire, those who are forced to deal with nails and the whips of an old rugged cross."[47] Whatever his flaws, and they were numerous, Tupac got this right about Christianity, how it attracted the poor and outcasts of history, how it offered hope to groups who have known the humiliation and horror of the old rugged cross. It was this intuition, of course, that lent his image of Jesus—as on "Black Jesus"—a darker hue, the color of blackness. Jesus was black, in his judgment, because he shared the suffering of the unloved and unwanted of history, ventured into their squalid hoods, knew their troubles and worries. He was black because he embodied compassion for sinners and the unclean, the poor and ostracized.[48]

In the end, Tupac's ghetto theology revolved on this point, the hunch that God dwells among the least of our brethren.[49] While there was much in his life and art, I admit, that is worrisome, confused, violent, and sexist, his music was also filled with honest and hard-hitting truths, ones that cut deep to the bone. "I like the look of agony/ because I know it's true," Emily Dickinson famously wrote. Tupac had this look of agony, in my opinion. And he was never more true than when he conveyed it in his music, when he fretted and agonized over his fate, when he poured out his soul to God, when he was raw with worry and sorrow, and when he opened himself to the beauty of life, baring his soul like the rocks on the shore when the tide recedes. He was never more real than when he closed his eyes to the false temptations and empty promises of the world, when he went blind and let God take over, as he puts on his "Ghetto Gospel": "Never forget that God isn't finished with me yet/ I feel his hand on my brain/ when I write rhymes I go blind and let the Lord do his thang." Always an unfinished product in this way, groping in the dark, reaching out for something undefined, fumbling for God, Tupac's life stands as a testimony not only to the imperiled and alienated existence of so many young black males throughout the world; it also bears testimony to the wisdom looming in blindness, to the beauty of blackness, and to the brilliant shafts of light that illuminate the motes of dust and experience that would otherwise remain invisible. So call Tupac, and souls in his mold, the sick, sinful, or mad; regardless, they are often the most explosively original and dazzling. "The only people for me are the mad ones," writes Jack Kerouac in a passage that could have served as an obituary for Tupac, "the ones who are mad to live, mad to talk, mad to be saved, desirous of everything at the same time, the ones who never yawn or say a commonplace thing, but burn, burn, burn, like fabulous yellow roman candles exploding like spiders across the stars and in the middle you see the blue center light pop and everybody goes 'Awww!'"[50]

CHAPTER 4
The Return of God in Hip-Hop

Kendrick Lamar's Street Theology

My partners in the hood right now, they listen to rap every day 'cause it's the only thing that can relate to their stories and tribulations. They live and breathe it. . . . And if you're not doing it to say the most impactful shit . . . then what are we doing here . . . I'm the closest thing to a preacher they have.[1]

Kendrick Lamar

Kendrick Lamar says, "God got Us" and the Us crawls out of the speaker and wraps its arms around the black people in the room. The way a good preacher might say "We" in a black church and the congregation hums.[2]

Hanif Abdurraqib

If the Black Lives Matter movement has an anthem, it's probably Kendrick Lamar's "Alright." Five years after its release, it's still chanted en masse by demonstrators and blasted from car stereos at protests, fluttering in the air like a liberation flag.[3]

Giovanni Russonello

Kendrick Lamar, the Compton native and first rapper to earn a Pulitzer Prize for music, tells us that he's the closest thing to a preacher for many of his "partners in the hood." The comment suggests, for better or worse, that emcees have now assumed the mantle of prophecy that was once enjoyed by preachers, priests, or imams, that rappers are today's voices of the disenfranchised, even mouthpieces of the divine.[4] There might be plenty of hyperbole in Lamar's comment (preachers, imams, and churches are alive and kicking in many parts of urban America), but I think it accurately registers some of the seismic shifts in urban religious landscapes. If religion hasn't disappeared in ghettos and barrios throughout the United States, it is, nonetheless, undergoing significant changes, shape-shifting to account for new predicaments and new threats to the soul.[5]

Kendrick Lamar's music, as I'll try to show here, is one of the best illustrations of such changes in hip-hop, a testimony to the ongoing vitality of religion in the streets, to its surprising ability to rise out of the ashes of urban life and speak to the spiritual and social anxieties of the twenty-first century. While he shares a common sound and purpose with his rap forebears in Compton—making art out of the simmering anger of the streets—Lamar is rarely satisfied with profane purposes alone, his soul too restless and uneasy to be content with fame and fortune alone.[6] In consequence, he has created his own unaffiliated version of "straight outta Compton," combining a wide variety of sources: the esoteric spirituality of East Coast rappers; the ethical-political righteousness of Public Enemy; the soulful, melodic, easy rhythms of G-funk; the storytelling of Scarface, Biggie, or Gucci Mane; the menacing street knowledge of N.W.A. or Compton's Most Wanted; the jazz-inflected vibes of Freestyle Fellowship, Guru, Digable Planets, or the Native Tongues; the soul-searching of Goodie Mob, DMX, Tupac, Lauryn Hill, Kanye West, and Chance the Rapper, and so on. He wanders widely across many rap styles: the sacred and profane, gangster and alternative, bass-slapped trap and the lyrically effusive East Coast stuff. Let's take a closer look, in this chapter, at the skillful arrangements and blends of Lamar's music, how he manages, in particular, to spin together a variety of filaments to make a rich variety of street theology.

Good Kid, M.A.A.D City

Good Kid, M.A.A.D City, Lamar's first major studio album, tells the story of a good kid in a fallen, dangerous world, a world beset by any number of perils. The album's cover features the rapper as a young child, on the lap of an uncle flashing a gang sign, surrounded by his grandfather and a second uncle. Baby formula and a forty-ounce bottle of malt liquor stand in front of him; innocence is juxtaposed with the poisonous realties of adulthood in South Central LA. Before we even break open the seals of the music, we are introduced to a part of California that is nothing like the dreamy, utopian land of American lore, its streetscapes much more jagged and treacherous, ruled by hostile sets of

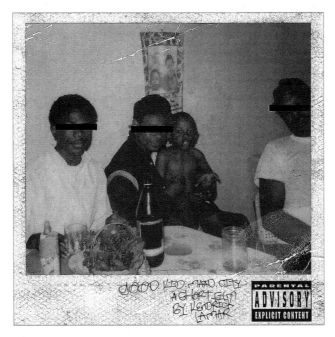

Figure 1 Cover of Kendrick Lamar, *Good Kid, M.A.A.D City* (2012)

Pirus, Crips, and militarized police. The child pictured on the cover will have to learn how to carefully navigate these traps and perils.

Though the album is a coming-of-age story, a bildungsroman, it swerves wildly away from Romantic versions of the genre. More realistic and street-smart, *Good Kid* is a day in the life of a Compton kid in the twenty-first century, following his cravings for girls, money, and status, his flirtations with alcohol, drugs, and gangs, and his narrow escapes from prison and death. These themes are, of course, common in hip-hop, but with Lamar they are subject to moral scrutiny, punctured of their hyped status and brought back down to earth. Instead of the highs of alcohol, drugs, or drank, he bemoans the lows and nadirs of altered states ("Swimming Pools," "The Art of Peer Pressure"); instead of the glory of gang life, he raps of the tragic waste of human lives lost to violence ("Sing About Me," "M.A.A.D City"); instead of the thrills of pimping, he satirizes the unfeeling and egotistical exploitation of women as a betrayal of Dr. King's dream ("Backseat Freestyle," "Sing About Me"); instead of "realness" as a trope of toughness and violence, it becomes synonymous with responsibility, faith, and love ("Real"); instead of the traditional preening and boasting in one's power and masculinity, he boasts in his weakness and vulnerability à la St. Paul. Through it all, Lamar advances as an artist, displaying significant progress over his earliest mixtapes, *Hub City Threat*, *Training Day*, *C4*, *The Kendrick Lamar EP*, and *Overly Dedicated*.

Only in his teens and early twenties, the mixtapes reveal a rapper still searching for his voice. He is too quick to claim the throne of hip-hop at this point, too cocky, too derivative. He already shows a talent for stringing words together, and for battling rival emcees, but he hasn't mastered the craft of songwriting yet and, more to the point, hasn't mastered himself. By the time we arrive at *Good Kid* (2012), however, a short year after his first studio album, *Section.80* (2011) (which, incidentally, had some fine songs in "HiiiPower," "Ronald Reagan Era," and "Poe Man's Dreams"), Lamar already sounds like a wise veteran of the game, a precocious young man who has grown up before our eyes. Not only has he honed his rapping and writing skills, but he also digs much deeper into his spiritual life, exploring parts of himself that he hadn't surveyed hitherto. As he has stated in interviews, he apparently underwent a religious transformation at the time, the change giving rise to a more mature and thoughtful artist.[7] Whereas his mixtapes show little introspection and soul-searching, *Good Kid*, and later albums, are now consumed by these things. A taste of religion, to borrow a phrase that the Dunham Jubilee Singers popularized in the 1930s, turned him inside out. Marcus Moore, addressing the transition between the mixtapes and *Good Kid*, touches on this exact point: "This is where he put God in control of his life and art, and where his work became therapeutic for himself and listeners at large."[8]

We might see the gradual transformation of the artist—the emergence of the butterfly from the chrysalis, to borrow a metaphor from his next album—by way of the name change that Kendrick adopted sometime around 2009. Instead of the childhood persona of K.Dot, the protagonist of his earliest mixtapes, he started using the name Kendrick Lamar, as if he needed a name change to mark the birth of this new self, the transformation as momentous as Jacob's experience in Genesis: "You shall no longer be named Jacob but Israel, for you have wrestled with God and man and your life has been preserved" (Genesis 32:28). Jacob, if you recall the story, only becomes Israel through a painful contest/struggle/*agonia* with God, an experience that leaves him wounded but blessed, lacerated but consecrated and set apart. His new name and epithet is earned by suffering, scrappiness, and preternatural guile (recall that in the womb, just before delivery, he grasped at the heel of his brother, Esau, so that he might seize the rights of the firstborn). He becomes his true and authentic self, this biblical hustler and trickster, through pluck and persistence, inventiveness and ingenuity and, above all, by way of this revelatory epiphany at the river Jabbok, as he comes face to face with God. Kendrick Lamar, as I see it, undergoes something vaguely similar on *Good Kid*.

Diverging from many of the common tropes of hip-hop, and consistent with this wrenching spiritual conversion, Lamar places the questions of God and family at the core of *Good Kid*; these themes, writes Jayson Greene, are the "fraying tethers holding Lamar back from the chasm of gang violence that threatens to consume him."[9] The rapper even includes the voices of his parents on the track of "Real," for instance, with his father warning him about the quagmire of gang violence, and his mother encouraging him to "tell your story to these black and brown kids in Compton," and to use hip-hop as a light in "dark places of violence." The entire album pays homage to this counsel.

Building on the warnings of his parents, and implying that spiritual needs are as imperative as social and political needs, "Sing About Me, I'm Dying of Thirst" turns the focus to the insidious and deadly circumstances of Compton life, how they can rob inhabitants of their bodies and souls. With a sample from the jazz guitarist Grant Green—a supple and bluesy guitar riff from "Maybe Tomorrow" fused with a kick drum rhythm, rim shots, and distant orchestral snippets—the song juxtaposes a smooth jazz aesthetic with rough ghetto scenarios, a cool and unhurried flow with the heat of the streets. (Grant Green, incidentally, has been widely sampled in hip-hop, including by A Tribe Called Quest, Wu-Tang, Digable Planets, Cypress Hill, Logic, and Public Enemy, to name a few.) The simple, plangent production clears the way for the dense and complex narrative that follows, delivered in an unhurried and meditative manner by Lamar, his words skipping nimbly through the verses. Often a ventriloquist in his raps, switching voices, pitches, or characters to tell a story, Lamar plays the role of a gangster in verse 1, the sister of a murdered prostitute in verse 2 (a verse that revisits "Keisha's Song" of *Section.80*), and finally introduces his own voice in verse 3. In the former episode, Lamar traces the arc of a man trapped in the swamp of ghetto violence, unable to escape the "Piru shit that has been in me forever" (the Piru gang, a set of the Bloods). Thrown into circumstances that he could neither fully control nor comprehend, the young man's life reads like the plot of a tragedy, a drama in which the protagonist is at the whim of forces beyond his control. What Michael Eric Dyson once wrote about Tupac Shakur's death applies perfectly to Lamar's character in this song: "He embodied the harsh, callous death of thousands of black males victimized by arbitrary violence, and, often, the violence they provoked."[10]

Ultimately, by situating the gangster in these tragic circumstances, Lamar humanizes him, an aimless, confused, and frightened young man; he is not malevolent. Never given the chance to be a child, or to learn and grow and change, he meets a violent end as gunshots ring out and interrupt his final words. As his voice falters and fades into silence, he beseeches Kendrick to tell his story. Lamar's rap, faithful to the plea, fills in the blanks and silences of this man's life. The rap eulogizes his life.

On the heels of this song, "I'm Dying of Thirst" quickly follows and continues the same story, but now with a spotlight on the temptations that can lead to ruin—he switches, in other words, from social to psychological struggles, addressing the threats of greed, sex, and depression in his life. At times, he confesses, he's a slave to these things, running in endless circles like a mouse on a spinning wheel, getting nowhere. Just as he's sinking further into the quicksand of his despair, however, he recalls the words of his mother, admonishing him on religious matters: "The truth will set you free," she says to him. "You dying of thirst, you dying of thirst/ So hop in that water, and pray that it works." Later in the song, a churchgoing woman, voiced by Maya Angelou, repeats the same message: "You young men are dying of thirst."

Synonymous with spiritual longing and desolation—a parched soul—the metaphor of "thirst" in the song draws from the symbolism of water in John's gospel: "Everyone who drinks this water will be thirsty again," Jesus says to the Samaritan woman at the well, "but whoever drinks the water I shall give will never thirst; the water I shall give will become in him a spring of water welling up to eternal life" (John 4:13-14). Caught in adultery, the woman is treated with forgiveness and compassion by Jesus, an act startling to his disciples. (As an unloved and isolated group—descendants of the Northern Israelite tribes who worshipped at Mount Gerizim instead of Jerusalem—the Samaritans were considered impure, and the adulterous woman was doubly impure.) Though there doesn't appear to be a redemptive end for the gangster (or for Keisha and her sister in verse 2), Lamar invokes the imagery of John's gospel in hopes that his listeners might bestow the same compassion upon such street figures—a gangster and a prostitute—as Jesus granted the woman at the well. It is invoked with the hope that his audience, if not the characters caught in these circumstances, may come to see (as omniscient readers/listeners) the possibility of redemption in the story. The water, hence, is a symbol of baptism: "The song represents being baptized," explains Lamar about the song, "the actual water, getting dipped in holy water. It represents when my whole spirit changed, when my life starts."[11] Thus, if a miasma of tragedy hangs over the world that the rapper sketches here, this rap is about the life-giving rain that can be extracted from dark clouds, about the possibility of renewal. Placed in a modern urban context, Lamar's rap turns the episode in John's gospel into a street parable for today.[12]

In terms of style and form, moreover, the labyrinthine narrative, psychology, and spirituality of "Sing About Me, I'm Dying of Thirst" is a good representation of a lot of Lamar's music. If crunk or trap prefers simple chants and memorable turns of phrase—attacked with a James Brown-like fervor—Lamar prefers wordy and hyperbolic abundance, his words rushing across the song like a swarm of bright, shooting comets. And behind this deluge of shimmering words, of course, there is almost always a lesson to be learned, a pattern to the wordy arrangements, a prophecy or augury in the comets.

Turning elsewhere, "Swimming Pools" is one of the standouts on *Good Kid*. Taking lessons from Houston's "chopped and screwed" music, or *Aquemini*'s dreamy and spaced-out acoustics, the song is a slow-motion and woozy groove, a reflection of the warping influence of alcohol and drugs on the mind. The rapper is a divided and twisted man in the song, torn between the angels of his better nature and the devils of his worst, the latter urging him to drown himself in alcohol and drugs, and his conscience urging resistance, stressing the poisonous consequences of alcohol in the lives of many, including in the life of his own grandfather. Various voices and pitches are used in his vocal performance: a vocoder-inflected singing delivery for influences that encourage debauchery; a high-pitched and nasal voice for his conscience; and a more natural, conversational language when he switches to the first person, speaking of the poison that oozes through his body as he starts to feel the mind-bending effects of the alcohol. Dazed and trippy, the music renders in sound and feeling an altered state of mind, while the lyrics probe the highs and lows of the experience. If relief or solace from the sorrows of life is desired, Lamar advises, without resorting to a moralizing sanctimony, that one look past alcohol and drugs.

Another musical standout on the album is "Bitch, Don't Kill My Vibe": it samples the gentle downbeat of Boom Clap Bachelor's song "Tiden Flyver" (a Danish electronic group), and then adds quivering percussion and bass, as well as resonant strings and flourishes of R&B à la Leon Haywood or William DeVaughn. Soulfully muted, the song dramatizes Lamar's inner jihad, his combat with an adversary that lurks within. The music video opens with Kendrick in the back of a Catholic church at a funeral, the camera panning to capture the image of Christ crucified on the altar as the rapper prays, "I am a sinner, who's probably gonna sin again/ Lord, forgive me. Lord, forgive me/ Things I don't understand/ Sometimes I need to be alone." Surveying his soul's terrain, and plumbing his subconscious mind, Lamar glides pensively through the verses, singing at moments, rapping at others. In oblique and subtle ways—the mode of communication is Kierkegaardian, allusive, not direct—he hints at the war that he is waging between his old self and the new Kendrick Lamar. He draws a contrast between drowning in liquor and drugs, on the one hand, and drowning in the waters of baptism, on the other— the former leads to death, the latter to life. At the end of the music video, in fact, the words "Death to Molly" (the drug ecstasy, MDMA) flash on the screen, and so we know that the funeral is, at minimum, for Molly, but also for the old Kendrick Lamar (K.Dot).

After the elegiac rhythm of "Don't Kill My Vibe," the music picks up speed and aggression with "Backseat Freestyle," a rap that can make any club get crunk. Lamar brings his big brass voice to this joint, sounding arrogant and brash like Lamar's sixteen-year-old self, his words recklessly flying through the lines like a car without brakes. Though he speaks in the first person, gloating and squawking like the Scarecrow before he got his brain, none of the vaunting verses reflect his current—more mature and awakened—state of mind. Following this shot of propulsion, the album returns to the mellow, cruising rhythms of G-funk with "M.A.A.D City." (MC Eiht cries out in G-funk fashion, "Ain't nuthin' but a Compton thang.") It has a slow, fat, reverberating bass beat, accompanied by an agitated synthesizer and then, at the end, a dash of Dr. Dre's high-pitched whine. (The production of Sounwave gives way in the second part of the song to Terrace Martin.) As the title suggests, "M.A.A.D City" spells out the madness of ghetto life, tallying the many pressures and stresses of the hood: the grilling of kids by gangbangers ("where are you from"); the sound of bullets in the air and "bodies on top of bodies"; projects tore up, gang signs thrown up; cluck-heads everywhere; regulators in the whip; drugs wreaking the destruction of young minds and souls, and so on. In the midst of so much chaos and conflict, Lamar's rap stardom—and specifically his spiritual vision—comes across as something of a miracle for escaping the deadening grip of these circumstances.

What Oliver Wang once wrote about Freestyle Fellowship applies nicely to Lamar's achievement on *Good Kid*: "They claimed South Central roots, but funneled the fury and frustrations of their physical space into the mental space of lyrical imaginations as expansive as the Southland's sprawl."[13] Lamar most certainly anchored *Good Kid* in the experiences of growing up poor in Compton, the son of a former gang member, but he also takes his listeners on expansive rides through the sacred landscapes of his psyche. In the journey of the album, outward and inward at once, spiritual matters come across as deeply consequential issues, matters of life and death, not to be neglected.

To Pimp a Butterfly

If *Good Kid* wasn't complicated enough, *To Pimp a Butterfly* (2015) is even trickier, more convoluted. Both albums are examples of California's post-gangster moment in hip-hop, but *TPAB* distinctly ventures into avant-garde territory, the rapper stretching himself out like a bird who first gets his wings. Made after an inspirational visit to South Africa to visit the prison cell of Nelson Mandela, *TPAB* reflects a deeper and more mature engagement with politics, art, and religion than what came before. This is mind-traveling rap, an example of Lamar's ability to explore the heights, depths, and breadth of hip-hop. If N.W.A. once put on wax the rage and defiance of ghetto youth at the outbreak of the LA riots of 1992, Lamar's music has done something similar for the disenfranchised youth of Trump's America. "His verses feel like pronouncements," writes Hua Hsu, "the words rushing out as though he had been tasked with conveying an entire community's joys and sorrows."[14]

The album's cover art—young shirtless black men from Lamar's neighborhood, posing, primping, and partying in front of the White House—also

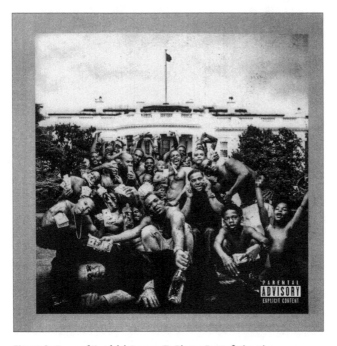

Figure 2 Cover of Kendrick Lamar, *To Pimp a Butterfly* (2015)

speaks volumes about Lamar's vision: youth who are consistently ignored and excluded by the White House are placed front and center, their lives rescued from invisibility. For never knowing the world beyond Compton, the young men wear an expression of excitement, elation, and smug defiance as they claim spaces that are not only unfamiliar to them, but typically unwelcoming and unsupportive of their lives. There's a white judge at the bottom of the picture, lying recumbent with his eyes X'd out (perhaps recalling Malcolm X), as the kids stand on top of him. He represents, according to Lamar, a judicial system and other forces of authority that have viewed young black kids as menaces to society, never giving them a real chance at life.[15]

In terms of music, *TPAB* is genre-bending, echoing the bohemian stylings of André 3000's *The Love Below*, the Roots' *Phrenology*, Souls of Mischief's *93 'til Infinity*, Q-Tip's *Kamaal the Abstract*, or D'Angelo's *Black Messiah*, if not older masters in Miles Davis, Sly Stone, and Parliament-Funkadelic. The influences of George Clinton and Dr. Dre bring the funk to the album (they both appear on the opening track, "Wesley's Theory"), while the horns of Kamasi Washington and Terrace Martin, the piano work of Robert Glasper, the crooning of Bilal, SZA, Jessica Vielmas, and Lalah Hathaway, and the be-bop splashes of Flying Lotus add the flavors of jazz and neo-soul. With few concessions made to radio-friendly tastes, the album is close in sense and sensibility to the alternative, underground vibes of "Project Blowed" in Los Angeles, the open-mic collective of abstract wordsmiths and jazz-accented beat-makers. It's the kind of sound that appeals to discriminating tastes—more like wine than malt liquor.

Thematically, too, the album is daring, experimental, and street savvy, a gospel where God makes surprising appearances in unlikely places: in the broken and scorned face of a beggar ("How Much a Dollar Cost"); among kids trapped in the ghetto ("Institutionalized"); in the struggle against the temptations of Lucifer ("For Sale?," "Mortal Man"); in the righteous, aggressive anger of black power ("The Blacker the Berry," "Alright"); or in the self-critical interrogations of an anxious, troubled soul ("u"). If mainstream American Christianity privileges decorum and respectability, Lamar is delightfully bedeviling on *TPAB*. He theologizes with a hammer, striking at creeds and dogmas that privilege the victors of history and diminish the victims. "What gives me inspiration," Lamar has said, "is giving expression and game to people who don't have it. . . . I want you to get angry. I want you to feel disgusted. I want you to feel uncomfortable."[16]

Written in the wake of Trayvon Martin's murder, "The Blacker the Berry" makes us feel uncomfortable in this way, thundering at the never-ending loops of racism in American life. With hints of James Baldwin's *The Fire Next*

Time, Tupac's "Keep Ya Head Up," and Ice-T's famous gangster rap "6 in the Mornin'," the rap invokes fire as a punishing and purifying force, fire as Pentecostal energy. "Six in the morn', fire in the street/ Burn, baby, burn, that's all I wanna see," Lamar chants at the beginning of the rap before launching into a fiery tirade of rhymes. Because black life is in peril, Lamar channels combinations of outrage, satire, and black pride in the song, rapping in a voice that is hoarse, impolite, and spitting mad, the words exploding through clenched teeth. "I'm African American, I'm African/ I'm black as the moon, heritage of a small village/ pardon my residence, came from the bottom of mankind." As if his emotions are tearing at his insides, yearning to be free, he races through the verses quickly and furiously, resulting in a harried sketch of his psyche.

And nothing is exempt from his fiery, blistering attack, including religion. He notes, for instance, the ways in which Christianity has played a part in American histories of discrimination and oppression: "Curse me till I'm dead/ church me with your fake prophesying that I'm a be just another slave in my head." Hinting at the curse of Ham—for centuries used to justify the subjugation of Africans and Muslims—Lamar excoriates the kind of religion that turns god into an idol of white supremacy, a god that would bless nativist-driven bigotry, a god that uses patriotism like a cudgel against black and brown lives. And Lalah Hathaway's backup vocals, in the intro, reinforce the point, urging resistance to "fake prophesying": "They want us ... To bow down to our knees ... And pray to a God. ... That we don't believe." Because the accent is almost entirely on the deconstructive, taking America to task for its history of racism, the song conforms to a variety of negative theology: we can only say what God is *not* (namely, a figure made in the image of white supremacy), not what God is. The image of "fire" in the song is, thus, purifying and liberating, a force that incinerates the false gods to ashes, and, simultaneously, reveals the true God as a name, YHWH, that must not be spoken.

Staying with the book of Exodus, Lamar's vision on *TPAB* also coheres with the emancipatory significance of the Exodus story, for the moment of the burning bush—when God is revealed to Moses like a spark from the flame—is also the moment when Moses receives the call to liberate the Israelites from bondage in Egypt, thus igniting the movement for freedom. "How Much a Dollar Cost" is written with these stories in mind, in fact, weaving together episodes of Exodus and the New Testament. The music here doesn't burst out of the speakers as in "The Blacker the Berry"; it bubbles and fizzes instead, a softer mixture of tambourine, piano, and pensive warbles with classic boom-bap percussion. Delivered in the first person, the rap describes the privileges of Lamar's current life, a rapper of great fame and fortune. No longer the hungry and hustling figure of his earliest work, trying to escape the claustrophobic conditions of Compton, "How Much a Dollar Cost" chronicles the anxieties of an artist who has made it to the mountaintop but is now lightheaded and dazed by his success. The song puts us in the driver's seat of his consciousness, a swirling vortex of fears and anxieties.

Driving up to a gas station in a luxury ride, Lamar recounts an encounter, first, with an African worker, whom he denigrates, and then with a beggar, whom he shuns. (This episode is based on Lamar's encounter with a homeless man during his trip to South Africa.) The beggar pesters him for money. And because he picks up the scent of alcohol, Lamar reacts callously, his thoughts running roughshod over the man's dignity, belittling and dismissing him. The verses detail Lamar's arrogance, anger, guilt, and queasiness when he is near the beggar, as if there were "parasites in my stomach." He feels accosted by his gaze. The beggar's first words invoke the Scriptures: "Have you ever opened up Exodus 14/ A humble man is all we ever need." Exodus 14, remember, details the episode of the Red Sea, with Pharaoh's army on the heels of the fleeing Israelites. Drunk with his power and privilege, Pharaoh sends his army to re-enslave the Israelites until God intervenes. Instead of identifying himself with the Israelites of the story, as we might expect, Lamar daringly makes himself out to be the villain, equating his own cruel and hard heart with Pharaoh.

And the beggar, on the other hand, turns out to be a manifestation of God, a theophany in the guise of a vagabond: "Know the truth," he remarks, "it'll set you free/ You're looking at the Messiah, the son of Jehovah, the higher truth/ the choir that spoke the word, the Holy Spirit/ the nerve of Nazareth, and I'll tell you just how much a dollar cost/ The price of having a spot in heaven, embrace your loss, I am God." In keeping with numerous episodes of the Bible and rabbinic traditions, God stuns the narrator here, appearing in the desperate guise of a beggar, a face leathered by the sun, diminished by suffering. In addition to numerous biblical texts (say, God appearing to Abraham in the guise of strangers at the Oaks of Mamre, or Christ among the least of history in Matthew 25), the rap echoes the great rabbinic legend of the Messiah (as recounted by Martin Buber in his "Three Addresses"): "Before the gates of Rome sits a leprous beggar and waits. He is the Messiah . . . and for whom does he wait? For you!"[17]

If the self-lacerating examination of "How Much a Dollar Cost" wrestles with the fears and anxieties that can accompany great wealth and fame, the rap "u" only intensifies the spotlight on Lamar's sins, this time verging on self-flagellation. He is a divided and damaged figure in the song, a soul that is cracked open, scrambled, and cooked right in front of the listener. In contrast to the cool music—jazzy, smooth, nimble, elegant—Lamar's bars are agitated and frantic, delivered in a wailing and howling voice, cracking and breaking as he accuses himself of failing his family and friends in Compton. (The tormenting guilt and feelings of unworthiness recall the *anfechtung* of Martin Luther before his breakthrough.) If he's striving to be a butterfly on the album, and to free his soul from its earthly fetters, Lamar is more like an agitated moth here, hurling himself at walls and lamps, banging into windows, blindly fluttering and charging in every direction. He's distraught and disturbed, delivering his lyrics in apoplectic and accusatory bursts. Like a hard-nosed prosecutor, his conscience piles on accusation after accusation, all of them related to the complaint that Lamar has deserted the struggling poor of Compton, that he has sold out. For a rapper who claims to speak for Compton and other ghettos, and who takes seriously biblical admonitions, this is a hard pill to swallow.

Meanwhile, the figure of "Lucy" appears on "For Sale?" to push him closer to the edge of despair. There is no doubt that Lucy is Lucifer in the song, the conniving angel of light. Whether a metaphorical figure (personification of the temptations and burdens that press upon him), or the devil figure of the gospels, Lucy seeks to poison Lamar's soul, depress his spirits, cloud his conscience, flatten his imagination, corrupt his will. A distressed voice is heard at the beginning of the song, a man gasping, wheezing, and panting for air, as if he is not only in danger of losing his breath, but losing his soul altogether. The music suddenly turns calming, however: soothing piano and horn riffs, a chorus of gentle alto voices, as if to remind us that music quiets the soul while Lucy agitates it, Christianity offers life while Lucy offers death: "Roses are red, violets are blue/ But me and you both pushing up daisies if I (want you)." (Falling for Lucy will put him, the point is, six feet under, to become food for worms, plants, and daisies.)

Lucy reappears on "Alright" as well, calling Lamar his "dog" and "chico." The rap recounts the particular charms that Lucy uses to ensnare the soul: greed ("ain't a profit big enough to feed you"), drugs and alcohol, the flash and fancy of material possessions, and, ultimately, the kind of depression that breaks the will and destroys the capacity for love. Lamar may be throwing shade at trap music here—or any form of rap that exalts money, drugs, sex, materialism—but the greater battle in the song is with his own compromises and bargains with Lucy, not with rivals in hip-hop. Lamar's devil wants the rapper absorbed by money, opiates, and women, wants the rapper adrift and aimless, lost in pleasure.

The most glaring motif on "Alright," however, is the battle with the legacy of prejudice and inequality in America. Moving from "u" and "For Sale" to "Alright" quickly changes the direction of the album, swerving from the private to the public, the personal to the political, the spiritual to the streets. The song, in point of fact, has been one of the most influential songs in recent hip-hop, a manifesto more than a rap. As a key anthem for Black Lives Matter, and hip-hop's equivalent of "We Shall Overcome," the song impressively captures the dissatisfaction and rage of underprivileged communities in America. To leave no doubt about the weight of the words, "Alright" opens with a line from Alice Walker's *The Color Purple*, "All my life, I had to fight." Right out of the gates, we know that we are treading on holy ground, a song that draws inspiration from past ancestors in order to face the struggles of the present.

And though he continues to be preoccupied with "Lucy" on the song, this figure is now seen as an external foe, a force that wreaks havoc, violence, and injustice on structural and systemic levels of society. The song, consequently, opens with a discourse on urban segregation and police brutality—a spoken-word delivery—before the music kicks in and Lamar begins to rap in a variety of flows, at turns staccato, singsong, and melodious, his verses musing over the social pressures and traumas of black life in a surprisingly buoyant key; the song, in other words, eases up on the dark existential mood of "u" and "For Sale." Now that he's wrestled with the griefs and troubles of life, the time has come for something comforting and cheering, and the chorus's refrain—"If God's got us/ we gonna be alright"—introduces a badly needed spirit of healing and hope. The music is now exultant and airy, "a psalm for street corners," says Marcus Moore.[18] The words and music translate Julian of Norwich's celebrated lines "All shall be well, and all shall be well, and all manners of things shall be well" into an urban, postmodern dialect. And the hook—not to mention the prancing, marching snare drums that accompany it—summons the community to the streets the way that Moses led the Israelites to the desert, or the way that New Orleans brass bands once called revelers to the parade; the urgency of liberation and justice coexists with the spirit of celebration. It's a vital, almost holy, rap.

At the same time, the song is nothing like a utopian dream: there is no chariot here to carry the black Israelites to freedom, no train that lights out for the territory, no bus that offers an escape from the indignities of Jim Crow. Lamar remains a troubled soul in the song ("I'm at the preacher's door, my knees gettin' weak"), a man too distrustful and cynical to believe that America will suddenly grant equality to people of color. At the end of the music video, accordingly, with Lamar floating on the top of a light post like a butterfly, a police officer shoots down the soaring artist. If Lamar is Icarus on *TPAB*, daring to soar into the stratospheres of art and society, daring to spread his wings and fly, the cop represents the heat of the sun, singeing and burning his wings, trying to keep him grounded and confined in Compton.

The final song on *TPAB*, "Mortal Man," returns to the image of the butterfly at the center of the album. The song was inspired by Tupac and Nelson Mandela. (Originally titled Tu Pimp a Caterpillar, or Tu P.A.C., *TPAB* was to be released at the twentieth-year anniversary of Tupac's *Me Against the World* [1995].) Lamar may rebuff the gangster tropes of Tupac's music, but he shares a strong bond with Tupac when it comes to the question of religion, both of them seeing rap music as a spiritual affair, a means of wrestling with God. And this brings us to the metaphors of caterpillar and butterfly on the album; for Lamar, the caterpillar is emblematic of a street-tough or hardened gangster, slithering and creeping through life, inhabiting the twilight zones of the city and doing what it can to survive. Since it is constantly shunned and demeaned by the world, it develops a cold attitude toward life. It feels cocooned and trapped. Its potential for contemplation and knowledge is stifled by its environment, and hence it lives to satisfy its most basic desires and urges. It lives by the codes of the warrior or hustler.

Though it's clear that *TPAB* defends the butterfly-like values of the Bible—gentle, compassionate, ethereal—we shouldn't be too quick to reject the traits and survival skills of the caterpillar, Lamar seems to imply. He knows that some of these harder and more callous attitudes can be necessary for survival in the streets; they are, as the word "callus" suggests, protective measures, the hard tissue that forms over a wound. When playing this role, a tougher and more visceral figure from the pages of gangster rap, Lamar's rapping will be aggressive, shrewd, and wily; it's closer, in fact, to a bull or shrewd serpent than a caterpillar, pure instinct, aggression, and cunning ("The Blacker the Berry," "Wesley's Theory," or "King Kunta").

And yet, in the end, there is no doubt that *TPAB* is primarily a schooling of the soul, an education in otherworldly and graceful attributes, a form of art that nourishes the wings of the butterfly that lies within us all. When not evident in the lyricism and storyline, Lamar's vulnerable tenor voice characterizes this, his pitch fluctuating and almost breaking at times to suggest tenderness, longing, and sublimity. Unbeknownst to the caterpillar, there is power and strength in these values. In this regard, the image of the butterfly on the album suggests an obvious spiritual preoccupation; the butterfly is, after all, a symbol of the soul in many religious and cultural traditions, a symbol of change, hope, and resurrection. The butterfly manages to break out of its cocooned existence, rising above its slithering existence, fluttering and sailing into the air. By appealing to this graceful creature, and choosing lighter jazz touches instead of bruising 808 beats, the music of *TPAB* aspires to be a catalyst for the metamorphosis of the human soul, helping facilitate the transition of the human person from larva to chrysalis to brilliant, colorful, weightless butterfly. Different from a reportage variety of rap, then, Lamar doesn't merely name things as they are on *TPAB*; he sees them, instead, for what they can be. "Wings begin to emerge, breaking the cycle of feeling stagnant," Lamar writes on "Mortal Man." "Finally free, the butterfly sheds light on situations that the caterpillar never considered."[19]

"Religion is a means of ultimate transformation," says Frederik Streng.[20] Whether or not religion is sized up accurately by Streng—and scholars in religion fight endlessly about the validity of any one definition—it applies nicely to Lamar's purpose on *TPAB* and elsewhere. His music is "religious" insofar as it is concerned with ultimate transformation, a metamorphosis of the human person into one's best and deepest self, into something transcendent and divine-like. In the case of *TPAB*, the metamorphosis at work is akin to Muhammad Ali's famous self-portrait: an artist that can sting, prick, and leave lasting welts like a bee, and then, just as quickly, turn into a butterfly, floating and dancing through the air.

DAMN.

Lamar's theological musings continue on his next album, *DAMN.*, even as the music changes registers. Compared with previous albums, the sound is spartan on *DAMN.*, stripped of the jazz riffs of *TPAB*. Gaining in force what it lost in complexity, the percussion—a return to fat 808s—is more pronounced on the album. Thanks to the trap flavors that Mike Will Made It brought to the table (famous for his Southern beats), and the loops of 1970s soul music, the beats are harder, fatter, and dirtier than Lamar's earlier music.[21] It makes for a soul-rattling experience, even more pleasing and electrifying than *Good Kid* or *TPAB*.

The new sound seems to have taken to heart the criticisms of *TPAB*: that too much musical complexity runs the risk of overwhelming the beats and rhythms that are elemental in hip-hop, draining the music of its kinetic energy. Jazz may confer an air of sophistication and profundity, and multisyllabic rhymes an air of erudition, but these things don't automatically make for good hip-hop. Simpler bass and percussion patterns, or monosyllabic rhymes, can be more musical to the ear and body than complex harmonies or a mouthful of multisyllabic rhymes. On paper, MF Doom's "Meat Grinder," Black Star's "Redefinition," or Lamar's "Rigamortis" are masterful displays of wordplay, dense verbiage, assonance, and internal and multisyllabic rhymes—and yet, rap is not played out on paper; rap is not the written word alone, not *sola scriptura*. It comes alive only in performance, when the emcee hits you viscerally. When missing this fundamental trait, it's easy to get lost in the thick woods and knotty jungles of some rappers' verses; sometimes you need a clearing and decluttering, an Occam's razor. Southern rap, whose minimalistic and beefy influence on *DAMN.* is unmistakable, has always known this.

I'm not saying that *DAMN.* is made entirely in the image of Southern rap, though. The music surely drifts in the direction of the South, like a migrating bird in the winter, but Lamar's lyricism remains tethered to his own erudite and contemplative habits. Lamar is a word-intoxicated emcee, after all, and he can't rap otherwise; words and ideas come to his mind in bounteous portions, pouring out of his mouth as if they were slick with oil, slipping and sliding, catching fire as they come off his tongue. This remains the case on *DAMN.*: the music fades out convoluted noises even as the rapper turns phrases, bars, and narratives into tricky, introspective journeys. As the title of the album suggests, a concern with the well-being of one's soul, and the corollary dangers of damnation, is a fundamental preoccupation. In interviews, Lamar has contrasted the concerns of *TPAB* (to change the world) with the concerns of *DAMN.* (to change oneself), but it seems to me that each album is more multifaceted than this suggests. It is, in my reading, splendidly unruly and unsystematic, torn between inward soul-searching and outward protest, animal wants and transcendent aspirations, cheap thrills and the possibility of damnation.[22] All these things, Lamar suggests, are revealing of a soul that is in the process of becoming, a soul that is always an unfinished project.

Before turning inward, though, he assesses the state of the American soul as a whole, its public and political condition. The rap "XXX.," feat. U2, takes aim at the "compulsive disorders" of violence, fear, and racism in American life. A symphony of male voices, suggestive of repose or innocence, introduces the song, but it's quickly interrupted by 808 beats, echoing pings, and old-school record scratching, which is fitting for Kid Capri's involvement on the song, as well as the classic nature of Lamar's bar-driven style of emceeing. In dazzling rhyme schemes, photographic images, and abrupt changes in tempo, the song captures the sights and sounds of contemporary life in the United States, with a special eye on the "soul-fracturing pressures of Trump's America," in Greg Tate's words.[23] Though he hardly excuses individual moral failings, he lashes out here against the bankrupt morals of the ruling elites, whether in the White House, on Wall Street, or among gun manufacturers and the NRA. Poor and desperate border-crossers are turned into rapists and drug dealers; children of our "barricaded blocks" are turned into pathological delinquents and villains.[24] To make matters worse, these prejudices are not only wrapped in the flag but shrouded in religious language—hence the references in the first bar to "Hail Mary, Jesus and Joseph." Here and elsewhere (as in "The Blacker the Berry" from *TPAB*), Lamar appeals to God against the sacred idols of Christendom, not unlike the way Jesus once invoked the Torah against the ruling powers of Jerusalem and Rome, or the way Dr. King's "Letter from a Birmingham Jail" turned the judgment of God against the church.[25]

As much as Lamar channels the prophets in such moments, he is always, as we've seen, quick to judge himself, as if Jesus's famous dictum "Let him without sin cast the first stone" is always playing in his head. The rap "DNA." is in this vein, with Lamar holding up a mirror to himself, shining an infrared light on the dark spots within. Everything hidden is exposed, the beautiful and the unsightly, the good and the depraved. "I transform like this, perform like this, was Yeshua's new weapon . . . I got millions, I got riches buildin' in my DNA/ I got dark, I got evil, that rot inside my DNA./ I got off, I got a troublesome heart inside my DNA." Matching the hard-hitting and thunderous trap beats—their low and rumbling frequencies sending a tremor through the bones, indicating judgment—Lamar paints a conflicted picture of humankind in the rap, a creature, as Basquiat famously rendered it, with a double identity, simultaneously royal and skeletal, aspiring to divinity, on the one hand, and subject to decay and death, on the other.[26]

"FEAR." is even more revealing of this, the song venturing deeper into Lamar's interior landscapes. The rap give us snapshots of the rapper at different stages of his life, first as a young child at home (fearing his mother's displeasure), then as a seventeen-year-old in the streets of Compton (fearing death by gang or police violence), and finally as a twenty-seven-year-old rapper (fearing the loss of his riches, or the loss of his faith). No matter the successes and achievements, fear holds him in its clutch, he confesses, grips and afflicts him. It stalks him like the figure of death in the Geto Boys' classic "Mind Playing Tricks on Me," or like the hellhound in Robert Johnson's ballads: "I went to the crossroad, fell down on my knees/ I went to the crossroad, fell down on my knees/ Asked the Lord above/ Have mercy now, save poor Bob if you please."

Accompanied by a mellow guitar riff, aching melismas, and a bluesy male croon ("I don't know if I can find a way to make it on this earth"), the music on "FEAR." is mellow and downcast, and Lamar's delivery changes tempo and timbre to illustrate the different manifestations of fear. Since verse 1 channels his mother's voice, and sees the world through her eyes, the bars have an agitated and aggravated tone, the pitch of a mother who has to fret about social workers coming for her food stamps, or worry about her son dropping out of school. Verse 2 then shifts registers, flagging and crawling through the lines, sounding defeated and depressed, emotionally aloof. It approximates the seventeen-year-old Kendrick Lamar, a young man crippled by fear, doubt, and death. His every third thought is with the grave, and he mentions as many as sixteen scenarios that could lead to his death. "Maybe die because these smokers are more than desperate/ I probably die from one of these bats and blue badges/ Body-slammed on black and white paint, my bones snappin'." Verse 3, subsequently, recovers Kendrick Lamar's animated, bouncing voice (now at twenty-seven), but his thoughts remain preoccupied with physical, moral, and spiritual ruin: the fear of losing creativity, the fear of losing humility, the fear of losing God.

Given the pervasiveness of fear and anxiety in this song and others, there is a palpable existential flavor to *DAMN.*, a theology in the tradition of Luther, John of the Cross, Pascal, Kierkegaard, or Paul Tillich, a faith burdened with disquiet and unease. While other rappers are happy to hug the shorelines and play in the shallows (Lil Wayne's metaphor), satisfied with empires of power and wealth (Jay-Z), or content to summon God out of the well of pure joy and gratitude (Chance the Rapper), Lamar swims in much deeper waters, far past the shoals. He belongs to a long line of brooding souls, tussling with God out of the belly of the whale like Jonah, from the confines of prison like Jeremiah, from the garbage heaps like Job.

For someone who shares these existential instincts, furthermore, it's almost inevitable that the problem of evil will arise at some point. *DAMN.*, for this reason, is not only about human sin and weakness; it's also about the more bewildering reality of evil, the problem of tragedy. Lamar introduces, toward this end, the voice of his cousin, Carl Duckworth, on "FEAR.," and turns the rap into an interrogation of suffering. With echoes of Jesus's cry of abandonment in Mark's gospel, the bridge gives expression to the seeming absence of God in the face of affliction: "Why God, why God do I gotta suffer? Pain in my heart carry burdens full of struggle. Why God, why God do I gotta bleed? Every stone thrown at you, restin' at my feet." And later, in the outro, his cousin tries to square these grievances with belief in God's providence. His cousin defends the Deuteronomic account of suffering, where the suffering of the chosen people is a consequence of their waywardness and wickedness, a form of punishment for disobedient and idolatrous behavior: "The so-called blacks, Hispanics, and Native American Indians are the true children of Israel," his cousin remarks. "We are the Israelites, according to the Bible . . . He's gonna punish us for our iniquities. For our disobedience, because we chose to follow other gods . . . So, just like you chasten your own son. He's gonna chastise you because he loves you." (Carl Duckworth appears again in the song "YAH," as a representative of this paradigm.)

In some ways, this position is related to Dr. King's vision of black lives as the suffering servants of the Bible: "Through the servant's suffering," Dr. King argued, "knowledge of God was spread to the unbelieving gentiles and those unbelievers seeing that this suffering servant was innocent would be conscious of themselves and thereby be redeemed."[27] In this perspective, civil rights' activists were regarded as agents in the redemption of the nation's soul, playing a part in the drama of salvation like a multitude of Simons of Cyrene, men and women summoned to carry the cross of Jesus. And yet, there is a crucial difference between Duckworth's and Dr. King's account of suffering: for the former, the suffering of the black and brown Israelites is related to their sin; for Dr. King, they suffer innocently, sharing in the blameless and redemptive suffering of Christ. Without dismissing the perspective of his cousin (for Lamar is too sensitive to the marring presence of sin in human life), it seems to me that *DAMN.* is closer to Dr. King's vision; the album complicates the Deuteronomic account of suffering.[28] Instead of laying the blame on sin alone, I hear Lamar implying that the modern-day Israelite has a unique historical destiny, that it has, as Jesse McCarthy has written about black intellectuals in American life, "a revolutionary role to play in the distribution of social equality, the form and tenor of a more egalitarian culture, and the nurturing of the intellectual foundations of a world destined in the coming years to shift away from several centuries of essentially European domination."[29] Using meter and rhyme rather than prose, Lamar makes a similar point, it seems to me, indicating that black artists, intellectuals, and common folk have not only suffered and writhed under the boot of oppression, but continue to play a redemptive and prophetic role in the Americas, alerting and trying to awaken the conscience of the hemisphere.

Keeping in mind the multiple masks and dramatic personas of his songs, the songs are often theater as much as autobiography anyhow, thespianism as much as realism, fiction as much as non-fiction. Split personalities abound in his narratives, and this makes it more challenging to identify his own voice, like trying to distinguish the voice of Socrates from Plato. We know that many of these characters are chips off his block (including his cousin's character), but there remains a deeper essence of his self that transcends any one of them. And so, on this matter of theodicy, while Lamar identifies with his cousin's theological position—"I'm an Israelite, don't call me black no mo'"—he hesitates to claim his cousin's explanation for suffering as his own. Compared with his cousin's attempt to square the circle of theodicy, Lamar is more uncertain and vexed, his theodicy a tangled labyrinth rather than a straight line.[30]

Besides, the Deuteronomic account doesn't even exhaust the Bible's own understanding of theodicy. Numerous texts can be recalled that contest the equation of sin and suffering: the Psalms, Lamentations, Ecclesiastes, Job, Jeremiah, Jonah, and so on. Lamar senses this, and thus orchestrates *DAMN.* with a variety of notes and emotions, from prayer and pleading to high-pitched howls of protest. The stronger stress may be on human sin, but the album also seethes with existential duress, with the puzzlement of bruised and troubled souls, with the anger of the streets. I interpret the scrambled and garbled voice of Lamar at the beginning of the song (the bridge of the song in reverse—"reffus attog I od doG yhw, doG yhw . . ."), for instance, as a way of breaking syntax down to its phonemes, reducing words to glossolalia-like sounds and broken syllables, like Sophocles's Philoctetes when he articulates his suffering with an untranslatable cry of anguish. (Bernard Knox suggests the line is best left untranslated, with only stage direction in its place: "A scream of agony, twelve syllables, three iambic metra long.")[31] Likewise, Lamar twists and inverts the line "Why God do I gotta suffer," the sentence now straining grammatical meaning until it breaks. The nature of suffering, the line implies, is twisted, nonsensical, and unintelligible, best translated by inscrutable and scat-like sounds.

The rap "FEEL." is in the same spirit of "FEAR.," delivered in a disconsolate state, sapped of energy and hope, a rap that hits a barren and nihilistic note, emitting a cold wind that you feel on the nape of the neck. He moves faster through the bars than on "FEAR.," however, and adds a tinge of anger and frustration to his speech; the sentiment nonetheless is similar, the words piled on top of each other to dam up his psyche against the deluge of empty feelings. He's trying to survive the dark nights of the soul. "Sometimes this experience," writes John of the Cross, "is so vivid that it seems to the soul that it sees hell and perdition open before it."[32] Something similar seems to be happening throughout *DAMN.*: hell and perdition opens before the rapper and threatens to consume him. The experience, harrowing and agonizing, leaves him edgy and restless, yearning for a redemptive truth, which, in his case, is a combination of music and religion, the two of them giving the rapper a shelter from life's storms.[33]

Surrounded by these gaping whirlpools of emotion, threatening to pull him under, Lamar also intensifies the frequency and quantity of his rhymes on the album, as if the search for order and harmony in the sound itself might beat back some of the chaos he feels. On *DAMN.*, in fact, he takes more and more delight in alliteration, consonance, and assonance than on the earlier albums. Like a liturgical rite or shamanic incantation, the repetitive phrases and bars on the album are not only mesmerizing for this reason; they're also medicinal and therapeutic. And this reminds us that Kendrick Lamar, like any rapper, is always searching for a syntax with sonic perfection—how it sounds matters as much as anything else. Rap, I can't say it enough, calls for the right combination of words, the right phonetic sounds. If it doesn't sound good, you won't feel it. "FEEL.," of course, illustrates this truth in its very title, the song striving to give the listener a particular *feeling*—in this case, of hopelessness. If one is unfamiliar with this sort of dread, Lamar offers metaphors and similes that provide an inkling of it.

Before I leave the reader with an impression of bleakness, however, it must be said that *DAMN.* is also filled with many moments of overflowing joy, the feelings of the album a richer spectrum of color than dark hues alone. "GOD." is a case in point, a song that is the equivalent, for all the non-mystics of the world, of a beatific and radiant vision. Lamar's entire demeanor is transfigured on the track: where the above songs are about crisis, his soul undone by angst, this rap is euphoric and epiphanic. Where he unravels on other songs, he pulls himself together here, the song acting as a counterweight to the heavy sinking moments of the album. Ironically, in a song with this title, the lyrics are not very theological; it's one of those rare songs in Lamar's repertoire where the meaning of the song is more apparent in the surface of the sound rather than in the lyrics, in the pure musicality and mellifluousness of the verses, in the froth. The chorus is the hermetic key, with Lamar singing in a honeyed voice, "This what God feels like, huh, heah/ Laughin' to the bank like, Ah-haa, huh, heah/ Flex on swole like, Ah-haa, huh, heah/ You feel some type of way, then A-haa/ huh, heah (a-ha-ha, a-ha-ha)." The website Rap Genius will tell you that the words suggest what it feels like to *be* God, swollen with confidence, flexing your clout, joyful in your command of life. Maybe that's part of it, but it misses the key point: that the vibes and emotions that the song elicits—exhilaration, euphoria, serenity, rapture, bliss—are what it feels like to *experience* God, what it feels like to be carried away by transcendent waves of emotion, caught up into the heavens like St. Paul. Lamar shifts from rapping to rhapsody on the track because ordinary language is inadequate when aiming at God. He requires a different tactic, more visceral, more tactile, more emotive. What does this line mean, for instance? "You feel some type of way, then A-haaaaa . . ." Answer: Nothing, really, nothing apart from the experience of the music, nothing apart from the way Lamar warbles and croons the phrase, soothing and calming the listener with the melody, climbing into sublime regions with his falsetto. No longer the frazzled and restless soul that frets over his salvation, he's found a measure of tranquility and peace here, as if he's achieved enlightenment.

In fact, there's almost something mantra-like in Lamar's recitation on "GOD.," the vowels stretched into a sweet-sounding refrain, where the meaning of what is said is not as important as the litany of sound itself.[34] Instead of merely informing, and plotting a clear narrative arc, a mantra, after all, conjures transcendence by the numinous sounds themselves, their efficacy felt in the pronunciation of the words and phonemes. That is to say, a mantra's impact is visceral, intuitive, and sensory, plucking at the cords of our emotions, acting as a salve for our wounds, and, in some cases, leaving us breathless like the prophet Muhammad at the first hearing of the Quran.

Each purpose is at work on "GOD.," but at the bottom of it all is that phenomenon, elusive and bewildering, that we call "feeling," an "amorphous, intangible, gut-borne thing that animates all music and gives it life," in the words of Amanda Petrusich. Her characterization is a fine crack at the meaning, but Petrusich gets even closer when she opens up personally, telling us what happened to her when first listening to the ghostly vocals of John Hurt's "Big Leg Blues," played on an old sizzling and cracking 78. Her account is rapturous and quasi-mystical: "I felt," she confesses, "like every single one of my internal organs had liquefied and was bubbling up into my esophagus."[35]

I'm not saying I feel the same way when listening to "GOD."—I'm more liable to liquefy when Lola Beltrán rips a melody out of her torn, tequila-doused throat, or when hearing Aretha Franklin reach a high note that gets as close to heaven as possible on this earth—but there is no doubt that the song stills and alleviates the distresses of the soul, making one feel less alone, less lost, a sudden surge of joy. I hear in Lamar's track a strong religious sentiment, of course, the rhythm and melody flush with an otherworldly significance that is spelled out in other raps but beyond words here. For those unable to relate to a religious experience, the song implies, the sway of the music will school you in such matters, speaking in an angelic tongue—"Everything I say is from an angel," as he puts it—rather than the standard stuff of speech. And, fitting for a song that touches on the theme of ineffability, the sheer number of words is drastically reduced in the song; it's spare compared to others. The spine of the song is a skittering computerized hi-hat and thumping bass beat (common in trap music), but the meat of it comes from Lamar's trilling vocals, rapturous but cool, ecstatic but smooth, bursting but contained. He sings in a language of pure exaltation, airy and breezy. Marks on the page—Lamar's or mine— are only hints and intimations that are meant to evoke, not expound upon, the experience of God.

"Music, by definition, begins where linguistic meaning stops," writes Ted Gioia, "yet critics earn their living by breaching the boundary, reducing melodies to words, and somehow convincing the rest of us to give credence to their judgments."[36] There is a mystical element in music that eludes intellectualization, in other words, but a critic is charged with defining and elucidating the sound anyhow, assigning value to the properties of music.[37] The same can be said about theology: by definition, it begins where linguistic meaning stops, and yet theologians earn their keep by naming the unnamable, attempting to reason (logos) about what exceeds pure reason (theos). Countless mystics through-out the ages have struggled with this conundrum.[38] When God spoke to Moses out of the burning bush, biblical writers recorded the encounter with fragmentary letters, missing in vowels, YHWH. The tetragrammaton, thus, is a Hebrew phrase of deliberate vagueness, an expression of what is inexpressible. Perhaps this is why the biblical authors sketched Moses as a tongue-tied and stuttering prophet: they were making a theological point commensurate with this revelation, namely, that all human language stammers and stutters when speaking of G-d, all language, post-Babel, is jumbled and confused. St. Augustine, speaking of the wordless chants of workers in the fields, makes this point beautifully:

> Do not go seeking lyrics, as though you could spell out in words anything that will give God pleasure. . . . Think of people who sing at harvest time, or in the vineyard, or at any work that goes with a swing. They begin by caroling their joy in words, but after a while they seem to be so full of gladness that they find words no longer adequate to express it, so they abandon distinct syllables and words, and resort to a single cry of jubilant happiness. Jubilation is a shout of joy; it indicates that the heart is bringing forth what defies speech. To whom, then, is this jubilation more fittingly offered than to God who surpasses all utterance?[39]

With this intuition in mind, the finest theologians and music critics have found ways to balance kataphatic speech (what can be said) with apophatic speech (what cannot be said), and bid the reader/listener to hear and taste for themselves. As for Lamar, it's true that he frequently storms the heavens with beats, rhymes, and an abundance of words, as we've seen; but with *DAMN.*, he has also learned how to use fewer words and fatter beats, fewer bars and more melodies, fewer noises and richer silences.[40]

With that said, as the chorus gives way to verse 1, Lamar now puts a greater spotlight on his lyrics. While his reedy warble soars into high altitudes with the chorus, it plummets back to earth with the rapped verses, the former marking an ineffable experience, the latter the banality of ordinary life. Approximating the pre-enlightened Lamar, verse 1 begins with a sluggish and faltering voice as he recounts the false desires of his youth: the instinct for violence and the coveting of guns, sexual sins, and the dreams of being a pop star (selling verses, handling "bars like a fade," and singing in the manner of El DeBarge). Verse 1, then, hearkens back to the circumstances of *Good Kid, M.A.A.D City*, where attention was on the tough predicaments and pressures of Compton life.

One moment rocketing into sublime heights, and then suddenly plum-meting back to the streets of Compton, this song alone illustrates the rapper's usefulness for a street theology, his music ethereal and mundane at once. If he's channeling God's voice in this song, letting it burn and scorch his throat, he does so to address many of the problems, both social and spiritual, that af-flict our contemporary world. His portrait of religion is nothing like, for this reason, sentimental varieties of spirituality, with sappy and shallow angels, empty of substance. When he invokes angel mediators, they have the likeness, on the contrary, of U2's "Angel of Harlem" (an homage to Billie Holiday), or the *duende* of Federico García Lorca—that mysterious figure that inspires the greatest poets, singers, and dancers, and that combines earthiness and sub-limity, sensuality and soul, awareness of death and an intense appetite for life.[41] There's a touch of the wicked and disreputable in the notion, in other words, a rough, raw, and rapturous sort of grace.

It's the sort of grace, moreover, that beats against the current of American life, advocating values that are endangered in Trump's America, as when La-mar riffs on the theme of humility for the most popular song on the album, "HUMBLE.," which won several Grammys for best rap song, best rap per-formance, and best music video in 2018. Jazzed up with hammering percus-sion and a riveting chorus ("Sit down/ Be humble"), Mike Will's production successfully bottles the turbo-charged sounds of Southern rap while infus-ing it with Lamar's soulful content. "Watch my soul speak, you let the meds talk," he says as a reproach of Americans addicted to the opiates of money, power, and phony conceptions of beauty. By rapping in a brisk and staccato flow, with a monotone and clipped delivery, Lamar hearkens back here to the lyrical virtuosity of East Coast rappers like Rakim, Big Daddy Kane, or the Poor Righteous Teachers.[42] The soundscape is Southern, but the content is righteous.

The rap, hence, is a study in contrasts between big, bass-rattling 808 beats, a pounding piano riff, and swipes of an electric guitar that sound like distress signals, on the one hand, and the simple, unassuming values of hu-mility and inner beauty. The music video opens with Lamar in a cathedral, dressed in the rich garb of a pope, as the light of the sun streams through the darkness, epiphany-like, to fall on Lamar, suggestive of the transfigura-tion scene in the gospels where Jesus appears radiant and luminous, but the disciples—Peter, in particular—misread the significance of the event. Just as the apostles misunderstand the path of discipleship—wanting power and glory instead of Jesus's vision of self-sacrifice and humility—the music video dramatizes the conflict between two different visions of art: one that wallows in money, power, drugs, and counterfeit beauty; the other composed of intangible and inner beauty, the stuff of the soul. Registering this conflict, the scene shifts from the vestment-clad Lamar at the beginning, a priest of the eternal imagination, to the rapper Lamar lying on a table of drug money, as if he is swimming and drowning in money, as if the abundance of Mammon has thoroughly swamped and choked his spiritual senses, rendering them dull and inert. As a reproach of rap's most hedonistic impulses, Lamar riffs once again on the sentiment of Jesus, "What does it profit a man if he gains the whole world and loses his soul?" Since the song gives voice to the language of his soul, as opposed to the simulated and fake images of popular culture (social media, music videos, the fashion industry, television, etc.), the song champions an offbeat view of beauty, deeper than the skin.

Additional criticisms of American commercialism are evident in the Last Supper scene, with Lamar playing Jesus, surrounded by his unruly and way-ward disciples gorging themselves on wine and bread, not heeding or com-prehending their master's lessons. Most interpretations of the scene read it as Lamar's indictment of other rappers, oblivious to anything besides gluttony and greed. Fair enough, but the satire also runs deeper, targeting everyone who brazenly ignores or misconstrues the words of Jesus, especially the in-ner circle of Jesus's disciples. In this respect, it is a scalding commentary on the state of Christianity in the United States, with the disciples representing Christians who are blind and deaf to the gospel values of humility, compas-sion, and justice. Like the disciples in the gospel of Mark, prone to flagrant misunderstandings and weaknesses of will, *DAMN.* constantly broods over the stunning failures of those ostensibly closest to Jesus. Just as the disciples in the video are seen as carousing and reveling in food and drink, unmindful of their teacher, each one jockeying for the better seat at the table, the song reproaches everyone in public or private life who betrays the lessons of the Messiah, a prophet who entered Jerusalem on a humble donkey. "Sit down, be humble!"

His adversary throughout the album, consequently, is clearly pride, a force that infects its victims with delusions of grandeur. Thus, the hard-hitting tonal palette on the album—booming beats, street swagger, tight lyricism—puts selfishness and vanity in its crosshairs, cutting the ego down to size. As he notes on the song "PRIDE.," and then repeats lest we forget again on "LOYALTY.," pride is going to be the death of us, and so he throws his weight behind the themes of humility, art, love, God.

After these hard-hitting truths, Lamar gives us sweeter and more gen-tle songs in "LOVE." and "LOYALTY." The whirlwind of beats and rhymes is stilled to give the listener relief. There are no exhortations to "parade

the streets with your voice loudly," as he puts it on "LUST.," or references
to American maladies like "barricaded blocks and borders," as he raps on
"XXX." Lamar comes down from Mt. Sinai and substitutes tender croons
for the squawking prophetic voice; think the Song of Songs more than Amos
or Jeremiah. Fitting for the subject matter, and for his collaborations with
Rihanna and Zacari, he switches cadences again, and adopts a syrupy singing
delivery, languorous and cool. Just as the singing voice suits his philosophizing on "GOD.," the singing voice is the ideal medium for the enigmas of love;
vulnerability and tenderness are better served by song than rap. Since the latter requires self-assuredness and bravura—necessities in a contest of wit and
wordplay—rap has a hard time conceding weakness. Song is freer in form, less
beholden to any one demeanor. It can ride a variety of emotions, aggressive
and sensitive, brash and broken. It's not surprising, then, that when rap has
sought to soften its image, it has frequently turned to melody and harmony
as conduits for a more searching, introspective style. If boast and brag are the
stuff of rap, and love is neither pompous nor puffed up, as St. Paul says, then
rap needs song to expand its thematic range.

Possibly the best music of the album, "LOVE." opens with the soulful and
longing soprano of Zacari Pacaldo, and then adds Lamar's pining refrain, "I
wanna be with you, ayy, I wanna be with you." This song, too, intertwines a variety of incongruent textures: clapping drumbeats, fluttering hi-hats, fat bass,
peaceful, gliding synths. It moves at a slow, easy tempo, and Lamar rolls with
the groove perfectly; he sounds warm, mellow, relaxed, and meditative in the
song, mirroring the gentle ocean tides that appear in the opening scene of the
music video. Filmed in slow motion, the video paints a contemplative mood
as Lamar chronicles, journal-like, his deep insecurities, his fears of loneliness,
his need for approval, his desire for his partner's affection, and through it all,
the joy that this particular woman—his longtime girlfriend, Whitney Alford—
brings to his life. "Don't got you, I got nothing."

For a rapper troubled by his sins, the romantic serenade on "LOVE." adds
a beautiful touch of warmth and grace to the album.[43] Since it's anchored
by the gravitas of *DAMN.*, the song is deeply satisfying sweetness, the kind
of rhythm that lulls and stills the soul after experiencing anxious, sleepless
nights. In contrast to the red-hot volcanic verses of other raps (especially
on "ELEMENT." or "DNA."), "LOVE." flows softly and smoothly, like lava
suddenly chilled. Lamar seems to be saying that hip-hop needs to try a little
tenderness; he seems to be saying that hip-hop is a noisy gong or a clashing cymbal when missing in love; he seems to be saying that the conventional emotions of rap music—pride, lust, anger, cupidity, envy, jubilation—

will cease and be brought to nothing, but love will never end. "All feelings go out," he croons, "this feeling don't drought/ This party won't end." Hip-hop, in this reading, is big and mature enough to contain the many manifestations of love: eros for romance, philia for friends and family, and agape for the love of God and love of neighbor.

After dwelling on eros in the song "LOVE.," as a matter of fact, he turns explicitly to the agapeic notion of love—love of God and love of neighbor—in the rap "LOYALTY." The producer of the song, Terrace Martin (along with DJ Dahi and Sounwave), described the song in these terms: "Loyalty represents some unconditional, agape love type shit," he said. "Loyalty to me is the first base of life. Real brotherhood. Real sisterhood."[44] The song samples the melody of Bruno Mars's "24K Magic" (a vocoder-modulated tune), enhances it with beefier 808s, and then simmers down the rhythm, making Lamar's version sound cooler and calmer—though ironically more anxious—than "24K Magic." If Bruno celebrates the flash and floss of living large, Lamar frets over these things. True to his brand, he wonders aloud about the vanity of human desires. "Tell me who you loyal to/ Is it money? Is it fame? Is it weed? Is it drink? . . . Is it love for the streets when the lights get dark?" And later, the thought continues: "Do it start with your woman or your man?/ Do it end with your family or friends?/ Is it anybody that you would lie for?/ Anybody you would slide for?/ Anybody you would die for?/ That's what God's for."[45]

The theme of the song, in my reading, echoes Paul Tillich's famous consideration of faith: "faith," Tillich explains, "is the state of being ultimately and unconditionally concerned about Yahweh and about what he represents in demand, threat, and promise."[46] The problem of idolatry arises when profane or finite concerns—money, fame, nation, race, reason, religion—are elevated to ultimate concerns, the idol now replacing God. Lamar may not possess the same philosophical and theological lexicon as Tillich, but he shares the theologian's fundamental presumption that loyalty to God renders all other commitments relative and finite.

As we've seen with *DAMN.*, though, such an absolute loyalty and dedication is hard to maintain—failure is inevitable. And Rihanna acknowledges the difficulty, too: "It's so hard to be humble," she sings in a rueful key. "It's so hard to be/ Lord knows is I'm tryin'/ Lord knows is I'm dyin', baby."

Take note of Lamar's rapping in the song, too: it slumps to characterize his mood of uncertainty and vulnerability, the tone itself bordering on prayer. In such moments, music, a vehicle of transcendent emotions, is equivalent to prayer. Indeed, throughout his catalog, and the comparison here with Tupac is obvious, Lamar's verses frequently bleed into supplication and contemplation, their sounds and words giving way to pleas, petitions, chants, praise, gratitude and, above all, submission. For whatever else it is, prayer is, in the end, a gesture of submission, the ultimate expression of vulnerability, as Hanif Abdurraqib wisely observes: "I have always been of the belief that the major function of prayer in our society was to allow for the idea of building vulnerability in the people who have least reason to be vulnerable."[47] Think of the act of prayer: forehead bowed to the ground, knees bent in surrender, palms upturned to the heavens, tongue silenced, and all members of the body and spirit surrendering to something greater than ourselves.[48] If you listen carefully, each of these gestures and sensibilities, now translated into the rhythms of sound, can be heard in Lamar's music.

As *DAMN.* spins to the end, finally, a gunshot rings out and appears to take Lamar's life, a denouement as grim as the beginning of the album. (The song, "BLOOD.," begins with Lamar getting shot.) When all hope seems lost, though, the outro sounds like a record spun in reverse, "as if he's speaking in tongues or trying to recover lost time," says Hua Hsu.[49] Could it be, however, that Lamar is also describing, besides this recovery of lost time, the hope of a public and communal redemption for the war-torn streets of Compton and elsewhere? The final song, "DUCKWORTH.," it seems to me, gestures in this direction, giving the album, ultimately, less the feeling of a tragedy than of a comedy. (Comedy, at least as it's understood in the Christian tradition, as the triumph of hope and love.) Coming on the tail end of the album, "DUCK-WORTH." narrates the serendipitous events that brought Lamar's father into contact with the founder of Top Dawg Entertainment, Anthony "Top Dawg" Tiffith. In their younger days, still strangers to each other, Anthony Tiffith had planned on robbing the Kentucky Fried Chicken where Lamar's father, "Ducky," worked at the time. After taking a liking to Lamar's father, however, Anthony let the plans go; peace prevailed over violence. In Lamar's telling, the relationship between his father and the founder of Top Dawg Entertainment— long before Kendrick would meet Tiffith—becomes a parable of the odd and surprising moments of grace that break through the smothering violence of Compton life. He imagines how different his life would be if Tiffith murdered his father: "Because if Anthony killed Ducky, Top Dawg could be servin' life/ While I grew up without a father and die in a gunfight."

With the record spun in reverse, then, Lamar is describing an alternative history for Compton, where grace breaks the cycles of violence and poverty, ending the curse of the streets . . . not unlike the train of events in Aeschylus's *Oresteia*. While the song's portrait of gang-driven violence and crippling poverty in Compton mirrors gangster rappers before him (N.W.A., Ice Cube, DJ Quik, the Game, MC Eiht), as well as the cycles of vengeance in Greek tragedy, Lamar takes this occasion to rap about the unexpected moments of grace in the history of Compton. Less a curse than a blessing, Compton emerges on "DUCKWORTH." as a place where miracles happen, where he learned how to "process and digest poverty's dialect," where he achieved real street knowledge, where he learned to "pray with the hooligans, shadows in the dark." Ruminating on Compton's deadly legacy of violence, Lamar considers the truce that occurred between his father and Anthony Tiffith as a sudden blessing in plagued circumstances: "One curse at a time/ Reverse the manifest." The album closes with the good news of this message, the belief that Compton's hooligans have gems of knowledge to offer the world, and that grace happens in the most troubled and forsaken of circumstances.

Educating the Sentiments

A final word: given the nature of *DAMN.*'s track list—BLOOD., ELEMENT., FEEL., PRIDE., HUMBLE., LUST., LOVE., FEAR., GOD., to name some—it's impossible to overstate the prominent role assigned to desire, sentiment, and imagination on the album. In these short titles—allegorically rich like characters in a baroque drama—Lamar is not only musing on these subjects like a philosopher or theologian; he is trying to school the emotions of his listeners, trying to offer, to borrow a phrase from Clifford Geertz, a "sentimental education," the kind of learning that would sculpt the sensibilities of his listeners.[50] Reminiscent of ancient philosophy or ancient poetics—"therapies of desire"—the purpose of *DAMN.* is not so much informational as it is transformational, aiming to move you, thrill you, change you.[51] "It's about stories you can feel," Lamar concludes about the purpose of *DAMN.*, "emotions you can feel, and emotions you can relate to."[52]

Thus, there is nothing like an *argument* for God's existence in this work and others in Lamar's collection; he persuades, instead, by rhetorical and musical eloquence, evoking joy and pathos, stirring up love, venting one's fears, shoring up faith, and even bringing one, as in the song "GOD.," into brief, immediate contact with the divine. For Lamar, as for any street theology, these experiences make for a more persuasive argument for God's existence than all the proofs and rational arguments that have taken aim at belief in God, presuming that the question of God is a proposition for the mind, as opposed to, as in Lamar's *DAMN.*, an affair of the heart and soul, an act of *credere*, the placing of one's heart in the Other.

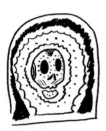

CHAPTER 5
The Dirty Latin South
Breaking, Reggaeton, and the Rise of the Global South

Anarchy moved in. For thirty years you couldn't possibly make it unless you were white, sleek, nicely spoken and phony to your toenails—suddenly now you could be black, purple, moronic, delinquent, diseased or almost anything on earth. . . . Under these rules, rock turned up a sudden flood of maniacs, wild men with pianos and guitars who would have been laughing stocks in any earlier generation but who were just right for the fifties. They were energetic, basic, outrageous. They were huge personalities and they used music like a battering ram. And above all, they were loud.[1]

Nik Cohn

Latin hip-hop and reggaeton are coming like a tornado.[2]

Domingo Ramos

A people cannot only see themselves suffering, lest they believe themselves only worthy of pain . . .[3]

Hanif Abdurraqib

What Nik Cohn has written about the anarchy of rock 'n' roll—its loud and outrageous personalities, its helter-skelter racial politics, its battering beats, its delinquent behavior—holds true for much of hip-hop, too, including the Afro-Latin subsets known as reggaeton and urbano. Think of Cardi B (Belcalis Marlenis Almánzar), the rapper of Dominican and Trinidadian descent, born and raised in the Bronx: she is a flesh-and-blood embodiment of many of hip-hop's signature traits. She plays the game of hip-hop with the authority of a

Bronx native, as if it is being played on her home arena and she owns the court. Her goal is not only to score, moreover; she wants to get there with poise, flash, and flair, weaving her way smoothly and elegantly to the hole. Plain and prosaic moves—the "fundamentals"—aren't exciting to her. She prefers the moves of street ballers and ABA legends, their nasty crossovers, their shakes and shimmies, their ostentatious spins and gravity-defying flights to the hoop. She prefers to dance, sway, and rumba as she delivers her lyrics, scoring points with flair and finesse, like Allen Iverson in his prime.

Important for our purposes, too, Cardi B—the "pan-Latin-unifier," in Jon Caramanica's words—exemplifies the rich collaborations between black and Latin American heritages in the South Bronx and Spanish Harlem (birthplaces of salsa, boogaloo, reggaeton, and hip-hop).[4] Her song "I Like It," for one, featuring the reggaeton stars Bad Bunny and J Balvin, is a compelling instance of this. A medley of thundering trap beats, exuberant salsa horns, reggaeton's sonorous vocals, biting and boasting lyricism, celebratory *gritos*, party noise, and the boogaloo of Pete Rodriguez (the song samples his 1967 classic "I Like It Like That"), Cardi B's song salvages numerous fragments of New York musical history and then tricks them out with house-wrecking 808 bass lines and brash verses.[5] J Balvin, in his opening verse, makes these heterogeneous debts obvious, too, invoking the iconic salsa musician Celia Cruz while dragging the music of old into the age of hip-hop. For her part, Cardi B, shining in resplendent headscarves and colorful Afro-Latin attire, struts like a flamingo in the music video, ruffling her feathers and warbling aloud about her love of stunting and shining, of fashion and fame, of the joy that she gets in beating up her lyrics like a piñata. Bad Bunny, to complete the powerful trio, boasts about having *mucha grasa* ("fat" or style), shouts out his love for Latinos (*que viva la raza*), and then gets in a line about Jesus (*El diablo me llama, pero Jesucristo me abraza*—The devil calls me, but Jesus Christ embraces me). The song is delightful, a feast of brilliant colors, booming percussion, and larger-than-life swagger. And it's a beautiful example of hip-hop's ability to squeeze new sounds and purposes out of lost and forgotten treasures (the boogaloo, mambo, salsa, dancehall reggae, Panamanian reggae en español, and Puerto Rican "underground," in this case).

Even a cursory glance at the flamboyant music video for "I Like It" will tell you additionally that there is almost nothing Puritan about the world of Cardi B. She is too bombastic to fit in the square pegs of Puritanism, too happy to feast on beauty to pay any mind to accusations of prodigality, excess, and sin. If there are traces of austerity in her work, one might point to her phrasing—tending toward clipped and punchy barbs, like a flurry of quick jabs—but even here the lyricism is usually hyped and puffed up, a rhyme style

Figure 3 An image of Cardi B from the music video for Cardi B, Bad Bunny, and J Balvin's song "I Like It," released in 2018, featured on her debut album *Invasion of Privacy*.

that cracks, pops, and snaps on her opponents. More like Medusa than Madonna, Cardi B practices hip-hop with stone-cold toughness, eyes that slay, hair that bites, a serrated tongue, a banging body. And, though explosive and irrepressible in this way, capable of turning her foes into stone, she also practices hip-hop as an act of prophetic defiance: "I think us bad bitches," raps Cardi on "I Do," "is a gift from God."

Whether or not the trope of "badness," or "dirtiness," is a gift from God—and, insofar as it represents a repudiation of repressive laws, customs, and mores, the claim should be taken serious—Cardi B's "I Like It" is certainly an example of the kind of aesthetic richness that engendered hip-hop and reggaeton. Consistent with any number of Afro-Latin artworks throughout the Americas, it celebrates the stuff of style, fashion, language, music, dance, gesture, and movement to claim one's humanity, and to contest the invisibility to which many black and Latin lives have been consigned.

The Iberian "Dirty South"

Long before the rise of hip-hop, and long before the rise of Cardi B, Iberian singing-poets proved something similar. Famous in Rome for their voluptuous dances and extraordinary poetic memory, the singing-girls of Cádiz combined, according to many observers, both grace and danger in their bodies. There's a remarkable discussion about such artists by Al-Gahiz (776–868): "An accomplished singing-girl has a repertoire of upwards of four thousand songs, each of them two to four verses long, so that the total amount of poetry contained in it, if one multiplies one figure by the other, comes to ten thousand verses. . . . They are mainly founded on references to sex, pimping, passion, yearning, desire and lust."[6] However narrow in substance, these singer-poets possessed remarkable lyrical skills, it seems, a capacity for acrobatically delivering a verse, making it coil, gyrate, bounce, and dance. Seemingly straight lines, without depth or profundity, were turned into vocal arabesques. And they would do the same with their bodies, making them bend and twist in elegant patterns of movement. The Roman poet Juvenal described them, with a disapproving tone, as dancing lasciviously by "shaking their booties down to the ground," and making noises with their "shells" (referring to the castanets).[7] In their writhing and quivering movements, hips dropped to the ground and hands snaking upward to the sky, they would cast spells on their audiences and turn them into pawns of their lyrical and kinetic charms, not unlike what Circe did to Odysseus's crew. Martial remarked that they were so beguiling that they would even seduce the paradigmatic figure of chastity in mythology, Hippolytus (famous for resisting his stepmother's advances).[8] These women, it seems, were the first rappers of the Dirty South, experts in the art of lyrical and carnal seduction.

And if the Romans were scandalized by the singing-poets of Cádiz, imagine the response of the church fathers. Likened to the dissolute dancing of Herodias's daughter in the gospels, the frolicking of the Israelites around the golden calf, or the meretricious lures of Jezebel of Tyre, these dancers concentrated all the glory and danger of paganism in their bodies.[9] Part fertility goddess, part Maenad, part sacred prostitute, these women were triple threats, capable of robbing your soul through the delights of language and the delights of the flesh. And if we recall that Jezebel was a Phoenician, and that Cádiz was a Phoenician settlement in ancient times, the judgment that these female rappers were descendants of Jezebel may not be too fanciful.[10]

Some of the panache and bravura of these women of Cádiz, at any rate, would spell trouble for later generations, giving rise to warnings and fears about the music and dances of "Oriental" and African-influenced traditions. By the sixteenth century, with the colonization of the New World, African percussion traditions would find their way to the New World by way of Spain, Portugal, and Cuba (Lisbon, Cádiz, Sevilla, and Havana). With the substantial black presence in these cities, the rhythms of Africa invaded Europe and the New World and left an indelible mark on Western music. Since drums were absent from medieval music—used exclusively in military marches in the fifteenth century—it wasn't until the sixteenth century that percussion would rock and roll into the music and culture of Spain. In the Corpus Christi celebrations of Sevilla and Cuba, for instance, two music and dance crazes ruled the land: the *zarabanda* and *chacona*. In both cases, the dances were associated with servants and slaves, and were reported to simulate sexual movements. Performed during Corpus Christi festivities, when blacks were permitted to dress, dance, and play music from their own cultures, the *zarabanda* sparked a fire in the general population, and caused religious authorities to fear a widespread inferno, an outbreak of hellish morals. Described by Covarrubias de Orozco as "lively and lascivious," it was apparently a sensual dance with "hips swaying and breasts touching."[11] Padre Juan de Mariana contended that the *zarabanda* was "so lascivious in its words, so ugly in its sway, that it was enough to set decent people afire." Another commentator associated it with a "circle of fire in which Satan occupies the center and the angels the circumference."[12] And Covarrubias de Orozco (1539–1613) even suggested, astutely, that the *zarabanda* was related to the same Gaditana dance and music that had once scandalized Rome (Gadir was the Punic name; the Romans called it Gades). Cádiz was the original Dirty South, but now it was resurfacing in sixteenth-century Spain!

Similar things were said about the *chacona* in late sixteenth-century Cuba: it was unrestrained, fast, and sensual, a dance that originated in the seedy and disreputable haunts of Havana. With a growing population of free blacks in Cuba (*negros curros*), and a rowdy mixture of sailors, adventurers, and peasants from Spain, Havana became a melting pot of musical and dance styles that would simmer, smolder, and eventually boil over, scalding everything it touched. In contrast to the composers of the church, who would erect sophisticated superstructures over the Gregorian chant and move music further and further away from dance, the *zarabanda* and *chacona* aimed straight for the body. The *chacona* used a repetitive bass rhythm known as the ostinato (basic to Arabic and African music), and this seemed to earn it a wanton reputation, so animating was it. In fact, the *chacona* inspired the Italian *passacaglia* and Spanish *pasacalle*, meaning "street songs," forms of music considered coarse, unrefined, and low class, and associated, as you might guess, with slaves, servants, and African peoples.

Thus, while church music of the sixteenth century sowed musical seeds for the symphony—with polyphonic vocal compositions for lute and organ, meant purely for listening—the popular music of the streets moved in another direction, toward dance rhythms and toward the Dirty South. With the exception of some remarkable mendicants, one might say that the music, dance, and fashion of the period spoke more eloquently and effectively on behalf of disenfranchised groups than much of the existing philosophy or theology. By imbuing the forbidden with grace and beauty—black and Indigenous bodies, the banging and thumping of drums, uninhibited dancing, the colorful and brazen fashions of the *negros curros*—the culture of the streets became synonymous with dissent and resistance, defiance through celebration.[13]

If reggaeton, Latin trap, and US Southern rap are not the same thing as the *zarabanda* or *chacona*, not the same as the Cuban son, Dominican salve or merengue, Puerto Rican bomba, or Colombian and Mexican cumbia (all products of African, European, and Indigenous collaborations), they are at least distant cousins, family members who share certain traits. And if one thing is certain, Southern rap, reggaeton, and urbano represent styles of music that update and remix many of the rhythms born at the confluence of African, European, and Latin American rivers of sound. Though there are clear differences—reggaeton and urbano are closer to salsa, disco, and merengue in their flashy costumes and elaborate choreography, while US Southern rap typically prefers a more scruffy and rugged aesthetics—they all converge when it comes to dance-centric sonorities, each of them attacking the body with their beats and phrases, prodding their listeners to dance, bump, rub, and lose oneself in the music. The goal, to borrow the term *pegarse* from reggaeton, is to produce music that "sticks" to the listeners, infiltrates the bloodstream, and elates the flesh. The goal is rapture.

The Soul Is the Form of the Body

In the aesthetic orientation of hip-hop studies, as we've seen earlier, it has been a common gripe that academic critics put the cart before the horse when it comes to rap music, narrowly focusing attention on lyrical analysis—with priority given to political lyrics—and neglecting, if not ignoring altogether, the horsepower that fuels hip-hop: the propulsive beats, the arrangement of sound, the poetics of language, the inventive dances, the dripped-out style, the art of it all.[14] I want to suggest here, though, that the mistake is also a theological lapse, a failure to account for the embodied nature of the soul. The soul may be transcendent in Jewish and Christian traditions, but it only becomes perceptible and palpable in the human body. The "soul" in the Christian tradition is not, as commonly presumed, a purely spiritual reality, which is why Maximus the Confessor described the soul as a boundary between material and spiritual realities, and Thomas Aquinas called it the "form of the body."[15] Associated with respiration and one's breath, the soul is, thus, the life-force of the body, and the essence of one's humanity.

Why is this relevant for hip-hop? For one, the act of rapping requires great breath control and lung capacity, an ability to deliver bars without running out of air. Part of the craft of rapping is knowing when to inhale and exhale, knowing when you'll need to come up for air in order to dive back into the flow of the verse. When one is working with complicated verses and multisyllabic rhymes, in particular, a deep reservoir of oxygen is required or else one risks running out of ammunition, shooting blanks. When and how one breathes "shapes the rhythmic possibilities just as much as an MC's lyrical imagination," writes Adam Bradley.[16] It influences the rapper's style, often dictating the particular tempo, rhythm, or cadence of the performance. On "Bodak Yellow," for instance, Cardi B begins her verses with a breezy pace, taking fewer but larger gulps of air, stretching out the syllables in a singsong fashion. When the tempo accelerates (roughly in the middle of the verses), she raises her volume and adopts a staccato flow, now stealing air in the middle of her bars, quickly snatching oxygen as she rushes through the lines, which lends a choppy and hiccupping quality to her phrasing. She seems to be pacing herself at the beginning, slowly winding herself up, getting tighter and tighter, until she snaps. At this point, she's huffing and puffing, blowing out her words and smashing the lines into small pieces. She's the big bad wolf, threatening the house of hip-hop with gale-like energy, whooping and hollering with her notorious nasal bleat and Spanish, New Yawk inflections. The result is infectious, and an example of how an emcee might bare her soul in the act of rapping itself, irrespective of what is being said (the gist of "Bodak Yellow" is that Cardi B is dope).

Rappers speak of "spitting" lyrics, in this regard; it's a nice choice of words, underscoring the way words bubble and spurt out of the mouth, the way saliva flies off the tongue, the way words assume a physical form in the act of emceeing. So, yes, the soul is invisible and incomprehensible—made in the image of the incomprehensible God—but it becomes incarnate in the act of breathing, speaking, and singing. RZA was getting at this point when discussing the meaning of chi, or life-force, in hip-hop: "It's something that can't be defined, but it can definitely be heard."[17]

The Catholic tradition, however, adds another dimension to this aural tradition: the soul, or life-force, can also be *seen* in the myriad manifestations of art, including the beauty of the human body. Think of how Michelangelo rendered the human soul in sacramental and visual forms. "Theologically," writes David Tracy about the art of Michelangelo, "a soul cannot be painted as such—it is, after all, invisible—but the soul can be painted or sculpted as it manifests itself in a visible ensouled body. . . . The human soul is an embodied soul; the human body is an ensouled body."[18] Instead of the word-centered focus of the Reformation, Michelangelo's theology was image centered, his vision shaped by a culture that celebrated the divine in a variety of visual and material forms, including liturgies and rituals; sculpture, architecture, and painting; processions and festivals; music, dance, and theater; nude human bodies; the marvels of nature; sacred vestments and fashion.

In a way, this legacy of Catholicism approximated the peacock, which was a symbol of the transfigured Christ in the Middle Ages. The bird's extravagant colors and picturesque feathers—its luminous blues and greens, its galaxy of iridescent stars, its noble bearing—were seen as visual signs of a redeemed world, resplendent and magnificent and holy. Without losing sight of the fallen condition of creation, and the image of Christ crucified in a world beset by sin and suffering, Catholic and Orthodox theologies would try to render in art, ritual, fashion, and philosophy the same splendor as the transfigured Christ, the same aesthetic glory as the peacock, the same beauty of creation. They sought to capture transcendence as it assumed incarnate form.

No wonder that the Met Gala of 2018, with Rihanna as chair of the gala and high priestess, adopted the theme "Heavenly Bodies: Fashion and the Catholic Imagination." (Andrew Bolton, head curator, enlisted David Tracy, in fact, as theological advisor.) Rihanna showed up in papal regalia, wearing a pearl- and jewel-encrusted robe, papal mitre and necklace, embroidered mini-dress, and long flowing overcoat. Ariana Grande chose a Vera Wang gown with imagery from Michelangelo's Sistine Chapel, and Cardi B was, well, Cardi B: she wore a gem-encrusted dress with a billowing cream-colored train, an ornate tri-point headpiece covered in pearls, rhinestones, and jewels, bedazzled gloves, and a thick, pearl-encrusted choker. If only bishops and popes looked as dazzling!

But then again, let's not forget that bishops and popes have, in fact, dressed with similar extravagances. In an essay on "Sacred Vestments: Color and Form," Maria Cataldi Gallo points to numerous biblical and theological precedents of blinged-out fashion: Jacob gives his favorite son, Joseph, a coat of many colors, the costliest garment of his time, and a father in the New Testament greets his prodigal son by ordering his servants to "bring out a robe and put it on him; put a ring on his finger and sandals on his feet."[19] In Exodus, the vestments of the high priest were rich in color (gold, blue, purple, and crimson), rich in material (byssus, or fine twisted linen), and rich in gems, embroideries, and even golden bells (lending an aural quality to the vestments). The mandate was established in Exodus 28:2–3: "You shall make sacred vestments for the glorious adornment of your brother, Aaron . . . to consecrate him for my priesthood." In observance of such decrees, the high priest's "investiture" (derived from *veste*, clothing), and later the pope's investiture, entailed the donning of vestments that lacked no refinement, with precious fabrics, showy colors, and expensive ornaments. "For millennia," Gallo remarks, "the church has hewed to its founding principles of sacredness and beauty, highlighting the role of the celebrant—and especially that of the pontiff—by garbing him in special vestments."[20]

The Body and Dance

If Catholicism managed to celebrate the glory and splendor of the world in such ways, thus honoring the fundamental goodness of creation, it has been more ambivalent about the role of dance.[21] As a grammar of the body, and poetry in motion, attitudes toward dance have often mirrored attitudes toward the body and sexuality, sometimes treated with uncompromising suspicion, and sometimes with religious, even mystical, value, its rhythms and pirouettes an expression, as Clement of Alexandria put it, of the longing for God.[22] Notwithstanding this latter conviction, dance was generally not integrated into formal liturgies in the Middle Ages however. For evidence of the role of dance in medieval religious life, one has to look to the streets, where dance was a prominent feature of pilgrimages, processions, and public festivals. It dotted the landscape of saints' festivals, musical dramas, and mystery plays, for instance, forming a crucial part of folk or street Catholicism. (Dance dramas, for instance, were used by the Franciscans in the New World as evangelizing arts.) In nineteenth-century Catholic Cuba, it is estimated that over 300 fiestas took place annually and dance was an integral part of the celebrations (e.g., the festivals of Caridad del Cobre; San Juan; San Jose; San Lazaro; Santa Barbara; Nuestra Señora de la Candelaria; Día de los Reyes; Nochebuena; Altares de Cruz; Promesa celebrations; Carnival before lent, etc.). Like the floods of hurricane season, one nineteenth-century critic warned that so many fiestas and dances in Cuba would eventually drown the island in frivolous gratifications: "Day dances, night dances, winter dances, summer dances, rural dances, urban dances, dances yesterday, dances today, tomorrow, late, early; dance of cachumba, cangrejito, guaracha, repiqueteo, rumba, chiquito abajo; dances modified by all the adverbs and qualified by all the adjectives in the dictionary."[23]

Sharing this same cynical attitude, the Cuban Revolution would try to strip the grammar of dance of all such adjectives and adverbs, aghast at so much bombast and pageantry, seeing these things as frivolous, unenlightened, decadent, and escapist, as so many opiates. In order to hew closely to Marxist ideology, they devoted themselves to demythologizing and desacralizing Cuban culture, pruning the verdant branches of the culture, casting off their blossoms and leaving it bare like a deciduous tree in the winter. (Alma Guillermoprieto describes teaching dance in the early years of the Cuban Revolution without

the benefit of mirrors—mirrors were a symbol of vanity and baroque decadence.)[24] Though they dispensed with the language of "sin," they treated the
abundance of revelry and merrymaking as a kind of sin against the Revolution,
inimical to the Sacrifices that were required by Revolutionary man and woman.
(The Sacrifice was Castro's initiative, known as *La Zafra de los Diez Millones*,
to harvest ten million tons of sugar.) There's a famous line, half-joking, by the
revolutionary *trovador* Carlos Puebla on this matter: "*Se acabó la diversión!
Llegó el Comandante y mandó a parar!*" (The fun or diversion/amusement is
over! The Commandante arrived and ordered it to stop!) In a new version, the
joke made its way to Mexico, but now with Fidel—notorious for his refusal
to dance—ordering the rumba to stop. As the people repeat the line—*Que se
acabe la rumba!*—they begin to swing and dance to the phrase, turning Fidel's
command into a rhythmic and spell-like mantra perfect for a conga line![25]

Jokes aside, the rumba and son came under suspicion by the Revolution
for their seedy origins, their lubricious values, their frenzied exuberance, and
their associations with the *santeros* of Catholicism and Santería. Too much
festivity became the stuff of heresy, punishable by excommunication, exile,
or imprisonment. Ironically, then, Communist verdicts on Catholic festivity mirrored the negative judgment of music, dance, theater, and the body
in some circles of Christianity: they were licentious and vain, occasions for
dissolute living. They were reminiscent of the Israelites' idolatrous dancing
around the golden calf (which was, for a Marxist, the sin of capitalism), or
Salome's lascivious dance before King Herod (which was, for a Revolutionary,
the sin of pre-Revolutionary Cuba's dark ages). They lacked a critical, emancipatory consciousness.

For Nietzsche, to think of someone outraged by such Puritanical thinking,
this (Marxist) outlook was tantamount to a repressive slave morality, renouncing as it does everything that is joyful and beautiful about life. "I could not believe in a god who would not dance," he would remark, seemingly opening the
door to gods who did, in fact, revel in dance—Dionysus, for instance. I'd like to
believe, thus, that he would have appreciated the Afro-Cuban traditions of the
santeros. Alma Guillermoprieto, in her beautiful memoir *Dancing with Cuba*
(2004), has a moving description of a dance in honor of Yemayá, the Yoruba
goddess of the oceans (associated with the black Madonna, Nuestra Señora
de Regla): "But just as the *tocadores* [the drummers who make the Batá drums
talk] began to mingle their voices in harmonies that were somewhere between
Tibetan and feline, a gigantic wave seemed to swell through her solar plexus:
crouching toward the floor as if a subterranean force had gripped her by the
ankles, she began undulating her torso, moving her arms as if they were made
of water, and shaking the blue skirt in ever broader waves until she herself had

become a sea" (my addition).[26] In the course of such graceful movements, with her torso riding the waves of the sea, her arms fluid and protean, the dancer becomes Yemayá and Yemayá becomes the dancer. This is surely a god who knows how to dance, who joins with La Virgen in rapturous gyrations, who merges into Nuestra Señora de Regla like the river emptying into the sea.

It's true, of course, that this joyful wedding of Yemayá to the Virgin Mary would evoke all sorts of theological anxieties in the minds of the authorities, for it smacks of idolatry. Fears of heterodoxy, in addition to the fears of sin and sexuality, influenced negative appraisals of dance, in other words, especially since dance often took on a more central role in the wild and unruly branches of religion: among Sufism in Islam, Hasidism in Judaism, and among the thousand and one syncretic varieties of Catholicism (e.g., Santería, Candomblé, Voodoo, and most Catholic-Indigenous hybrids, such as the rites of the Yaqui and Mayo peoples, the Tarahumara, et al.).[27] No wonder that the character of the devil, in many of the mystery, miracle, and morality plays of the Middle Ages, was given so many choreographed parts—dance seemed to be his favorite way of waltzing into the lives of good Christians. Casting the devil as a figure of dance made it clear that dance was a dangerous business, a source of waywardness, mischief, heresy and, God forbid, pleasure.

Breaking

And if the critics of black music in America are to be believed, the devil would continue to ply his trade in genre after genre, snaking his way into the blues, jazz, rock 'n' roll, R&B and, most recently, hip-hop. Each of them, at one time or another, have been tagged with a diabolical reputation, held responsible for sexual license, moral ruin, senseless irrationality, the mad abandon of fleshly pleasure, and everything, in sum, that would profane what was good and holy. If b-boying has generally escaped similar accusations, it's probably because it is not primarily sexual in nature, and does not require a partner. Instead of revolving around the thrills of sex, romance, and love (as in disco, salsa, or reggaeton), breaking has been a means of claiming one's territory and turf, combating invisibility, and carving one's name and legacy on city street-scapes. It moves centrifugally, not centripetally, outward rather than inward, employing public spaces and street corners as its stage rather than dance halls and theaters. There is a clear contrast, in this regard, between the work of, say, Martha Graham (famous for dances that reveal the inner landscapes of the psyche) and the street-centric work of b-boys and b-girls (famous for revealing the social and cultural struggles of the barrio). Breaking always included, of course, the cravings of the soul, and the desire for self-transcendence; but it always pointed back to the hood, combining the floating grace of a butterfly with the earthbound attack of a hawk.

As much as it simulated street struggles and conflicts, though, breaking ironically represented the power of dance to transform violence and aggression into something graceful and peaceable. It's probably too naïve to say that it always overcame the violence of the streets—there are countless examples of breakers' pugilistic postures leading to fights—but the aim, in the final analysis, was on the battle of style and skill, not on something as artless as blunt-force trauma.[28] These things, as I have been insisting, are about the growth of the soul as it tries to break out of its cocoon: "Regardless," Jeff Chang writes about the various elements of hip-hop (breaking, deejaying, emceeing, writing), "they shared a revolutionary aesthetic. They were about unleashing youth style as an expression of the soul, unmediated by corporate money, unauthorized by the powerful, protected and enclosed by almost monastic rites, codes, and orders."[29]

The "break," in any case, is the fundamental building block of both b-boying and rap music, the percussive and rhythmic core of the song, the section boiled down and stripped of all extraneous vocals and instruments. B-boy songs, writes Joseph Schloss, "tended to feature Latin percussion (especially bongos), have relatively fast tempos (110 to 129 beats per minute), use horns and guitars in a percussive way, use stop-time at various points in the song, and feature a formal structure that builds to decisive musical peaks. But, most important, they have breaks."[30] More cyclical and repetitive than linear, the break is the explosive moment of a song when the drumbeat or bass line attacks the listener with big wallops of sound, the rhythm rousing the body and loosening up the hips. Instead of moving in one direction (from beginning to end), however, it spools backward in endless loops, picking up force as it spins round and round. "The break," Will Ashon writes, "is where the music explodes, where rhythm in particular starts multiplying and complicating and copulating—where there is almost too much information for the body and mind to deal with. . . . Dancing, on this reading, becomes an involuntary response to this sudden data overload, this tsunami of information, which causes not so much a slaying in the spirit as a bumping and grinding in the spirit, an unchosen twitching and twisting to the beat, as if Saint Vitus and not the Devil had all the best tunes." (Saint Vitus, incidentally, is the patron saint of actors, dancers, and entertainers.)[31]

When the rhythm hits the body in this way, overloading the mind and tripping the body, music and dance can be vehicles of transcendence, giving one a taste of eternity, in T. S. Eliot's sense: "Neither flesh nor fleshless, neither from nor towards; at the still point, there the dance is," writes Eliot. Dance, in this mystical rendering, is a taste of the still point, the sudden union of the body with the rhythms and orders of the universe. It's stillness in motion, the moment when the mind loses self-consciousness and operates without intention or aim, like a basketball player "in the zone." If one can quiet the mind, center the body, and find the zone, dance can be a transporting experience, a break from the grind and drudgery of life, a loss of consciousness, an immersion in the music to the point of union.

If you think this sounds too sublime for the street art of b-boying, you're wrong. B-boying is a combination of the spiritual and street, the transcendent and earthly, an art that integrates the movements of the body with the pulses of the soul—hence, the common comparisons with capoeira or kung fu. Like the martial arts, b-boying requires much more than the strength of muscles, the balance of the torso, the rocking of the body, the flurry of feet, the fluidity of arm waves and strikes; there are gnostic elements that must be learned as well, including spiritual and breathing techniques, a history of the forms and movements, strategies for improvising, a general understanding of dance, and so on: "Foundation," Schloss remarks, "is a term used by b-boys and b-girls to refer to an almost mystical set of notions about b-boying that is passed from teacher to student."[32] To learn the "foundations" of breaking is to be initiated into a cloistered society, which is why Cuban rappers, for instance, use the term *fundamento* to refer both to the foundations of breaking and to the foundations of Santería.[33]

As best can be determined, b-boying began with top-rocking and up-rocking before descending to the floor. In 1960s Brooklyn, young Puerto Ricans began dancing to rock and soul music with the trappings and frills of their parents' music: mambo, bomba, boogaloo, salsa. After adding tough and belligerent moves from the streets—burns, jerks, warlike poses—they called it up-rocking. As it spread to the South Bronx and other parts of New York, it merged with African American styles of dance, as well as elements of kung fu, capoeira, and gang war-dances. At this point, in partnership with the pioneering deejays of the South Bronx, the dancers began to exploit the longer breaks and openings in the music. As Kool Herc, Afrika Bambaataa, Grandmaster Flash, Grand Wizzard Theodore, and other pioneering deejays extended the grooves of the music, prolonging the rhythms and sonic booms, b-boys were given more time and space to play with, more room to experiment. Breakers now started taking to the ground, growing more creative with backspins and head-spins, flying footwork, twisting bodies, acrobatic flips, soaring helicopters, and taunting freezes that served as exclamation points. In the spirit of competition, limits were increasingly pushed as breakers sought to best their opponents, becoming more inventive and creative, and daring anyone to underestimate them. They battled their opponents with their bodies the way rappers battled with their tongues, the way graf writers battled with the visual tags and pieces, the way deejays claimed private and public property. "Starting upright in the top-rock," writes Jeff Chang about the various fragments of b-boying, "hands up and stabbing like a gang-member in motion, feet moving side to side like Ali in a rope-a-dope, dropping down like James Brown, turning hurricanes of Spy's boricua footwork, exploding into a Zulu freeze, tossing in a spin and punctuating it all with a Bruce Lee grin or a mocking Maori tongue—the entire history of the hip-hop body in a virtuoso display of style."[34]

My brother's b-boy group, the Royal Rockers, borrowed bits and pieces of these things. In their prime, 1983–1984 or so, they studied, trained, and battled rival groups with the seriousness of a heart attack. Andy and I both studied Shaolin kung fu, so many of the acrobatic moves came quickly to him, especially the kick-up, windmills, back bridges, freezes, sweeping kicks, pretzel-like twists, and the thumping flip on one's back that they called a suicide. Each member of the crew had their own expertise: one or two were imaginative choreographers; others good at handstands, head-spins, and pikes; one had a dope centipede; another was skilled at popping and locking; and almost all could contort their torso at improbable angles, legs fluttering in the air, weaving arabesque designs in the air. Popping was my favorite: the move started at the extremities of the hands, folding in at the joints of the fingers and then rippling inward, like the thawing of a frozen lake in springtime. It combined robotic and dispassionate coldness with the fluid shuffles and glides of a dancer on ice, wildly incongruent and wildly graceful. And, while each individual would have to throw down at some point, independently and separately, the crew usually ended their routines with some crazy coda that gathered everyone together into one aggregate. I recall one routine, choreographed to the robotic and vocoder-modulated catchphrases of "Egypt, Egypt" by Egyptian Lover, that had the architectural scaffoldings of a pyramid.[35] Once everyone was in place, they began to rotate and turn as if they were an alien spacecraft that was now unfurling its propellers to fly away. Who knows what inspired it (perhaps it dramatized the Afrofuturism of P-Funk, Afrika Bambaataa, and Egyptian Lover), but it was imaginative, grand, and soaring, the b-boying equivalent of the high-flying rhetoric of rappers. It reminded me of one of the prancing floats in a Mardi Gras parade, all theater and kinetic energy.

The only thing that fired our interest as much as hip-hop at the time was Chinese kung fu. Kung fu, as we practiced it, was a close cousin of breaking; however violent and bellicose it seemed to outsiders, it was something supple and spiritual to us, an exercise in physical, aesthetic, and moral discipline. Unlike karate, which we perceived as inelegant and stiff and only good for a fight, we studied kung fu because of the lithe beauty of the forms, the sophisticated choreographies, the phantom leaps and strikes, and the mimetic aping of cranes, tigers, snakes, monkeys, praying mantises, drunken boxers, and so on. We studied it because of the esoteric knowledge and power that it offered, as though what we were really after was the Tao. And since the "Tao that can be named is not the Tao," to invoke the first line of the Tao Te Ching, we sought the Way through an art form that philosophized with the body, an art form that was part martial technique, part dance, part spiritual exercise. "Kung fu," writes RZA, "is less a fighting style and more about the cultivation of the spirit."[36] "Wu-Tang," he goes on to say, "was the best sword style. But with us, our tongue is our sword."[37]

For rappers, as RZA suggests, the tongue is the primary weapon of choice; for breakers, it's the body and dance; for graffiti writers, the combat is visual, chromatic, and graphic, guerilla warfare with paint; for the deejay, the war is waged sonically and rhythmically, the search for the perfect beat. Regardless, in each case, the artist in question is tussling with insignificance, flipping situations of adversity into opportunity, somersaulting the realities of poverty, monkey flippin 'em, as Nas famously described it on "N.Y. State of Mind" (*Illmatic*, 1994). Just as Nas employed the rhythm of language to snap on his opponents, b-boys used the rhythmic stylings of the body, not to mention hip gear and regal names ("*Royal* Rockers"), to battle chaos and gain a foothold in their world. Their struts and dances and nicknames were a cry for esteem and respect, a refusal to remain silent and invisible, a refusal to believe that their music, dances, cultures, and lives were low class and inferior. Making due with makeshift stages (cardboard taped to hard concrete) and marginal locations (street corners, parks, and skating rinks), they shared the unspoken conviction that these beats, rhymes, and dances were somehow—if only from the sound of the bongos and Afro-Latin percussion in the breaks of "Apache," "Planet Rock," Jimmy Castor's "It's Just Begun," James Brown's "Give it Up or Turn It Loose," and so on—tied to black and Latin roots. And that by participating in the culture, they were claiming their ancestry, leaving their mark, and narrating their lives in this brave new world.

So, while breaking lacks the deep allegorical, biblical, and mythological allusions of modern dance, it has its own codes and closely guarded secrets. If a parable is a teasing and enigmatic story, often subversive to conventional values and best understood by the outcasts and underdogs of society, breaking is probably closer to the spirit of a parable than an allegory. Afrika Bambaataa's

"Planet Rock" (1982), a sacred anthem for breakers, is the quintessential example, a parable that spoke volumes to the insiders of the culture but mystified outsiders. But the song was parabolic in another way, too: it contained a utopian ideal consistent with biblical dreams, one that would integrate people of different races into one nation under a groove, all differences fading away on the dance floor, all cultures and classes melting into one as the revelers sweated, sashayed, and partied the night away. In its kaleidoscope of fragments—Kraftwerk's "Trans-Europe Express" and "Numbers," Babe Ruth's "The Mexican," electronically distorted vocals, a Japanese-made Roland 808 drumbeat, synthesized orchestral stabs—we were offered an alternative vision of America, a future that welcomed difference and strangeness, a poly-cultural pastiche of sound, dance, poetry, and culture.[38] In contrast to life on earth, where patterns of division and inequality were the norm, planet rock provided space and opportunity for everyone. "'Planet Rock' was hip-hop's universal invitation," writes Jeff Chang, "a hypnotic vision of one world under a groove, beyond race, poverty, sociology and geography."[39]

I'm tempted to say that Afrika Bambaataa and the Zulu Nation's beautiful prophecy failed (especially as the benign neglect of urban communities turned malignant in the 1980s and 1990s), but it's more accurate to say that the prophecy is yet unrealized. The rise of reggaeton and urbano indicates to me a recovery of this spirit, the passing of the torch to a new generation. From one perspective, the popularity of reggaeton and Latin hip-hop represents a sea change, with the tides of the Global South crashing and carving their identities onto the shores of North America and Europe; but at the same time, it's also a return to some of the earliest inspirations in hip-hop, a recovery more than a revolution. Whatever the case, whether old or new, the winds that propel the sails of reggaeton are variable and rowdy; they blow in swirling patterns, from the north and south, east and west, as though they are powered by Urakán, the Caribbean god of tumultuous air who whips the ocean into a frothy, rambunctious riot and turns life on its head. Though notoriously apolitical—tending toward windy words and festive, dance-centric grooves—reggaeton is a blustery and extravagant aesthetics, whipping across land and ocean without any regard for borders. In so far as it embodies the "promise of a convivial, cosmopolitan multi-culture," reggaeton is a fulfillment of Afrika Bambaataa's prophecy.[40]

Reggaeton and the Global South

Jon Pareles has called reggaeton "a Caribbean party with a hip-hop beat," and a "spicy mix of salsa, hip-hop, and reggae."[41] In either portrait, reggaeton has shifted hip-hop's center of gravity to the Global South, ushering in a resplendent, upbeat, and sun-drenched soundscape. It usually lacks, consequently, the dark and overcast atmosphere of gangster rap, where one gets the impression that the sky is not only menacing, but about to fall and flatten the people below. Think of Nas's *Illmatic*: the album's cover art superimposes the Queensbridge Projects onto a picture of Nas as a young child; the ghetto is literally on his mind, troubling and vexing it, forcing him to grow up quickly if he wants to survive this tough, brutal world. His eyelids droop over the outer layer of his sclera like curtains, veiling the white of his eyes, hiding any trace of vulnerability, preserving a sense of distance and aloofness. His head is held high, and his gaze comes across as stony, intimidating, and guarded, as fierce as a raging fire. It's overstated to say that the light in his coal-like eyes is extinguished (the miracle of the album, and of hip-hop in general, is the unceasing Hanukkah-like burning of the soul's candles), but nonetheless it's remote and distant, as if his eyes act as dark sunglasses that shroud what is behind them. And the grim and sunless metaphors throughout the album—dungeons, trenches, mazes, black clouds, wintry climate, crack spots, prison cells, war zones, death traps—all expound on the disaffected

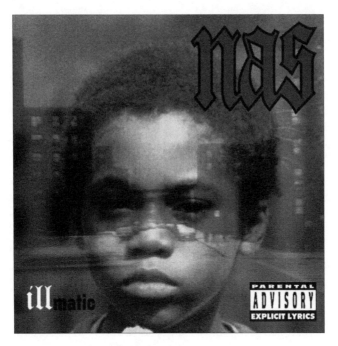

Figure 4 Cover of Nas, *Illmatic* (1994)

glare of the young Nas: "I need a new nigga for this black cloud to follow," he raps on "Life's a Bitch," "'Cause while it's over me it's too dark to see tomorrow." Life's a bitch for a young black child in the ghetto, and Nas registers its challenges and dangers in brilliant and brooding lyricism.

There is little of this in reggaeton: besides the fact that the lyrics are relatively insignificant—relative to the music, catchphrases, and dance-centric rhythms—reggaeton is explosively exuberant, a carnival of life. I wouldn't say that minor chords are always absent (they emerge when the producer riffs on gangster rap, for instance), but they are nonetheless rare, a momentary calm before the ensuing cyclone of dance rhythms and breakneck bars. Reggaeton has eclectic and varied roots, drawing from Jamaican dancehall; the Panamanian reggae en español of Renato and El General; Puerto Rican bomba and "underground" (*música negra*); the creative mixtapes of DJ Negro and DJ Playero; the quickened, fever pitch dembow of the Dominican Republic; Brazilian funk; the sensitive poetry of Colombian vallenato; and a variety of other Latin musical elements: the timbales and congas of salsa, the trebly guitars of bachata, the improvisations of a sonero, heavily synthesized drum patterns, electronic echo and reverb, the syncopated clave rhythm, sentimental ballad singing styles, Andalusian nasal timbres, the bombastic sounds of house- and techno-infused dance anthems, and the melodious blend of rapping and singing in dancehall reggae. By marrying itself to the rambunctious and reckless spirit of "dancehall reggae"—and not to its liberationist and conscious-minded cousin in "roots reggae"—reggaeton fell head over heels for the sound of revelry more than revolution, for grooves that attacked the body and snubbed the mind. "Whereas roots reggae," writes Wayne Marshall, "preached pan-African liberation and consciousness raising, often couched in the millenarian language of Rastafari, dancehall reggae embraced more earthy and local concerns, themes resonant and in close conversation with contemporary hip-hop: crime, drugs, violence, sex, poverty, corruption."[42]

Stealing some of its attitude and identity from "reggae"—with semantic echoes of ragamuffin, rough, rude, raw, rebellious, rangy—reggaeton almost immediately grated on the tastes of the middle and upper classes in Puerto Rico and Panama, where it first came into the world. Such critics would judge it harshly, seeing it as a noisy din, full of sound and fury, signifying nothing. Not unlike Southern rap, it was considered ignorant, hollow, vulgar, and crude, unworthy of the lofty values of jíbaro music, for instance. And to be honest, they weren't necessarily wrong—this was, indeed, the kind of music that concentrated on the primal desires of the body, the flesh set on fire and sent careening straight into the flames like a moth. It was music that screamed for more gas and energy—más gasolina, in the words of Daddy Yankee—and called for the listener's participation in down-to-the-floor dips, spins, bumps, grinds, and booties shaking like a castanet.

Shabba Ranks's version of the dembow rhythm has been key to reggaeton: basically the classic habanera figure of Latin music—present in dancehall reggae, mento, soca, calypso, salsa, son, merengue—the groove is created by a steady bass drum (4/4 measure), and a rapid-fire tresillo cross-rhythm pattern with snares, hi-hats, and bells that strike on the downbeat of the kick drums (3+3+2 measure). It makes for a compulsive dance tempo, full of the kinetic vitality of so much of Latin music. Much like bomba, plena, bachata, cumbia, or timba—all once described as "grotesque rhythms," and "expressions of primitive frenzy"—reggaeton concentrates most of its energy on the business of dance and having fun.[43] Its popularity in Cuba, to take one example, represents a disillusionment with the Revolution's never-ending calls for sacrifice, discipline, and self-renunciation. Exhausted by penitential appeals to bear the cross for the Revolution, by the 1990s or so Cuban youth began to long for something more redemptive, something that had the triumphant joy of Easter in it. For communities long expected to play the part of suffering figures—like a St. Sebastian, body riddled with arrows—music was increasingly sought for its jubilant and ecstatic pleasures, its ability to transport one to another dimension. Geoffrey Baker puts this trend in its proper global context: "After the period of protest and politically engaged music of the 1980s," he writes, "South African kwaito music focused on pleasure principles, a departure from the ideology of social sacrifice and asceticism in the past; Brazil's funk carioca also represented a break from the protest music of Brazil's military rule, 1964–1985, and a celebration, carnival-like, of individual pleasure, dance, and aestheticism; Jamaican dancehall was a rupture with the religious and politically engaged 'roots reggae' and a revolt, subversion against the standards of decency, law and order in Jamaican society."[44]

In each instance, a seismic shift displaced the axis mundi of music, moving it away from logocentric, word-centered approaches (prophetic-ethical in nature) and closer toward body- and dance-centric genres (mystical-aesthetic in nature). It was an upheaval that seemed to jar open the repressive cages of the body, allowing it to stretch its wings, take flight, and soar. Part of this freedom was sexual in nature: unlike the individual stylings of b-boys and b-girls, usually without a partner, reggaeton dancing is meant for couples. Its most infamous dance is dubbed *perreo*, a back-to-front form of grinding, shimmying, and twerking; it echoes any number of dances that simulate erotic movements, from the rump shaking of the Jazz Age's hootchie-kootch and shimmy-shake to the game of pursuit-and-capture, driven by the congas, known as the guaguancó (a subset of the rumba).[45] Ivy Queen's classic "Quiero Bailar," from the album *Diva*, 2003, is a paean to the style; the song celebrates the sensual contact of *perreo*, the rubbing, sticking, and sweating on the dance floor, the surging electricity created when two bodies collide. One of the pioneering figures in reggaeton, also known as La Diva, La Caballota, or La Potra, Ivy Queen enjoys the mating game on the dance floor, she declares, all the teasing and wooing and bumping, but this doesn't mean that she's easy, much less a plaything of male desire: "Eso no quiere decir que pa la cama voy." (That doesn't mean that I'm going to bed with you.)

Delivered in a thick and throaty voice, scraped for shouting, demanding to be heard, the rap manages multiple feats, celebrating the euphoria of dance, on the one hand, while asserting sexual liberation for and by women. "It allows us," writes Isabelia Herrera, "to enjoy a *perreo sucio* and remind men that we can be the masters of our own desire."[46] While Ivy Queen, who first got her start in DJ Negro's club "The Noise," could deliver sharp, jagged barbs in honor of her rough-and-tumble origins—say, on "Mi Barrio," a tribute to her roots in Añasco, Puerto Rico—she really thrived when she roused her listeners to dance, whipping and whirling them about like grains of sand in the wind. "But it's when the album heads to the dancefloor," Herrera continues, "that *Diva* excels; this is where La Potra most convincingly asserts her power, where she invites us to lay siege to hypermasculine posturing, to revel in sex and refuse the conquest of our bodies."

Notwithstanding these feminist digs—Ivy Queen was an exception in reggaeton's boys' club, after all—it's tempting to reduce the genre's boisterous energies to a matter of pure entertainment, devoid of any social value. Though one can marshal evidence for this perspective from any number of artists in the genre (especially since songcraft matters more than social theory), the criticism is overstated. It overlooks the way that reggaetoneros employ vocal artistry in the service of personal and cultural freedom; the way they can make music out of yelps, ululations, and onomatopeiac sounds; the way the dembow riddim shocks the flesh into motion; or the way they throw their arms around the barrios, slums, and projects from which they come, conferring value and grace upon what is despised and lowly in the eyes of the world. As in hip-hop, most of the pioneering figures of reggaeton came from the poorest barrios and caseríos, the dark side of the city.[47] If they didn't always wax political or poetic, a black consciousness, nonetheless, almost always oozed out of the speakers, spilling onto the dance floor, and infecting the walk, talk, and style of these artists.[48] "In a place where racism purportedly does not exist," writes Petra Rivera-Rideau on this point, "reggaeton provides a language, sometimes verbal, sometimes visual, and oftentimes aural, to speak about the unspeakable black presence on the island."[49]

If more subtle and indirect than other forms of rap music, dancing around social issues more than tackling them head-on, reggaeton rarely leaves it up to the lyrics alone to address social and racial injustices, often reveling in the stuff of dance, fashion, and sound to strike a rebellious note. And yet, at the same time, many of the key figures of the genre—I'm thinking of Vico C, Ivy Queen, and Tego Calderón in particular—never believed that party tunes were incongruent with social and spiritual messages; they braided these themes together, sounding their displeasure at racism and inequality at one moment, and then turning sybaritic at another. Known as "El Filósofo," the Philosopher, Vico C earned the tag by his thoughtful and meditative lyricism, for instance. His early works, "Underground," "Soy de la Calle" (I'm from the Streets), and "La Recta Final" (The Final Stretch/End of Times), covered a broad sweep of themes, everything from political and economic corruption to the soul-stealing power of money and drugs. In the scenario of "La Recta Final," for instance, the world is falling apart, groaning in these last days. With the mounting chaos and tumult on the earth, the rapper stretches out his vocals with a mixture of anxiety and longing, hoping for a cure in the midst of a pandemic. In his case, the cure is religion: "*Pero para tener una vida mas pura/ Creer en Cristo es la mejor cura*" (But to have a purer life/ believing in Christ is the best cure). The music, meanwhile, signals the apocalyptic emergency with a harsh and grating metallic rasp on the surface, an ominous bass line groaning below, and the rapper's conversational flow somewhere in the middle, musing over the world as he sees it. A seismographer of the streets, Vico C registers all the disturbances and tremors in his world, and then turns to God for respite and repose, searching for calm in the eye of the storm.[50]

If not as religious as Vico C, Tego Calderón was just as deep. The pantheon of his musical models—Vico C, Public Enemy, Bob Marley, and the *salsero*, Ismael Rivera—speaks loudly about his own Afrocentric and conscious inclinations. Where others in reggaeton indulged in loud and flashy appearances, whether with cars or clothes, Calderón embraced plain street styles, an aesthetic that ran against currents of conspicuous consumption. For his celebrated work, *El Abayarde* (produced by Luny Tunes, DJ Nelson, Noriega, and others), Calderón sported an unkempt Afro as well as Santería-inspired wardrobe (cotton pants, beaded necklaces, baggy shirts), and he claimed the *abayarde* (a fire ant that has a powerful sting for its small size) as some kind of spirit animal. Calderón's lyrics bite, the simile implies; they get under your skin, produce an irritation, and cause an itch that can only be scratched by dance. The single "Pa' Que Retozen" is a fine example of this, a song for romping and rollicking, a song for pleasure and enjoyment. The dembow rhythm, a syncopated boom-pa-dum-dum beat, is central to the song, thrusting it forward with the force of a charging bull, stabbing the listener directly in the gut. In fact, consistent with the metaphor here, the rhythm echoes the stampeding bullfighting music of "Pasodoble" (e.g., the España cañí of Pascual Marquina Narro), as well as the polka's oompah bass line.[51] The song is less rambunctious than other reggaeton hits, but it's compulsive and energizing nonetheless, a cooler and more collected way to get bodies on the dance floor.

Throughout *El Abayarde*, the sounds of Puerto Rico are unmistakable. There's a clear nasal patter to Calderón's vocals, with echoes of the Spanish that came to Hispaniola from Andalusia and the Canary Islands. Traces of bomba are clear too, with lilting melodies, stretched-out vowels, and consonants that are consistently unpronounced (hablado becomes habloa, dedo becomes deo, etc.). Calderón doesn't carefully chew and spit his words so much as he swallows them whole, like a snake eating a mouse. In terms of lyrical content, Afro-Latin cultures and histories are front and central on *El Abayarde*, as on the chilled, boom-bap rhythms of "Los Difuntos" (The Dead), "Loiza" (a tribute to the black barrio that dates back to the slave trade), or "Guasa Guasa," where he boasts that his flow is "antiguo como el voodoo" (ancient like voodoo). In a kind of Manichaean balance, Calderón holds opposites together on the album, delivering banging, dance-centric joints, on the one hand, and then offering pensive pieces meant for contemplation and self-scrutiny. With "Los Difuntos," for instance, he turns spiritual and meditative, his words now messages from a sacred source, *"una voz que me hablaba/ una sensacion sagrada"* (a voice that spoke to me/ a sacred sensation). Keep it raw, the voice says, and speak on behalf of the dead, speak on behalf of the exploited poor, the victims of violent death, and all the mothers who grieve over their deceased children. On the single "El Abayarde," too, he mixes together—with a sample of the muted, fuzzy trumpet riff in Cab Calloway's "Minnie the Moocher"—boasts about his smooth lyricism, declarations of black pride (*agradecido de esta negrura*), and gratitude for the divine grace that sustains his life (*tengo la prida de mi vida por gracia divina*). In each case, Calderón seems to enjoy confusing the boundaries of the sacred and profane, mixing sacramental wine with a bootlegger's brew and drinking it out of a paper cup.

Whether righteous or wildly indulgent, sacred or profane, in any case, Calderón has consistently maintained that reggaeton comes from the streets, a claim that is almost literally true if you consider that some of the earliest mixtapes in Panama, by Renato, were sold and distributed on tricked-out buses known as *diablos rojos* (red devils).[52] Since the music is known for its synthetic textures, heavily synthesized drums, electronically filtered vocals, dense samples, and programmed grooves (all the effect of the digital revolution and the use of Fruity Loops software in the early aughts by DJ Blass, Luny Tunes, Noriega, DJ Nelson, et al.), the claim is counterintuitive, a boast that seems—at least sonically—to ring false. Ironically, though, reggaeton's realness and authenticity is an expression of artifice and affectation. As in Jamaican dub or hip-hop, reggaeton doesn't require live instruments and doesn't sweat the anxiety of influence; it makes music by raiding, chopping, and remixing a variety of musical fragments, pushing the music into the future without forgetting the past. And it has been wildly aggressive in this regard, pirating Jamaican dub and dancehall reggae, stealing from salsa, bachata, merengue, bomba, and plena, adopting rap's verbal virtuosities, and employing the sacred language of Batá drums, timbales, bongos, palitos, snares, kick drums, and so on. Its collages are crowded and jumbled, a sonic style that mirrors the polychromatic palette of the New World, a *mestizaje* of sound.

Daddy Yankee is another example of this bright sonic carnival. He hails from the Villa Kennedy projects in Barrio Obrero, San Juan, and was shot in the leg at sixteen years of age when he was visiting DJ Playero, a friend and pioneering producer of reggaeton. It was a gang-related incident and had a life-changing effect. He still carries the bullet as a reminder of his origins: "The street is my inspiration," he says. "If I got disconnected from this, I'd lose my music."[53] Echoing this sentiment, his debut album, *El Cartel de Yankee* (1997), opens with a poem by Gallego, "Chamaco's Corner," a thoughtful consideration of the plight of youth stuck in the corners and cracks of society. When his mind wanders back to these places, Daddy Yankee turns philosophical and political. In "Corazones" ("Hearts") from *Barrio Fino* (2004), he laments the broken conditions of his barrio, where the schools are underfunded and the air is saturated with *"un espíritu de muerte que devora lo que vive"* (a spirit of death that devours the living). He wishes he could gather the *caseríos* and shelter them under his wings. He wishes that politicians had more heart and soul, that they had eyes for the unseen and marginalized. He wants to squeeze more out of his own heart, sculpt it in the image of the bleeding heart of Jesus, *"un corazón mas poderoso que nos pretege/ que jamás y nunca será vencido"* (a more powerful heart that protects us/ that never will be defeated).

After speaking from the heart on "Corazones," Daddy Yankee shifts gears and speeds up the tempo on "Dale Caliente," his words—or better, his whoops and hollers—now about igniting dance, making the arms and legs move like pistons, the hips like a tree in a storm. "Gasolina," his most famous song, is in this vein as well, a high-octane track, music for the party. Lyrically frivolous and scat-like, Daddy Yankee employs primal shouts, catchy phrases, and bumping rhythms to whip the audience into a frenzied joy, pumping more and more gasoline into the body's engine.

Música Urbana

However capable of shifting gears in these ways, reggaeton, in Daddy Yan-kee's estimation, is ultimately about bringing Latin@s together: "It's unified the Latin masses," he remarks. "The music makes them feel Latino."[54] If be-coming Latin@ is like a born-again experience (you become Latin@ once you cross the US border), reggaeton is something similar in Daddy Yankee's reading, baptizing various Latin communities in the same river of music and dance. No longer Mexican, Colombian, Salvadoran, Guatemalan, Cuban, Dominican, Boriqua, or Peruvian, we all become one in reggaeton, different members of one larger body.

"Urbano" has become an umbrella term for such kinds of fellowship, an ark that contains the many species of Latin music: reggaeton, trap music, rap en español, dancehall, dembow, bachata, nu cumbia, urban champeta, et al. If hip-hop and reggaeton are guilty of violating musical borders, urbano is even more culpable. The boundaries between genres are hard to trace in ur-bano, so porous and jagged they are, like the edges of spilled oil in water. Even when the genre is hard to define (as they say about religion), you know it when you see and hear it however: it contains, at minimum, Jamaican dancehall vibes, the thunderous 808s of trap, stuttering hi-hats, and the kind of viscous and slurred lyricism that sounds as if the syllables are melting in the rappers' mouths.

The popularity of urbano is undeniable: at the time of my writing, 2021, the three most-streamed artists on YouTube worldwide are Ozuna, J Balvin, and Bad Bunny. Picking up where salsa left off, these artists substitute street-tough motifs for the nostalgic and rural imagination of classic Latin music. Bad Bunny and Héctor "El Father," for instance, turned Eddie Palmieri's clas-sic "Vamonos Pa'l Monte" ("Let's Go to the Mountains") into "Vamos Pa'la Calle" ("Let's Go to the Street"). This new rendition is unmistakably barrio-centric, driven by call-and-response catchphrases ("*vamos pa' la calle*"), hol-lers and shouts about barrio life ("*Esto es cosa nuestra de barrio*"), stabbing orchestral strings, crashing cymbals, fluttering hi-hats, screeching car tires, and marching snare drums. The snare drums, in particular, evoke the feel of a parade, march, or rally, their drumrolls guiding the throng of revelers through the streets in a pride march of sorts. The rhyming pattern in the song is heavy with assonance and consonance as Bad Bunny stretches out the vowels, giv-ing them a slightly higher pitch at the end of each bar. The key to the song is these stylistic and vocal manipulations, a rap style that is melodic and martial at the same time, with the rappers both singing and barking out commands like drill sergeants. Even here, though, theological convictions cast a shadow over the song—Bad Bunny tosses in a line about Christ being the helm of his boat, saving it from going under: "*Que en mi barco no se hunde mientras Cristo sea quien lo guíe*" (My ship does not sink as long as Christ is the guide)—and Héctor "El Father," now looking past this song, threw himself into the deep end of Christianity in 2008 or so; after getting religion at the time, and renouncing the gangster persona for which he was famous in reggaeton, he became a Christian pastor.

It should be said, though, that neither this inclusion of religious desires nor the street-centric aesthetics is altogether new in Latin music. Salsa had already paved the way on both of these scores: belligerent, shrill, and contrapuntal horn lines were introduced to signify the cacophony of the streets; snare drums to emulate machine guns; aggressive, attacking rhythms to echo civil rights protests; and lyrics, often in honor of the saints, Jesus, Mary, and the Orishas, to give voice to spiritual and sociopolitical aspirations alike. Ismael Quintana, the co-writer of "Vamonos Pa'l Monte," claimed that the lyrics "were about trying to cope with the injustices of the world. It meant let's get out of this crazy mess and so much negativity that we live in, and let's go to the mountains."[55] The feeling is the same with hip-hop and urbano, only the party has shifted decisively to the streets. The aim remains as playful and celebratory as salsa—a music for dancing in the streets—but these younger artists are also willing, like their ancestors, to take to the streets in the spirit of protest, as when Bad Bunny, Residente (of Calle 13), and half a million Puerto Ricans shut down a major highway to protest government corruption and demand the resignation of the governor, Ricardo Rossello, for his overt sexism and homophobia. The resulting protest song, "Afilando los Cuchillos" (Sharpening the Knives), had 2.5 million views on YouTube within a day of its release.

Bad Bunny is currently leading the way in the urbano trend. He names the salsero Héctor Lavoe, in addition to Daddy Yankee and Vico C, as key influences and, thus, seems to cherish the conscious roots of his family tree. Latin trap, nonetheless, is rarely woke. Like its cousin in the Dirty South, it's more likely to engender joy and relief, sometimes stupor, than vigilance or revolutionary action. The music and oratory—gut-bucket beats, molasseslike flows, echoing vocals, rhyming consonants and vowels—take precedence over lyrical meaning; form masters content. The way in which rappers execute a verse is the key to the style: syllables embossed with a particular accent, stress, tempo, or vocal timbre; the dialect ragged and yet aspiring to the condition of music. Since many fans of reggaeton and Latin trap cannot understand the Spanish lyrics anyhow, the music often does not "mean" anything. It can sound divine even when unintelligible to the listener, a glossolalia of soul. Myka 9, from Freestyle Fellowship, made this point about rap in general: "It's kinda gibberish if you're just writing and putting stuff down that you don't really understand, but even in that sense, gibberish is a style. . . . We call that wild style, where you're just putting random words together because you like the way the syllables and the consonants ring."[56]

Bad Bunny's raps have this gibberish quality, his words discharged in low-slung, slurred, legato, and thick flows, part song, part rap. They seem to come from somewhere deep in his chest, resounding from guttural and sepulchral depths while remaining, ironically, lighthearted and nasal. He has sonorous, operatic vocals that carry through the airwaves like a sonic boom. They are loud and rebellious in the way that carnivals and fiestas throughout Latin America have been rebellious: subverting class and racial apartheids, melting and dissolving identities, and lumping everyone together in one heated mass of humanity. Urbano may not always rely on the dembow rhythm—trap beats often replace the dembow—but it remains heated by the same fiery sun, the music slicing through wintry moods, thawing frozen and gloomy temperaments. Notice Bad Bunny's sartorial extravagance, for one: he wears a wild blend of prints and pastels, as though springtime is breaking out over his wardrobe itself. He clothes himself the way an impressionist uses sunlight and vibrating colors, or the way a surrealist wields shocking images and concepts. To the 2018 American Music Awards, for instance, he rolled up to the red carpet with a third eye on his forehead, a sign, he boasted, of his musical and spiritual clairvoyance. Other times, he wraps himself in Catholic symbols and icons, dangling gold cherubs around his neck, flashing pendants of the Virgin Mary, rocking a Jesus piece.

Raised in Puerto Rico, in a devout Catholic home, Bad Bunny's musical breadth—reggaeton, cumbia, boogaloo, trap, bomba, salsa, et al.—owes a lot to the baroque culture of the island, a heritage that is visually and aurally fecund. Like so many musicians in Latin American and African American heritages, he changes looks quickly when it comes to religion, slipping on church sentiments and then dropping them for bawdy ones, changing his mood hurriedly like a stage performer between acts.[57] He started singing in a church choir as a child, but once the viral energy of salsa, rap, and reggaeton got to him, he succumbed to its charms. He named his first major tour "La Nueva Religión," a fitting name for the eccentric combinations of spirituality, sexuality, dance, and pan-Latin motifs in his music. Since the tour in 2018, the term has endured, and has come to define not only Bad Bunny's passionate fans (devotees of this new religion), but an entire generation of woke millennials who are questioning traditional gender roles, chasing new spiritual experiences, and joining the struggle for equality and justice.[58] Different from white rock groups—I'm thinking of R.E.M.—Bad Bunny hasn't exactly lost his religion as much as he's reformed it, adding a host of dance rhythms, folk motifs, and barrio experiences to orthodox theologies. He'll take you to church in the charged atmosphere of the concert hall, he implies, he'll electrify and thrill you, he'll get you to lose yourself in the ocean of sound and people.

Which brings me to the album *Oasis* (2019): Bad Bunny describes it as "a rescue, a relief. An oasis helps you supply yourself with what you're missing and to find what you lack spiritually; this is what the album represents."[59] I'm not convinced that the album delivers everything that he promises, but I agree that it offers spiritual relief. If not revelatory music, it's surely exhilarating. It stays on the frothy surfaces of the music, surfing on the waves, gliding on the shallows, sticking to the shores.

"Yo Le Llego" is a nice illustration of urbano's composite sound. (Most of the production on the album is by Sky and Marco "Tainy" Masís.) The song proclaims the arrival of Latin@s in the contemporary landscape, declaring their presence with dazzling colors, stentorian phrases, and rich Afro-Latin percussion. If Run-DMC's "Walk This Way" once fused metal guitars and rock choruses with hard beats and raps, urbano is doing something similar with Latin percussion and US Southern rap, cutting and splicing them together to represent the entire hemisphere of the Americas, north and south of the border. The percussive polyrhythms in the song—an elegant acoustic bass, pulsing timbales, snapping synthetic claps, salsa rhythms, steady hi-hats, and chunky trap beats—root the song in earthy sonorities, while Bad Bunny and J Balvin provide melodic polish with their wafting, singing vocals. The song is a *grito* of independence, a war of independence for Latin@s. We're here, they sound off, we cannot be ignored. "La Canción" is also very fine, a romantic ballad that employs the dembow riddim in an unusually cool and serene tempo. The tender piano vamp, plaintive horns, and unhurried reggaeton rhythm in the song match the wistful and nostalgic theme of the lyrics, a portrait of love lost. "Un Peso," finally, continues in this same vein of love's regrets and disappointments, with a ukulele and acoustic guitar wringing sensitive emotions out of the hard material of reggaeton. The soft underbelly of urbano is bared to the world as Bad Bunny speaks of his former partner with a loving and sentimental intensity that smacks of religious worship.

Once anathema, revelations of this sort are now tolerated, even encouraged, in contemporary hip-hop, as I suggested in chapter 2. (The delicate and emotional lyricism of Colombian vallenato played a role in this evolution, too, the folk music lending a more romantic and velvety touch to reggaeton—

apparent in Nicky Jam, Maluma, or J Balvin's music, for example.) It's a welcome trend, especially since it has generated more nuanced and thoughtful attitudes toward women. If not as angst-ridden as "emo rappers"—a Kid Cudi, Lil Uzi Vert, Lil Peep, Lil Xan, Yung Lean, XXXTentacion, Juice WRLD—the younger minds of urbano are certainly more exploratory with their feelings, more self-aware. On Bad Bunny's "Solo de Mi," for instance, he allows a woman to mouth the words "Don't call me baby again. I'm not yours or anyone else's. I only belong to me." After the song's release, he took to social media to reinforce the song's concern for women's rights, and to assail the persistence of domestic violence in our time. His latest work, *Yo Hago Lo Que Me Da La Gana* (2020), continues in this vein, but now with a stronger stance taken on behalf of the LGBTQ community. (The record is also the highest-charting Spanish-language album in the United States.) He also puts on drag for the music video of "Yo Perreo Sola" (I Twerk Alone), dressing in women's clothes as a way of expressing solidarity with marginalized identities. An anthem more than a song, it deliberately throws a gigantic wrench into the normal, often sexist, business of hip-hop, the equivalent in hip-hop of Luther's ninety-five theses on the church door. In the background of the video, in fact, there's a neon sign that announces his stance: it reads "Ni Una Menos" (Not One Woman Less), a rallying cry used throughout Latin America to protest gender-based violence. Bad Bunny has joined his voice to the struggle.

Indeed, ever since Hurricane Irma and Hurricane Maria in 2017—when over 300,000 homes were destroyed, and many left homeless—Bad Bunny seems to have grown more and more conscious, turning political, engaging in protests, and using his platform to express his commitment to the poor and marginalized in Puerto Rico and beyond. "It's no coincidence," writes Suzy Exposito for *Rolling Stone*, "that Bad Bunny's Latin-pop revolution has dovetailed with a time of upheaval across Latin America—where women rally against rampant femicide; where LGBTQ people combat hate by upping their visibility in pop culture and the streets; and where people of all stripes challenge emboldened, authoritarian politicians and their cronies. As Latinos, Latinas, and those in between fight for a much freer society, Bad Bunny is writing songs to light their path."[60]

One gets the impression that Bad Bunny, flaws and all, is willing to learn and change. He is comfortable with a broad range of roles in hip-hop, far beyond the conventional tropes of cocky masculinity and gangster ruthlessness.[61] And, more significantly, he and others in his generation are now making room for women's voices, which is causing a drastic reshuffling of the mental furniture of earlier eras of hip-hop. There's a host of promising female voices now emerging out of the underground, inspired by figures as diverse as Celia Cruz, Selena, and Frida Kahlo: Tomasa del Real, the Chilean rapper and reggaetonera, working under the tag "neoperreo"; Mare Advertencia Lirika, the Zapoteca rapper, for whom rap is a voice of Indigenous rights, gender equality, and social justice; the half Puerto Rican, half African American Nitty Scott, rapping about mental health, sexual abuse, and women's empowerment; the Brasileña Zuzuka Poderosa, addressing the history of race and colonialism; Bia, the Puerto Rican rapper who claims Ivy Queen, Selena, and Jay-Z as role models in hip-hop; Nani Castle, "the Frida Kahlo and Zach del la Rocha of the rap game," addressing overlooked themes in hip-hop, backed by collages of Latin music, rock, soul, and hip-hop; the Mexican American Snow Tha Product, claiming Lauryn Hill, Celia Cruz, El General, and Big Pun as her inspirations, and using her voice to illuminate the history of discrimination experienced by Mexicans in the United States; the Dominican American rapper Maluca Mala, who shuns any one name for her music, calling it Latin-dance, ghetto-techno, hip-hop, and rave all at once; or, finally, the singer/rapper/novelist Rita Indiana, dubbed *La Monstra*, who combines electro-merengue, rap, metal, and reggaeton, while addressing a variety of social issues, especially concerning themes of immigration, gender, and queerness. The list goes on and on, and it seems to me that it won't stop, can't stop.

The times are changing, in sum, and hip-hop and reggaeton are changing their tune accordingly, finding the right note to represent the "blab of the pave," the right lyric to speak for the plight of women, the right fury to characterize the voices of the incarcerated and undocumented. Pop music is becoming more sensitive to the power of words to injure or heal, degrade or elevate. And it is learning that the concept of "liberation"—as in the Christian tradition—means not only freedom *from* all the systems and attitudes that oppress and degrade a race or culture or gender; it also means freedom *for* others, a willingness to use one's voice in the spirit of solidarity, justice, and compassion, a willingness, as Dr. King put it, to remain awake and alert and, when necessary, to take to the streets.[62]

CHAPTER 6
Native Tongues

What is a DJ if he can't scratch to a ranchera?
Ozomatli, "La Misma Canción"

Angelica Garcia, the singer-songwriter of Mexican/Salvadoran descent, born and raised in El Monte, California ("the Greater Eastside"), complains in her song "Jícama" that Latin@s are rarely seen in their fullness in the United States, the images usually monochromatic and two-dimensional, not fully developed: "I see you but you don't see me, nah/ Jícama! Jícama! Guava tree/ Dichotomous-Guadalupe-Angeleno breed, ya/ Jícama! Jícama! Guava tree," she sings, driving her point home in a constrained but bellowing soprano, a voice that pleads, urges, and bemoans all at once. An exuberant synth melody, handclap beats, brass splashes, and bold Mexican horns complement the lyrical message, an account of living in the United States with a split identity and being invisible as a result, a shadow that's only seen in its shady and sinister guises, if at all. Mexican Americans are ghosts in California, Octavio Paz once noted in the 1950s, neither quite existing, nor quite vanishing, and Garcia, now seventy years later, bewails the same point as if little has changed.[1]

As we've seen throughout this study, hip-hop emerged in the 1970s as a reaction to such a predicament; it was a bright splash of sound and color in a drab environment, representing a desire to be seen and heard, a wish to leave one's mark on a society that treats you as if you're invisible, beneath notice. Garcia announces herself on "Jícama" in this way, her music a bright mural of multicolored, pied beauty, of all things "counter, original, spare, strange."[2] Whether in her sound—a constellation of 1990s indie, reggaeton, dancehall, and traditional Mexican ranchera music (her mother was a mariachi singer)—or in her person—she's part-Salvadoran, part-Mexican, part-American, all Angeleno—Garcia is perfectly emblematic of "Nuevo LA," a region where the lines of identity are constantly being erased and redrawn. An avatar of this brave new world, she brings us face to face with the changing landscape of California and the nation, forcing us to notice things that are right in front of our eyes.

Angelica Garcia's "dichotomous-Guadalupe-Angeleno breed" is now the majority in Califas, and you wouldn't necessarily know this by listening to mainstream hip-hop. Compton, for instance, a city mythic in hip-hop, is now 65 percent Latin@ and 32 percent African American. To be straight outta Compton in 2021 is to be, more than likely, Latin@. If it's a common cry of all disenfranchised groups ("to be poor," as Simone Weil once said, "is to be invisible"), Garcia's musical theme—"I see you but you don't see me"—does what all good art does: it transforms an ordinary insight into something inspired and wise, adding depth and complexity to representations that are hastily drawn, as if with a pencil for a cartoon.

Garcia's complaint, then, hits home with regard to hip-hop as well. If Tupac once acknowledged the presence of Mexicans on the West Coast—"It wouldn't be LA without Mexicans," he memorably rapped on "To Live and Die in LA"—mainstream rap has been silent on the topic lately, seeing the world only in black and white, missing the nuances and tinges of color, ignoring the shades of brown.[3] How can one accurately rep Compton when these hues remain invisible to the eye, inaudible to the ear? The time is coming when a deejay, emcee, or producer will have to notice the likes of Angelica Garcia, when they will have to learn how to scratch or rap to a ranchera. Music is always pushing ahead in such ways, straining to break free of existing conventions, improvising to change with times, heralding the new and surprising. And all of this will entail a greater familiarity with the great polyphony of sound throughout the Americas, beyond the borders of the United States. For those deaf to it, as Josh Kun warns, fate will not be kind. "The DJ who's been schooled on funk break beat or jazz bridges or Roland 808 kick patterns, who can scratch to the Watts funk of Charles Wright or the South Central electro of World Class Wreckin Crew but who can't scratch to the accordions and rural romance of a Mexican ranchera is a DJ who will become obsolete."[4]

I'd like to consider here this greater polyphony of sound in hip-hop, then, beginning with some of the pioneering figures in Latin hip-hop, and then turning to other brown voices of the new millennium.

East Coast Origins

The story of hip-hop's origins has been told many times before, but one fundamental fact continues to bear repeating: Latin@s were always partners and allies in the culture of hip-hop.[5] Almost fifty years into the game, this fact is still overlooked, if not easily forgotten. Truth is that Latin@s, particularly Puerto Ricans and Cubans, shared similar spaces, similar dance and music crazes, similar street arts, and similar feelings of alienation and exclusion in the South Bronx of the 1960s and 1970s. Hip-hop was one of the products of these bonds, a culture that was spliced and grafted together in the South Bronx out of various seedlings of sound and style.

Besides the crucial contributions of Latin@s in the history of b-boying (say, Salsoul, Crazy Commandos, and the Rock Steady Crew), graffiti writing (say, Lady Pink, an Ecuadorian New Yorker; Lee Quiñones, Puerto Rican; and Basquiat, Puerto Rican and Haitian), or deejaying (DJ Charlie Chase of the Cold Crush Brothers or DJ Disco Wiz), for instance, the heavy bass and percussion rhythms in funk and hip-hop owe a lot to the history of Afro-Latin music. For one, the use of "breaks"—the rupture in the pattern of the song highlighting the clave beat and bass line—was a common feature of mambo and salsa music. As early as the 1930s, Cuban dancers referred to an extended percussion break as a mambo, and it was this portion of the song that seemed to light the dance floor on fire. Hip-hop deejays would quickly learn the power of this secret, exploiting and extending the breaks in order to move and rock the crowd and, eventually, in order to give the deejay space to shout out his or her phrases, slogans, and rhymes without interference from the other instruments.[6]

Even salsa music, as distant as it might seem to hip-hop, was born in the same barrios and the same decade as hip-hop, as I suggested earlier, and it reflected the circumstances of these times and places, taking on the color of its surroundings in the so-called Caldera del Diablo ("the devil's cauldron" of the South Bronx and Spanish Harlem). Aptly named, the South Bronx had indeed turned into something of a cauldron in the 1970s: smoldering buildings, raging turf wars, scorched physical surroundings, dying embers of opportunity, a wasteland in the eyes of many. It may be a "living hell," rapped Grandmaster Caz of the Cold Crush Brothers on "South Bronx Subway Rap," but "look past the garbage over the trains/ under the ruins through the remains/ around the crime and pollution" and you'll discover, buried under the ruins, signs of hope.[7] Instead of seeing the world as it was, like a realist, Grandmaster Caz dared to dream and imagine a different world than the one he inherited, more like a visionary. Where others saw death, Grandmaster Caz saw glimmers of life:

the drab subway cars turned into moving murals of color and wild-style lettering, the old turntables converted into musical instruments, forgotten song
fragments cut and remixed, the geometric patterns of b-boys creating mathematical order out of chaos, broken concrete turned into projectiles to hurl
at the powers that be.

And salsa arose out of similar circumstances. It had much of the same vitality and flamboyance as hip-hop culture, the kind of tenacity that enabled
it to flourish in the mean conditions of the South Bronx and Spanish Harlem.
A melting pot of various Latin ingredients—the Cuban son, above all—salsa
was a "music full of street odors, raspy trombones that sounded like car horns,
barrio stories of aggressive rebel youths," writes Leonardo Padura Fuentes.[8]
The vocals were rough and unpolished, the trombones or trumpets raw and
dissonant, the repetitive vamps bitter and violent, the stomping rhythm section compulsively kinetic and dance-driven, and the tales, revolving around
rebels of the barrio, distinctly street-tough and confrontational. It was urban
folklore, said Ruben Blades, an art made for the asphalt.[9] It was a music of the
city, chimed in South Bronx native Willie Colón, a collection of street stories
about guerilla fighters, outlaws, rogues, and runaway slaves.[10] Even the figure
of Jesus in salsa—say, in "El todopoderoso" and "Rompe saraguey" by Willie
Colón and Héctor Lavoe, or "El nazareno" by Ismael Rivera—took on barrio
nuances, his appearance resembling the black Christ of Panama, "Cristo Negro," a God who took the "form of a slave" (Philippians 2:7). Though almost
always festive and dance-centric, and never synonymous with politics, salsa
music was, in short, the Latin sound of civil disobedience, which is how Willie
Colón sized it up: "The music, although it wasn't explicitly social or political,
had a connotation almost of civil disobedience."[11]

Eventually, though, much of this original spirit was lost in the commodification of salsa, turning a spicy aesthetics, with a serious kick, into a ketchup-
like product that was bottled to be sold, full of sugary and frivolous Latin
stereotypes. (Similar things, of course, have been said about hip-hop.) Whatever the case, early hip-hop and salsa had strong family resemblances, the
two of them dancing to the same percussion-driven rhythms, speaking the
same street vocabularies, collecting and fusing similar aural fragments, and
always insisting on the primacy of the barrio in the culture. In dance, music,
or graffiti, they captured the restless energy and constant motion of black and
brown youth aching to be seen, aching to be free.

By the 1990s, several rappers on the East Coast would begin to add more
and more layers to these black and brown collaborations. The Afro-Panama-
nian El General, the Boriqua Vico C, and La Reina of reggaeton, Ivy Queen,
brought their own distinctive backgrounds, styles, and cadences to the booming dancehall and rap en español scenes in New York, helping to give birth to

a distinctive Latin custom of hip-hop. And though generally sticking to the English language, the two Bronx-born Puerto Rican emcees, Big Pun and Fat Joe, would also join their voices to this stream of sound and culture. Both rappers made a large splash in the genre, adding Latin flavors and experiences to the mix, and peppering their lyrics with Spanish words and phrases—not unlike the way Basquiat splashed Spanish on his walls and canvases. They were both big in stature and big in lung capacity, but Big Pun was the better rhyme-spitter; his flows spilled off his tongue in torrents of alliteration and assonance, rarely pausing to take a breath or gulp, as if he didn't require as much oxygen as other humans. Orotund and extravagant with his rhetoric, he orchestrated words as much for the sheer pleasure of the sound and jingle of the syllables as for their thematic content. Whether delivering rapid-fire, tongue-twisting bars, or more relaxed, teasing ones, his flow was always smooth and effortless, never straining or tripping as he ran through the song.

And by way of message, he styled himself a "street professor" and "ghetto scholar," his knowledge and grammar learned on the tough blocks of the South Bronx's Soundview Projects (a neighborhood that was ravaged by the crack epidemic in the 1980s and 1990s, seeing some of the highest murder rates in the city). He rapped about the curses and dangers that haunted these streets, a state of affairs that compelled him to "hold my rosary as tight as I can" ("Twinz"). Punitive and callous, the streets that he knew swallowed the weak whole, which is why Big Pun and his rap influences—Big Daddy Kane, Biggie, Fat Joe, N.O.R.E., Nas, Wu-Tang, and Mobb Deep—would almost always project images of strength and oversized badness, playing the predator, not the prey. Weakness might leave you for dead, and so they invented images that were as big as the image of Godzilla on drive-in movie screens. Willie Colón had done the same thing, posing as a gangster for numerous album covers—El Malo (1967), Cosa Nuestra (1969), La Gran Fuga (1971), Lo Mato (1973), et al.—and dreaming of a time when Latin@s, powerless and subordinate as they were, would have more clout, more weight, more equality. In this sense, Big Pun gazed backward and forward at once, looking to his Boriqua ancestors in salsa or bomba while paving the way for a new generation of Afro-Latin@ rappers, and presaging a time when they would become more and more visible: "'Cause everybody's checkin' for Pun, second to none/ 'Cause Latins goin' platinum was destined to come" ("You Came Up").

West Coast Origins: Pachucos, Low-Riders, and the Eastside Sound

If salsa music, reggae, and other tropical Afro-Caribbean sounds were thick in the air in the New York of the twentieth century, the West Coast had its own musical climate. Mexican folk traditions, classic corridos, Chicano rock 'n' roll, jump blues and jazz, pachuco street culture, and LA's own salsa style (faster tempos, more theatrical choreographies) gave the region its own distinct weather pattern, its atmosphere heavily influenced by rhythms from south of the border.[12]

As early as the late 1940s, several Mexican American musicians had pioneered a syncretistic aesthetic on the West Coast, part Mexican folk, part Afro-Caribbean, part rhythm and blues, part barrio. Two figures stand out, beginning with the Don Tosti Band, from East LA, and his hit "Pachuco Boogie" (1948), and the work of Lalo Guerrero, born in Tucson, with "La Pachuquilla," "Los Dos Carnales," "Los Chucos Suaves," "Marihuana Boogie," and "Vamos a Bailar."[13] Differences aside, these songs all reveled in one of the most reviled groups in Los Angeles, the pachucos. Identified by their loud and garish clothing, and their brash slang known as caló, the pachucos became objects of abuse in the notorious Zoot Suit Riots of 1943, an event that began with violence against pachucos in LA and later snowballed into widespread anti-Mexican violence in other US cities.[14] Seeing the zoot suit—tacuche or "drapes"—as the garb of delinquent hoodlums, sailors and vigilantes took it upon themselves to punish, humiliate, and assault those draped in the style, purging the streets, as they saw it, of anti-American attitudes and postures. And the police, if they didn't look the other way, sometimes joined in the fray, carrying out campaigns to profile, abuse, and imprison Mexican Angelenos.[15] Speaking for the War Production Board, Frank Walton summed up the attitude: the zoot suit was, simply put, unpatriotic.[16] But for African Americans and Mexican Americans, the zoot suiter, with his exaggerated and overstated style, had the dignity of a peacock, strutting and carrying himself as if he not only had a train behind him but a retinue to attend to it, as Flannery O'Connor once described the bird.[17] In its billowing pants, its killer-diller coat, reet pleats, dangling keychain, padded shoulders, wide-brimmed hat, pinstripes, and conspicuous colors, the zoot suit represented a pageantry of attire, its excess and extravagance flying in the face of white America's plain and austere aesthetics. It was as superfluous to mid-twentieth-century America as baroque architecture—marble folds, spinning angels, colorful icons, excessive altars and vaults, twisting columns, gilded facades, flying creatures, anguished saints, suffering Christs—was to Puritan tastes.

Keep in mind that as early as the Reformation, and certainly by the time of the American and French revolutions, fashion had shifted away from the ornate and ostentatious toward bourgeois inconspicuousness. "As they gained economic power," writes Kathy Peiss, "a bourgeois merchant and manufacturing class set new norms of proper appearance . . . thus inconspicuousness became the hallmark of the well-dressed man."[18] Faithful to the radical wing of the Reformation—where iconoclasts sought to undress Christianity of visual splendor, aesthetic grandeur, and material excess—the bourgeois revolutions of the Western world stressed minimalism and austerity as the appropriate garb for the Protestant work ethic and spirit of capitalism.[19] Instead of retreating from Protestant criticisms of Catholic extravagance, however, the baroque went the other way; it doubled down on its love of aesthetics and celebrated the arts of painting, sculpture, drama, music, rhetoric, and fashion with unparalleled intensity. And the same can be said about the baroque in the New World: in Havana, for instance, the *negros curros* of Seville—a class of free blacks and mulattos—were famous for their flamboyant clothing and dialect, a vogue that was derived from the underworld of Seville. Once transplanted to Havana in the sixteenth century, they established the first black street fashion in the Indies.[20] They used their walk (a swinging and rocking swagger), their talk (peppered with slang, vocal inflections, and private codes), their dress and jewelry (thick gold earrings, jackets with tails, straw hats with silk tassels, finely embroidered shirts), and their extraordinary dances, parades, drums, and theater (let loose on the streets of Havana during Día de los Reyes and other Catholic festivals) as forms of lively, animated resistance to the widespread indignities and abuses of daily life.[21] Dress, style, music, and festivity became forms of nonverbal dissent, a way to contravene or flout racial and class subservience by turning an oppressive social world on its head.

African Americans, now skipping to the 1940s or so, would fashion the zoot suit for similar purposes. If not necessarily political, the zoot suit's style, dress, and gesture symbolized the kind of defiance—or deviance—that became associated with the cool, a countercultural chic that challenged bourgeois norms behind a mask of stoic detachment, aloofness, and inner confidence. The suit and attitude quickly spread not only to Mexican Americans, but to young Japanese Americans, Filipinos, Jews, Italians and, in fact, to enthusiasts throughout the world, appealing to youth who longed for an alternative to mainstreams customs, who invited excess into a repressive and square world. The French *zazous* wore elements of the suit in defiance of the German Occupation; black South African youth known as *tsotsis* embraced it as the secret code of the streets; Russian youth known as *stiliagi* welcomed it as a striking counterstatement to the sartorial dullness of the Soviet Union; the Hungarian *jampec* and Polish *bikiniarze*, and I suspect many other disenfranchised youth, threw it on like a costume that would finally render them visible.[22]

Stealing their colorful slang and barrio idioms, and adopting their oppositional and defiant postures, at any rate, the Don Tosti Band and Lalo Guerrero turned Mexican American feelings of exclusion and estrangement into a code of coolness, their music into a tribute to barrio culture. "Pachuco Boogie" features a twelve-bar-blues chord progression with boogie-woogie piano by Eddie Cano, a brush shuffle beat on the drum set, tenor sax, scat vocals and, most famously, Don Tosti's spoken dialogue in pachuco extolling the merit of looking and dressing sharp.[23] The song's flamboyant Spanish-caló lyricism—a mellifluous singsong lilt—is the highlight of the song, burrowing into the listener's memory to stay long after the song ends. (Castilian Spanish, by contrast, is usually clipped and precise.) Lalo Guerrero's "Los Chucos Suaves" (smooth/cool pachucos) is even more energizing and irresistible, a shot of adrenaline to the body with its habanera bass line, cowbell clave rhythm, piano montunos, rippling trumpet, maracas, and the singer's exhortations to dance the rumba, guaracha, and danzón. As in "Pachuco Boogie," Lalo Guerrero sprinkles pachuco slang throughout the song, swinging between sung Spanish verses, exclamatory *gritos*, and a spoken-word delivery when he switches to caló, the speech and accent of the streets. Combining archaic words with a roughshod, lawless, and urban diction, caló functioned as a secret, cryptic code, a language by which Mexican American youth expressed their bonds with one another. If these barrio idioms turned inward, communicating in private languages, the music itself—a mixture of Mexican corridos, Afro-Caribbean rhythms, jump blues, and jazz—turned outward, absorbing African American culture and music until it became part of its own tongue. For Don Tosti and Lalo Guerrero, the result was a buzzing, vibrant polyphonic sound and style, a constellation of fragments that spoke to the divided, *mestizo* identity of Mexican Americans, and that envisioned a more inclusive and heterogeneous America.

The Eastside Sound, or the Eastside Renaissance, came to embody this spirit in the 1960s. Swept up by a maelstrom that spun and tangled various sounds together, artists of the period were increasingly attracted by the forbidden lure of miscegenation, whether in music or in daily life. "Masters of musical blending, mixing, and retooling, these innovative young people braided together R&B, soul, traditional Mexican music, doo-wop, country-western, Afro-Caribbean and Tex-Mex. . . . The Eastside sound was defined not so much by particular instruments or styles as by an approach, a lively negotiation with multiple cultures, and a knack for connecting disparate musical traditions."[24] What others considered incongruent, dispensable, and obsolete, the Eastside Sound cherished like lost treasures, stitching together what seemed incompatible, salvaging what seemed old and dated.[25]

Even the low-rider in black and Latin@ cultures of Los Angeles in the 1960s and 1970s illustrated this spirit: it was not only a restored and salvaged car (frequently vintage); it was a piece of art, valued for ornament over anything more practical. True, it shared the dream of mobility and freedom with the classic American car, giving its occupants the delicious and, in some cases, forbidden taste of freedom. For communities that were boxed in their neighborhoods, in particular, the car became a means of liberation, allowing a person to transgress the fixed boundaries of the barrio or ghetto, granting the driver a provisional freedom. With this said, low-riders, like the ostentatious zoot suit, were non-utilitarian in the extreme, more mobile murals than simple rides. Instead of driving fast, loud, and elevated like a hot rod, they moved at a snail's pace, slow and low to the ground (*bajito y suavecito*), a bearing that was contrarian and cool, running against the demand for speed, efficiency, and functionality in consumer-driven, capitalist culture.[26] Embossed with glossy images of Guadalupe, pachuc@s, or Chicano folklore, and accessorized with hydraulics that made the car bounce, dip, and dance, everything about the cars was hopelessly impractical, a garish display of ethnic pride, a carnivalesque capsizing of American social and cultural tastes. Just as words were more than sounds to graffiti writers—they had color and flesh and contour and movement and attitude—cars were more than cars, coming alive when splashed with flecks of paint, interior chandeliers, chain steering wheels, chrome trimmings, plush upholstery, polished rims, pimped-out interiors, twin mufflers, baroque rosaries draped over the rearview mirror, and chrome exhaust pipes that blew out smoke like Melville's Moby Dick, "spouting his frothed defiance to the skies." Whether they documented Mexican American existence, or simply imagined a brighter and more brilliant existence, the cars became cultural icons to Chicano barrio youth in Los Angeles and elsewhere. And many bands—Tierra, War, Thee Midniters, and El Chicano, to name a few—would make music that mirrored the swagger of such cars, gleaming and growling with cultural pride. In the case of Thee Midniters' "Whittier Boulevard" (1965), Bardo Martinez, lead singer of Chicano Batman, summed up the song in this manner: "The key to the song's aesthetic is the bass—a heavy thump you can hear half a block away. You show off how loud your car bumps. You're just bumping it, saying, 'Look at me. We own this street. This street is us.' And this is, sometimes, all that we've got."[27]

As for the band El Chicano, the group's name speaks loudly of the age, a time of civil rights marches, cultural nationalism, and struggles for racial equality. Originally a derogatory word for Mexican American underclasses, "Chicano" was flipped into a badge of pride by young activists (like the Brown Berets and MEChA), transforming something inelegant and demeaning into a dignified expression. One of their most famous songs, "Viva Tirado," is particularly important for the history of Chicano rap. The song has a fascinating genealogy: it was written by Gerald Wilson, an African American jazz trumpeter and composer, in honor of a Tijuana bullfighter by the name of Tirado.

(Wilson was also married to a Mexican American woman, Josefina Villaseñor, for more than fifty years.) The song, like the bullfighter himself, seems to have constantly shifted, bended, and changed hands in order to avoid a violent death, going on to live many lives at the hands of El Chicano, the 5th Dimension, the Fania All Stars, Augustus Pablo, Tim Weisberg, Nico Gomez, Los Mozambiques and, of course, as we'll see, Kid Frost. Through it all, it became a soundtrack for black and brown alliances. Oliver Wang says it nicely: "'Viva Tirado' is at the center of a rather remarkable, multi-generational conversation between LA's Black and Brown communities. After all, here's a song, originally written by a Black composer in honor of a Mexican bullfighter, covered by a Chicano band steeped in Black R&B and jazz, then sampled by the first major Chicano rap artist. It seems no matter where the song goes, it's always a bridge between cultures."[28]

If Wilson's original version didn't immediately conjure up these mixed legacies, El Chicano's sample left little doubt. It featured electric guitar and organ—a growing hallmark of Mexican American music—a Cuban-styled bass line, conga drums, and bossa nova clave on the snare rim.[29] Anticipating the skills of hip-hop later, El Chicano cut, revised, and reworked the original, adding stronger Latin accents and a trendy cool vibe to approximate the tempo and pace of a low-rider cruising down Whittier Boulevard. Less feverish than some of the gut-bucket grooves of Johnny Otis, or the honking tenor saxophone of Cecil "Big Jay" McNeely (both of whom played at Angelus Hall in Boyle Heights, and were very popular among Mexican Americans), the song complemented the mellow, lounging, and laid-back spirit of a driver in a low-rider, slumped down in the front seat of a '57 Chevy. It fit the West Coast like a glove.[30]

But there's a less obvious reason why "Viva Tirado" is important for my consideration of hip-hop: in Spanish, the term "tirado" refers to a person, place, or thing that is tossed or thrown aside, a castaway, outsider, misfit, or displaced person. In Tucson, there's an old street shrine in the heart of the old barrio (where my father's family once lived before being forced to move for the building of the Tucson Community Center), "El Tiradito," the only Catholic shrine in the United States dedicated to a sinner buried in unconsecrated ground. Dating to 1871 or so, the shrine pays homage to a young man caught in an adulterous love affair and refused burial on church grounds, his soul forced to wander in the afterworld. Votive candles, ex-votos, prayers, and petitions dot the shrine, offering prayers not only for the young man, but for all lost and outcast souls. The sanctuary is, in short, dedicated to all outsiders, wayfarers, and pariahs, souls that are beyond the pale of the church, tossed into the streets.

Figure 5   Photo of author at "El Tiradito" shrine in Tucson, Arizona

Accordingly, the shrine is reminiscent of many legends in Catholic history, none more obvious than the lore of St. Jude, the patron saint of lost causes, last resorts, desperate cases. Among the poor in Mexico, San Judas is one of the most popular saints, second only to Our Lady of Guadalupe. For lost, desperate, and wayward souls, those whom the church might overlook or casually toss aside, San Judas is seen as a refuge and advocate, a saint who rescues the rejected and abandoned, who redeems discarded and secondhand lives, saving them the way a deejay saves recycled beats and rhythms.

Seen in this theological light, the history of the song "Viva Tirado" and the shrine "El Tiradito" are tributes to the experiences and lives that hip-hop would eventually privilege, the ones forsaken by the gatekeepers of Christendom, "the lowly and despised of the world, those who count for nothing" (1 Corinthians 1:28).

West Coast Chicano Rap

Built on the soundscape of "Viva Tirado," Kid Frost's "La Raza" (1990) is the next step in the song's history, a more hard-core and barrio-centric version than anything hitherto. It opens with a funky drum sample from Graham Central Station's "The Jam" before El Chicano's "Viva Tirado" kicks in. Once Kid Frost starts emceeing, though, we're immediately dragged into the world of hip-hop, the rapper now syncopating his bars with the beat, boasting about his toughness and valor, and extolling the glory of Chicano culture. For a song named "La Raza"—a term that refers, says Ilan Stavans, to the masses in Mexican street Spanish—the latter is a key theme in the song, of course.[31] "I'm tired of dudes gettin' over on la raza," he vents in the intro. If different in tenor and timbre from El Chicano or Angelica Garcia (more aggressive, intimidating, gruff), Kid Frost's rap, appearing twenty years after El Chicano and twenty years before Garcia, shares roots with both of them.

Consistent with the gangster rap of the late 1980s, however, Kid Frost's music was locked and loaded with martial and macho ammunition, his narratives framing the pachuco, cholo, and vato as heroic rebels of popular resistance, *bandidos* in the mold of Gregorio Cortez or Juan Cortina. In a way, Kid Frost was reprising the classic corrido—a narrative poem and song that thrived along the US-Mexico border 1836-1930s—for the hip-hop generation, channeling its combative and fugitive protagonists, a cast of characters who, as the ballad of Gregorio Cortez notes, defended life and liberty with pistols in their hands.[32] The corrido, says Américo Paredes, was a serious genre, telling of rebels and rogues who lived by the motto "I will break before I bend," and who sang with "deadly serious faces, throwing out the words of the song like a challenge, tearing savagely with the stiff, callused hands at the strings of the guitar."[33]

Kid Frost neither sings nor plays the guitar, but "La Raza" and other raps are surely slung out "like a challenge," his words slow and sinuous but biting and poisonous at the same time. His style of rapping, casual and cool with his chest puffed out like the big bad wolf, matches the demeanor of the unflappable cholo, a cousin of sorts to the pachuco but without the latter's formal and tailored chic. In consequence, Kid Frost rarely gets excited, rapping in a low-key manner and swerving between English and Spanish-caló lyrics. Even his movements in the video are slow and easy, as if he's too cool to dance. His eyes, glaring and surly, tell this same story in the music video for "La Raza"; when not shielded by dark sunglasses, his gaze is stern, beady, and hooded, a look as mean and intense as the desert sun. Since he's never introspective or meditative on the album (such things were generally forbidden in gangster rap), his character is as elemental as a force of nature, driven by pure instinct, tribal loyalty, and animal passion, like a warrior out of Homer or Mesoamerica. For all these shortcomings—the hyper-masculinity, belligerence, lack of inwardness—when Kid Frost plays the part of Chicano bard or griot in the song, the rapper finds his voice and purpose; he gives us something more nutritious to chew on.

Even more than the verses, the images in the music video make this clear: colorful Aztec calendars with Indigenous pictographs (jaguars and the plumed serpent Quetzalcoatl, for instance); murals of skeleton figures, recalling the art of José Guadalupe Posada; a fresco of Che Guevara, as well as young men donning brown berets; graffiti-like icons of Guadalupe, reflecting the Catholic identity of the barrio; calligraphy in *placas*, throw-ups, tags, and murals; positive messages—"Be Proud of Your Roots"—spray-painted on public spaces; and, finally, derelict street landscapes, all of these things paint a vibrant picture of the barrio, the postindustrial setting in which migrants and the urban poor must fight for their livelihood.

The strongest current of the song and video, touched upon in the video frames, is Kid Frost's identification with Indigenous identity, a central theme in Chicano folklore. Countering middle-class tendencies to claim Spanish or European roots, or to disappear into the melting pot of North American culture, the Chicano movement went the other way, stressing Native American ancestries, claiming the bloodline of Aztecs and Mayas, identifying with the underclasses. It honored the victims of American history, looking with suspicion at attempts to "pass" as one of the victors. Kid Frost's embrace of the term "cholo" is suggestive: like the term "Chicano," it has disreputable origins, originating as an Aztec word for servant, and then later picking up connotations of a street cat, rebel, or hustler. Instead of the slick and colorful clothing of pachucos, however, the cholo embraced simpler styles: high-waist khaki pants ("chinos"), ribbed-cotton muscle shirts, military web belts, black leather shoes or black canvas slip-ons, flannel shirts buttoned up to the throat, black sunglasses, and tattoos with Old English lettering.[34] If more rugged and minimal than the zoot suit—with sartorial indications of the working classes and prisoners—the cholo turns the condition of a servant, and later barrio dweller, into a source of pride.

For all the Native motifs running through Kid Frost's street figure, we might see his music in light of David Alfaro Siqueiros's famous mural on Olvera Street in Los Angeles, *América Tropical* (1932). Subtitled "Oppressed and Destroyed by Imperialism," the mural placed a crucified Indian in the center, dead on a cross, with Mayan pyramids and pre-Columbian sculptures in the background, all in a state of wreckage and ruin. The tortured position of the man's gaunt head and neck really stands out, running almost horizontal to the cross-bars, lolling to the side as if it had been fractured like the neck of a bird, or else, to borrow an image from the *Iliad*, like a poppy under the weight of the spring rain.[35] The iconography hits you between the eyes with a cudgel, evoking shame for centuries of abuse and oppression. Gazing at the image,

I can't help but recall the famous line of Las Casas: "I leave, in the Indies, Jesus Christ, our God, scourged and afflicted, buffeted and crucified not once but millions of times."[36] Till the day he died, Las Casas would earn unrelenting scorn for seeing Christ in the racked bodies and lives of Native peoples, his theological vision unnerving to the powers that be. And Siqueiros's mural did something similar, provoking the ire of the political and cultured elites in Los Angeles to such an extent that they ordered the mural to be whitewashed. The whitewashing was fitting, in a way, an ironic fulfillment of Siqueiros's prophetic witness. His point was that imperial powers have long sought to erase the lives and cultures of Indigenous peoples, and the act of whitewashing proved him right. Unable to tolerate such glaring exposés of Western sin and aggression, they responded by trying to cover it all up with blinding white paint, like Adam covering up his shame with a fig leaf.[37]

Whether he was conjuring Las Casas, or anticipating Malcolm X and James Baldwin, in any case, many of Siqueiros's murals seethed and sermonized in this manner, howling on behalf of human rights and racial equality, demanding change. And many of these themes would reappear in the music of the 1960s. Decades of pent-up energy were released in the music, surfacing in songs like Thee Midniters' "Chicano Power" (1967), Lalo Guerrero's "El Corrido de César Chávez" (1968), and Little Joe y La Familia's "Las Nubes" (1972), the latter an anthem for the United Farm Workers that begins with a *grito* and then a shout, "Órale raza, here's my brown soul!" I mention these artists, including Siqueiros, not only to point out forerunners to Kid Frost, but to also highlight what Kid Frost is not. Kid Frost belongs to the hip-hop generation and, more specifically, to the N.W.A.-influenced variety of hip-hop in the early 1990s; he is not nearly as politically conscious as the artists above.

I'm tempted to say that he gives us rage without prophecy, but that's not entirely right. There is, in fact, prophecy in Kid Frost, but it tends to be limited to cultural motifs, lacking in the sharp ethical and political edge of Las Casas or Siqueiros. Marcus Reeves's comment, contrasting Public Enemy and N.W.A., is helpful: "If Public Enemy fought white fears and black stereotypes with black pride, N.W.A.'s defense was to embrace the fears and myths, flipping them into a source of strength and power."[38] There are elements of both in Kid Frost, cultural pride and hyped gangster tropes, the former confronting white fears and prejudices with the resources of culture, the latter fighting with blunt and violent instruments, an eye for an eye, a tooth for a tooth. If a moral compass is missing in the latter (especially when it comes to the representation of Chicanas, most of whom dance and flit about in his videos lacking in clothes as much as dignity), his battle cry on behalf of Latin@ culture remains important to this day. Whether in 1990, when Kid Frost released "La Raza," or in 2020, when Trump associated brown lives with violence and criminality, the simple decision to claim one's humanity can have a prophetic, even revolutionary, value.[39] Flaws and all, Kid Frost built on the legacy of the Chicano movement in this way, exercising self-determination, bolstering self-respect, and trying to instill a sense of pride and dignity in Mexican American communities.[40]

"Viva Tirado," at any rate, presents a snapshot of these exchanges, a song that continues to grow and change, its history still unfinished. In 2016, the group Brownout remixed it yet again, the song seemingly surviving decay and oblivion like the bodies of the saints after death. Their version is called "La Raza," too, but now includes a wider variety of Latin voices, with Mellow Man Ace, El Dusty, Mexstep, Niña Dioz, and the Afro-Cuban MC Kool A.D. Arriving twenty-six years after Kid Frost's rap, the song has aged well, sounding more mature and ripe for making it into the new millennium. Though I prefer the music of Kid Frost's version—especially the languorous, dreamy saxophone riff that winds through it—the production and lyricism of Brownout's "La Raza" dragged the original into the year 2016, striking a more progressive, enlightened, and psychedelic vibe. (Adrian Quesada, formerly of Grupo Fantasma, the Austin-based Latin funk orchestra, added honking horn stabs, old-school scratching, a keyboard refrain, and pinches of indie rock in the new version.)

Each of the emcees adds their own distinctive color and texture, but they're all working with the same thread of experience, the same bilingual and bicultural experience of Latin@s in the diaspora. As I hear it, they envision a Latin@ identity that is achieved and adopted as much as found, one that joins together a rich variety of members in one larger body. As part of such a nation, under siege at the moment, they each take their turns shouting out their verses, trying to drown out the loud cries of bigotry unleashed in 2016 by MAGA and Trumpism. As if their message is urgent, water in a burning building, they all return to the fundamental theme of cultural dignity, doing what they can to counteract what Trump and his allies say about immigrants, Muslims, Blacks, and Latin@s and, if the self-hatred has already been internalized, to help such lives vomit it up. Like the original, then, the song is a tribute to Latin@ identity, but it wades into the tumultuous waters of racism, sexism, political injustice, and economic inequality in ways that Kid Frost generally avoided.

Out of this interesting collection of emcees, which includes the pioneering

Mellow Man Ace (famous for one of the earliest bilingual raps, "Mentirosa," 1989), one voice stands out above the rest: Niña Dioz, a Mexican rapper.[41] She raps in Spanish about the resurgences of racism in our age, corrupt governments, police brutality, violence against women, gender politics, and a host of other social issues. Here and elsewhere, Niña Dioz plays the prophetess in her music, putting oracular powers on display like Cassandra, warning of impending ruin, calling for social change, and urging compassion and tolerance. Leaving more frivolous topics for others, her primary material tends to be the pressing social, cultural, and political issues of the day. Because she's working within confined parameters on "La Raza," however, she is much more creative and exciting on some of her own raps, such as "Dale," "Salsa," "La Cumbia Prohibida," "Magdalena," or "Tambalea." Considered by some a feminist anthem for Latin American hip-hop, the latter song, for instance (featuring the Colombian artist Lido Pimienta and Tijuana-born Ceci Bastida), is one of her best, its marimba-spiced melody, programmed beats, and soft mariachi horns irresistibly contagious. And her rapping on the song is second to none, the lyricism choppy and staccato one moment, poignantly melodic the next. Everything staggers or wobbles, she sings in the song, as if to say that the center cannot hold, and that the narratives that once excluded marginalized groups are shaking and tumbling to the ground. In this time of crisis, with the world trembling underneath and hope flickering, faith is the only thing, she insists, that "keeps me on my feet" (*la fe me pone de pié*).

To make the point, colorful statues of Guadalupe appear throughout the music video, shadowing the song with a touch of the sacred feminine. Nothing like conservative images of Mary, however, Guadalupe is for this young queer Mexican rapper the merciful mother of women, natives, misfits, and all other marginalized groups. Instead of meek and submissive, she's strong and bold; instead of docile, she is capable of sorrow, anger, and outrage too, her heart pierced with a sword for having witnessed not only Jesus's death, but the horrifying violence against women in the United States and Mexico, where over 23,000 women over the past decade have been killed at the hands of men (*el feminicidio*, it's been called in Mexico). These atrocities have haunted Niña Dioz's conscience: "I decided that if I wanted things to change," Dioz remarks, "I have to be part of that change. I can't just cross my arms and expect someone to do it...."[42]

Which brings us back to the legacy of "Viva Tirado": with Niña Dioz's voice added to the mix, not to mention the conscious-minded verses of the others, the song has changed with the times, now speaking to an age that is increasingly hungry for voices that howl in the desert, voices that proclaim a thought-provocative and meaningful Word. Ironically, though, "La Raza" is timely not only for pushing ahead, but for circling back around to the age and spirit of Gerald Wilson and El Chicano, proving that the recovery of the past can be radical as much as reactionary.

And the kind of change that it registers is striking, especially when the song is seen in light of the gangster rap of the 1980s. If you recall, gangster rap emerged out of the smoldering embers of civil rights aspirations, when the founding gods were dead and faith in the promises of America started to break and buckle, ravaged by evidence—unending racism, oppressive conditions of poverty, a harsh carceral state, militarized police forces, segregated blocks, drug wars, dwindling social services, deadly gun violence, the crack epidemic—that contradicted the American creed that all men and women were created equal. Given the grievous conditions of urban America, most gangster rappers came to see the pious and proper attitude of civil rights as sentimental and naïve, an attitude that, when it wasn't chasing after windmills, would leave the poor and oppressed impaled like a butterfly on a pin, or a neck under the boot of a cop. Even beloved civil rights songs like "We Shall Overcome," as Eddie Glaude has remarked, sounded like minstrel tunes to the Black Panthers, corny and tired, a Kumbaya-like ditty that may prepare one for the afterlife but does very little to change life on earth.[43] White folks didn't give a damn for morality—racism doesn't even register as a moral concern for many—and so, the Panthers argued, let it be damned. Let's turn our focus to the business of power, let's substitute the will-to-power for caritas and humility, Nietzsche for the gospels, Zarathustra for Jesus, Marx for St. Paul. To avoid a tragic fate, forever on the cross, black, brown, and Indigenous folk will need to fight for power by any means necessary.

Gangster rappers, in my estimation, embraced this position and took it in a more ruthless and individualistic direction than the Black Panthers. Their minds became fixated on the clout that came with money and material capital, an ambition that was driven by a Darwinian, dog-eat-dog code, the strong ruling the weak. This attitude was merciless, needless to say, when it came to the losers of such ventures. When boasting on "La Raza" about being strapped, and pulling out his *cuete* (gun) on some sorry *chavalas* (punks), Kid Frost was not only channeling the spirit of black and brown nationalism, therefore; he was also playing the part of the hardened and ruthless gangster, quick to flash his gun, quick to resort to violence. He was playing with firepower, in other words, and this while South Central, Compton, and East LA was caught in a conflagration of homicides and vendettas that claimed the lives of thousands of youth. This was a time, after all, when LA was as saturated with urban violence—not excluding the state-sanctioned violence of the LAPD—as it was with smog and fossil fuels. Kid Frost breathed this air, spitting it out in his raps and, in some ways, adding to the pollution of violence. His conception of brown power, simply put, lacked the spirit of love that, according to Dr. King, prevents power from corroding the soul and society alike. "Power without love is reckless and abusive," he wrote, "and love without power is sentimental and anemic." And James Baldwin complemented the sentiment: "There is absolutely no salvation without love . . . Salvation does not divide. Salvation connects."[44] In both versions, love and justice have equal weight, the latter demanding radical social change—to the point of civil disobedience, if necessary—and the former uniting various clans and tribes together in the same battle. Without love, Baldwin insisted, we risk imprisoning ourselves in totems, taboos, races, and blood sacrifices, getting hung up on "some mystical black bullshit."[45] The same has been true, of course, about the Chicano movement.

In my first faculty position, immediately after graduate school, I served as the faculty advisor to MEChA—the Chicano student movement, *Movimiento Estudiantil Chicano de Aztlán*—on the campus of Seattle University. Many of MEChA's founding documents, which my students and I carefully scrutinized, read exactly as James Baldwin described black power: full of Manichaean oppositions between good and evil, the pure and impure, heroes and villains, macho Aztec warriors and frail princesses, noble Aztec deities and the ignoble Christian God. Conceptions about identity and race—*la raza*—were generally fixed and unchanging, devoid of nuance and complexity. Identity was a thing of the blood, and MEChA was intent on reconnecting blood ties that were severed by the history of imperialism, calling the lost tribes of Aztlán back to the homeland.[46] When Baldwin warns us about the imprisoning nature of totems, races, and blood sacrifices, I often think of this kind of legend and lore, especially in light of the tribal gods that the Chicano movement revered and enthroned—Huitzilopochtli, Quetzalcoatl, Coatlicue, and the like.

On the one hand, I still believe that there was, and still is, something vital and urgent in this vision, a message that binds *mestizo* cultures to their Indigenous roots, and stands in unity with farmworkers, undocumented laborers, and all deprived communities of the Americas. (Our club was particularly involved with the United Farm Workers in the state of Washington.) On the other hand, the kind of loyalty that it inspires is often naïve, parochial, tribal, and sexist. Instead of flesh-and-blood Indians and *mestizos* (like the members of our club), MEChA seemed to prefer the mythological Indian of legend and lore, a figure who is frozen in the prehistoric past, a noble savage. Even their gods seem to have been shrouded in the mists of time: though they were quick to take a knife to the Christian God, sacrificing him on the altar of Indigenous religion, they tend to be uncritical, romantic, and credulous when it comes to native deities, attributing to Indigenous gods a mystical power and moral innocence that they denied to the Christian God (not unlike, in fact, the New Age spirituality of Carlos Castaneda's *The Teachings of Don Juan* [1968]). Never mind that Coatlicue had an insatiable lust for blood sacrifices, as Marie Arana writes: "Her skirt is a mantle of writhing snakes. Her fingers and toes are clawed. Her neck is festooned with skulls, human hearts. Spiders, scorpions, centipedes are her companions. She is life and death in one; our birth mother with an insatiable lust for human sacrifices."[47] Never mind that Xipe Totec, ruler of war, was known as "the Flayer," since he wore masks or capes of flayed human skin. Never mind that the Aztecs "were past masters at genocide," Arana again, "memorializing their truculence in vast, fearsome walls of severed heads. The skull towers at Tenochtitlán alone were said to number as many as 136,000 decapitated crania, embedded into the stone. One can only imagine the carnage in the killing fields of the Mexica, the horrific stench of death, the deranged cries of victory as one head after another was ripped from its trunk and borne high."[48]

The Christian God, I will be reminded, has plenty of blood on his hands, too, his followers responsible for turning the virgin rivers of the New World into rivers of blood. No doubt, I would be the last person, student of Las Casas and Gustavo Gutiérrez as I am, to deny such a thing: the Christian record, marred as it is by grievous sins, is disappointing; every great achievement of Christian civilization is, it seems, also a work of barbarism. I mention the violent history of Mesoamerican gods, nonetheless, only to make sense of Baldwin's warning about totems, races, and blood sacrifices, about the mystical bullshit that he detects in ethnocentric forms of nationalism. He was hardly against black pride, hardly against the dignity of African American ancestries and cultures, but he feared that a dogmatic, superstitious, and metaphysical identification with a particular family, clan, lineage, or tribe—and this is what he meant by the "mystical" reference—risked duplicating the kind of racism that he had spent his life contesting. Thick with illusions, including the self-delusions that prevent knowledge of self, the ideology of blood ties and pure races obscured for him the bonds that unite all members of the human race. It obscured the ability to see oneself in others, thereby thwarting the work of solidarity among all oppressed groups: Native Americans, Africans, Latin@s, Syrian refugees, Chinese Americans, Palestinians, Jews, Muslims, and so on.[49]

Believer or not, Baldwin's universal vision—where there is neither Jew

nor Greek, slave nor free, male nor female—pays explicit homage to Christian thought. He was, in fact, steeped in Christianity since childhood, and
it saturated every pore of his body. He may have tried to sweat out some of
the more troubling legacies of American Christianity, like a bad flu; but the
rudimentary elements of Christianity were present in every atom and cell of
his body. His vision of human brotherhood and sisterhood remained, hence,
deeply Christian, and was inspired by a faith in a common condition of man
and woman beyond the color of skin and the category of race. The black and
brown power movements, he was right to say, neglected this fundamental
truth, just as they tended to neglect, even denigrate, women and queers.[50]
What Eddie Glaude says about Eldridge Cleaver, an early leader of the Black
Panthers, holds true for what I discovered about MEChA: "His was a world of
hypermasculinist politics, full of virile black men slaying enemies and defend-
ing distressed damsels."[51] If true about the world of the Black Panthers, and
I think it is, it's not surprising that Cleaver was particularly tough on Baldwin's
queerness; it unnerved him and other Panthers; it threatened their rule, their
command, their muscle.

Brownout's "La Raza," and in particular Niña Dioz's participation on the
song, does something similar to Kid Frost's version of "La Raza," I'm suggesting—it unsettles his muscular and hyper-masculine understanding of
"la raza," tones down the violent gangster threats, and shatters the frozen and
fixed identity of Chicano myth. For all their efforts to play the role of the shaman or medicine man, the Chicano movement, including Kid Frost on "La
Raza," lacked the gifts of a great shaman: the ability to see both the surface
of things and their inner mysteries and complexities. Brownout's version is
an advance in this regard; it remains "brown and proud," for sure, but without the toxic, priapic masculinity, and without the narrow ethnic and gang
affiliations. Like an older and wiser king, chastened by the years, the vision
of Chicano power is more fragile and compassionate in this latest iteration of
"Viva Tirado." By including an Afro-Cuban in MC Kool A.D., a Cuban-born
Californian in Mellow Man Ace, the Tejanos Mexstep and El Dusty, and the
Mexican lesbian rapper Niña Dioz, it captures a more diverse grain of Latin@
life in the new millennium, still raw and radical, but more inclusive, noble,
and conscious, too, the past, present, and future tenses of Latin hip-hop all
compressed in a song.

Migrating Rhythms

I've tried to tell the story of Chicano rap through the reception history of "Viva
Tirado" up to this point, but this is only one short chapter in a larger book,

of course. There are many other figures who deserve mention in the genre of Chicano rap: Lighter Shade of Brown, Cypress Hill, Brownside, 2Mex, Baby Bash, Delinquent Habits, Funky Aztecs, Krazy Race, Proper Dos, Psycho Realm, Jae-P, Akwid, Ozomatli, Shystie, Snow Tha Product, to name a few.

It's always dangerous to reduce such a diverse group of voices and styles to one musical theme, but I don't think it's unfair to say that the experience of migration is a common refrain. Exile and alienation, bilingual raps, Afro-Latin rhythms, temporal shifts between past and future, the urban barrio and rural campo, the plight of migrants, all of these things surface in Latin hip-hop, the music capturing the struggles and possibilities of uprooted lives in the Americas. Instead of moving from the East to West Coast, Latin hip-hop has typically revolved on the North-South axis of the Americas, following the passage of sounds and peoples traveling by bus, train, or foot in search of the promised land. For this reason alone, Latin hip-hop may be one of the best examples of cultural displacement, miscegenation, and *mestizaje* in popular music, a blending that gives us a view of the world from the margins, "where you see things that are usually lost on minds that have never travelled beyond the conventional and the comfortable."[52] It shouldn't be too surprising that music can be an unconventional vehicle of this kind, taking us to places we've never been. Music is much freer in its nature than human beings, after all, traveling below the radar of border sentries and sensors, gliding across countries like a bird or the wind. A stealthy and unseen force, and a harbinger of change and otherness, music can steal into the life of a nation or culture, exerting a sway over it. And it can, as the case of Latin hip-hop proves, help one see the world from the perspective of an outsider.

Consider, for example, the group Ozomatli, a live band that trespassed all sorts of genres, blending rap vocals, funky bass lines, rhythm guitars, exuberant horns, turntable scratching, Spanish and English lyrics, and the rhythms of cumbia, salsa, merengue, bachata, samba, polka, and reggaeton. The product, a wild and danceable squall of sound (with a socially conscious message), was a perfect match for the multiracial Nuevo LA of the late 1990s and early aughts, a music that celebrated difference and that brought together Chicanos, African Americans, Salvadorans, Basques, Jews, Japanese, and Filipinos to be members of this American band, a group that was one of the roughs, a kosmos.[53] Or, moving into the early 2000s, give a listen to the group Akwid, consisting of the brothers Francisco and Sergio Gómez, born in Michoacán and raised in LA. They championed a new style that they called "banda hip-hop," a fusion of rap with the throbbing tubas, bleating trumpets, snare drums, tamboras, and the marching oompah rhythm of *banda sinaloense*. The result is a compulsive, kinetic sound, full of high voltage rhythms and rhymes.[54]

Or what about Delinquent Habits, a trio consisting of El Güero Loco, Kemo the Blaxican, and DJ Invincible—they also looked south of the border for inspiration, but in their case toward the brass and mariachi traditions of Tijuana, Mexicali, and Guadalajara instead of the banda sound of Michoacán. They never offered school knowledge, much less righteousness, only a variety of street wisdom, a view of America from the shadows of American life, where hiding from the police, ICE, or the border patrol is a way of life.[55] El Güero Loco's phrasing recalled B-Real's vocal style (of Cypress Hill), while Kemo the Blaxican, ethnically Mexican and African American, concentrated in his person the sonic fusions that I have been discussing in the chapter, the prolific union of black and Latin cultures, the hyphen in Afro-Latin blends. "Hittin' hard like an Aztec, swift like a Zulu," Kemo boasts on "Tres Delinquentes," a song that sampled Herb Alpert and the Tijuana Brass as well as "3 Lil' Putos" by Cypress Hill, while employing a Spanish/English/caló dialect, the language itself capturing Kemo's mixed, polyglot identity.

Sure, they strutted and pounded their chests as much as any gangster rapper, threw up *placas* to mark their territory, and struck intimidating demeanors with furrowed brows, scowling mouths, and eyes glowing red with menace. They wanted, no doubt, to make themselves bigger than reality, like a shadow in an alleyway at dusk. Nonetheless, the stronger emphasis in their music fell less on violence than on partying, fun, foolishness, peace, and smoking *grifa* or *yerba buena*. "Bass gets to thumpin', rucas get to pumpin'/ Who's that rockin', got the party to start jumpin'" (rucas or jainas is slang for women). When they weren't rocking the party in this manner, they extolled the pleasures of marijuana, like their homeboys in Cypress Hill, or like their pachuco ancestors, offering to the hip-hop generation what a Los Angeles mariachi corrido of the 1950s called the "poesia del tírili," poetry of the marijuana-smoking pachuco. (Lalo Guerrero's song "Marihuana Boogie" [1949] and Don Tosti's "El Tírili" [1950] are examples.)[56] It's true, of course, that by celebrating marijuana they flirted with degrading stereotypes, perpetuating, rather than contesting, the bigoted image of the lazy, indolent, criminal Mexican. But, like so many gangster rappers, and like their zoot suit-wearing *tíos*, they turned the fears and myths of Chicanos into a source of humor and strength and style, appealing to marijuana as a taste of harmless fun, illicit behavior, and playful rebellion. Maybe it was pure escapism, and an homage to an opiate that dulled revolutionary instincts, but the mood of the music became decidedly peaceable and laid back under this influence, a blunting of violent tendencies.

Jae-P, another rapper from the Greater Eastside, also made important contributions to West Coast Latin@ rap (sometimes called "urban regional," suggestive of both urban rap and regional Mexican/Latin music). His album *Ni De Aquí, Ni De Allá* (Not from Here, Not from There, 2003) speaks to the conflicted identity of Latin@s in the United States, the condition that leaves one feeling, whether in the United States or Mexico, like an outcast and stranger in thine own house, a perpetual alien, an internal exile. Born in LA, he's the son of Mexican immigrants, and makes beats and rhymes to give voice to the fears, anxieties, and restlessness felt by many immigrants and undocumented workers in the United States. He grew up on a mixed diet of Mexican music (Banda el Recodo and the corridos of Chalino Sánchez, for instance), and socially conscious hip-hop (Public Enemy and KRS-One, among others). He draws upon both heritages not only to address his own divided psyche, but also as resources for survival in a multicultural, postindustrial LA.

Latin pride, social problems, and the plight of immigrants in the United States are consistent themes in his music, including on "Ni De Aquí, Ni De Allá," which begins with the cry *"que onda raza"* (what's up, my people). The music video captures Jae-P and his family and friends in the barrio, giving the viewer a glance of an ordinary day on the Greater Eastside: the community gathering around him in a festive spirit, men and women flirting with each other, and low-riders bouncing and leaping in the streets like sprung jack-in-the-boxes. Though a US citizen, he puts himself in the shoes of an undocumented immigrant in the song, following the trail of someone who was forced to cross the river as a child, brought here by his father. The young man learns English to survive in the United States, but no matter what, *"para el gringo soy un wetback"* (for the white man I'm a wetback). Still, he's determined to persevere, doing what he can to navigate the dangerous labyrinths of the barrio. He's tough and spirited, finding his voice in company with other immigrants and learning from their example. Though his opportunities are severely circumscribed (as an "illegal," he's part of the underground economy, of course), he is motivated by the thought that other Latin@s have thrived here, and that *"el latino hoy en día no es un simple lavaplatos"* (the Latino of today is not only a dishwasher).

As real as the experience of Latin@ dishwashers and service industry workers may be in today's America ("essential workers," as we call them in 2021), the reference here recalls an old stock character in Mexican American music, going back to the classic corrido "El Lavaplatos" (1930), by Los Hermanos Bañuelos. This plaintive ballad follows the plight of a disillusioned Mexican immigrant in the early twentieth century, his dreams dashed on the rocky shores of Southern California. He migrates to Hollywood in search of Eden, eyes swollen with a sense of wonder and promise. After working numerous menial jobs, and encountering the sneers and scorn of discrimination, he decides to return to Mexico, however, his experience of Eden less a paradise than a wilderness, filled with dangerous serpents and insurmountable barriers that exclude him from the tree of life. Los Hermanos approximates his downcast mood, their subdued melodies tearing at one's heartstrings with solemn and sentimental chords: "Good-bye my dreams/ Good-bye movie stars/ I'm returning to my beloved country/ Poorer than when I came." And many of their corridos struck a similar chord, narrating tales of discrimination, exploitation, and violence against Mexicans in the United States. They addressed issues of migration and deportation ("El Deportado"), wrongful imprisonment ("Los Prisioneros de San Quentin"), and abusive police authorities ("El Corrido de Juan Reyna," about a Mexican man brutally beaten by the police, handcuffed to a black man, and eventually sentenced to prison). In the latter case, Juan Reyna manages to grab a policeman's gun and strike him with it as he is being arrested. The song celebrates his courage and strength, his ability to bend without breaking: "*Adiós Juan Reyna, supiste defender tu dignidad*" (Good-bye, Juan Reyna, you knew how to defend your dignity).

In 1981, the Chicano punk rock group Los Illegals offered a punk version of "El Lavaplatos" as well, calling it "El-Lay" (a homophone referring to both Los Angeles and *el ley*, the law). In tribute to "El Lavaplatos," the song recounted the plight of Mexican immigrants in LA in the late twentieth century, returning to the classic corrido as a parable of the mistreatment and abuse of migrant laborers, their lives treated like mules or cart horses more than human beings. Adding a personal touch, Willie Herrón, on vocals, sang and shouted about his stepfather's arrest while washing dishes in LA, using this anecdote as a gloss on the corrido, a story within a story. Needless to say, the rock group updated "El Lavaplatos" culturally and musically, adding punk's wild, feverish, and anti-establishment sensibilities: crashing, frenetic drums; shredded electric guitar chords; screaming, half-intelligible lyrics that move so fast that they can only be understood in snippets, like the view of a billboard from a fast-moving train. And the fact that the group consisted of Mexican Americans, neither fully Mexican nor fully American, added a postmodern flavor to the music, the sound capturing the bifurcated, edgy, and stressed experience of Chicanos in the late twentieth century. The song, in all, chronicled the stalled progress in race relations, as if the angel of history was caught in a storm and unable to move forward. As they told it, as a matter of fact, the troubles facing Mexican immigrants in 1981 were more dangerous than in 1930, the times bringing militarized policing, threatening gangs, growing anti-immigrant sentiment, and more deadly guns and weapons. "We didn't go home to our bedrooms after playing punk shows and jumping up and down and spitting beer at each other," says Jesus Velo, bass player for the band. "We came home to the barrio and you heard gunshots."[57]

Hip-hop, of course, has always registered these things—gunshots and sirens, crisis and clamor, minor keys and violent beats. You can hear it in Jae-P's "Ni De Aquí," the music minimalistic but forceful—a classic boom-bap beat, an eerie G-funk synth line, pounding piano keys, and a soft flute or clarinet that has a folksy quality, like the wavy sound of wind through bamboo. Though Latin music is understated here, Jae-P turned to Norteño music for other raps, as in "Un Pandillero Más" (one more gangster), a cautionary tale about the dangers of gang life. The accordion is the star attraction of this sound, its rhythms meant for bopping and dancing. Frequently considered low class and coarse, *"la musica de la gente pobre"* (the music of the poor), as Manuel Peña has called it, Norteño developed in the peripheries of northeastern Mexico and southeastern Texas, appealing to millions of working-class Mexicans.[58] Different from the melancholic nostalgia of the corrido, the accordion adds a lilting upbeat rhythm to Mexican music, the mood decidedly more buoyant than the downcast emotions of a corrido. If the corrido is a mournful cry under the storm and stress of life, Norteño (a Mexican incarnation of cumbia) is a cry of delight, its melodies meant for lightening the burdens of the working poor.[59]

For sharing these humble origins, *música norteña* and hip-hop make for an interesting marriage. Both partners, of course, are changed as a result, hip-hop becoming more Latin and Norteño becoming blacker, more urban and, as in "Un Pandillero Más," more sensitive to the threats of poverty and violence in countless black and brown communities. Speaking from the eye of such storms, Latin hip-hop has been as prescient as any art form in the new millennium. Jae-P only scratches the surface, truth be told; other rappers dig much deeper. I think of Chhoti Maa's "Dejame Entrar," where she employs an angelic, beseeching voice in pleading, like a Greek supplicant, for asylum; or Olmeca's "Define" and "Browning of America," where the Los Angeles rapper switches at ease between English and Spanish to chronicle the movements of the Mexican and Latin American diaspora; or Mare Advertencia Lirika, the Zapotec rapper from Oaxaca, who uses hip-hop, in her words, "as a way to speak about the injustices that we all faced growing up"; or Calle 13's "Atrévete Te, Te," where the Puerto Rican group tells a middle-class girl to reach into her guts to find the native Taino in her; or Mexican rappers like Bocafloja, Jezzy P, Akil Ammar, and others.[60] The examples are numerous and only building in intensity, a swelling chorus.

Straight Outta Compton Circa 2020

If America is browning, then, hip-hop is browning too. Compton in 2021 is not the same as it was when N.W.A. released "Straight Outta Compton" in 1988. Some have registered these changes, and others haven't bothered noticing, preferring the Compton of myth and legend over the Compton of today.[61] What Peter L'Official has written about the South Bronx—the legendary city of hip-hop par excellence—holds true for Compton too: "They are symbols that may or may not have root in fact, and their symbolic language is as visual and cinematic as it is literary . . . Thus do urban legends become facts, facts become symbols, and cultural representations inspired by both spiral out in an endless strophe, far beyond the realities that produced them."[62] Something like this has happened to Compton, the facts becoming symbols, the symbols becoming fables and fictions. Whether the city has become synonymous with urban crisis—drugs, nihilism, poverty, violence, decay, blight, the ghetto, and so on—or synonymous with the black underclasses, such representations be-lie the reality, ignoring the thumping heartbeat of such places as well as the many shades of brown.

As far as mainstream rappers go, YG, an African American rapper from Compton, has been unusually perceptive in this regard. He may not be the finest rapper to hail from Compton, but he's a good barometer of the global shifts that have altered Compton's landscape, culture, and sonic customs. Retrospective and prospective at the same time, his music echoes vintage gangster rap (with samples from Funkadelic, Fatback Band, Mack 10, and Ice Cube, for instance), while chronicling the present and future of the city.[63] On raps like "FDT" or "Police Get Away Wit Murder," he uses curses and hexes to denounce the bigotry that black and brown communities face in Trump's America, his voice rising in pitch like steam blowing through a spout. In oth-ers, like "Blacks and Browns," feat. the Chicano rapper Sad Boy Loko, or "Go Loko," feat. Tyga and Jon Z, he pays explicit tribute to the changing demo-graphics of Compton, now mapping parts of Compton that have remained under the radar of most rappers, hidden in plain sight. For the latter rap, in fact, he put on charro attire for the video: wide-brimmed sombrero, bolero jacket, silk tie, silver trimmings, and so on. And DJ Mustard's production on the song—the bolero rhythms, the gentle ripples of a mariachi vihuela and guitarrón, the sound of squeaking hydraulics, a restrained drum-machine clap and, at the end, a blast of mariachi horns that bray and neigh in the man-ner of ranchera music—matches nicely YG's garb. The rap has the flavor of a rural bolero that has been uprooted and transplanted in the urban jungles of the city, capturing the city's cultural and music life, everything from the working-class genres of ranchera and *banda* (made famous in California by Antonio Aguilar, the ranchera idol who has a statue dedicated to him in the city) to the contemporary aesthetics of hip-hop. The video, too, is colorful and vibrant, with bobbing low-riders, charro horses in the middle of the barrio, and Chicanas with thick mascara, coiffed hairdos, tall bangs, Guadalupe-embossed t-shirts, Aztec jewelry, and eyebrows shaped into thin arches. In lieu of gang warfare, blacks and Latin@s dance, flirt, and party with each other, and YG's music logs the alliances, building bridges between various cultures instead of border walls.

While it remains true that a lot of gangster rap of the 1990s, or gangster bounce and trap music of later years, drank the Kool-Aid of American greed and violence, and in many cases renounced political and cultural criticism, threads of dissidence and protest in hip-hop are returning to favor, as I've tried to show throughout this study. Whatever the exact provocation, political sentiments are showing signs of life, buzzing again like a swarm of killer bees. Though there will always be party-centric hip-hop, and any rapper worthy of the name has to be able to rock the house, or at least make the foundations quiver and vibrate, hip-hop lives and dies by its ability—unlike disco, for instance—to reflect the decayed streetscapes of barrio life, its congested and smoggy air, its troubles and burdens, its gaping poverty, its deficits of resource and opportunity, its spirited dreams. Almost from the beginning, hip-hop embraced a ragged and grimy aesthetic, picking up sounds, styles, and struggles that it found in the meanest streets of America and making them speak for black and brown youth in urban America. The earliest figures of hip-hop culture—say, a Rammellzee, Lady Pink, or Afrika Bambaataa—established a precedent on such matters, highlighting the experiences of misfits and marginalized kids, cherishing what many had cast off and treated as waste material, rescuing dishonored and excluded things. In the process, hip-hop responded, perhaps subconsciously, to the injunction of Jesus in the gospels to go to the streets and alleyways in order to welcome the people, places, and things that are unclean and disparaged, judged worthless, a vision, in the end, that is at the heart and soul of a street theology.

NOTES

Introduction

1. Christopher Tirres describes the shift nicely: "Whereas first generation liberation theologians approached 'liberation' as an ethical and political category, a subsequent generation of liberationist thinkers in the US have often highlighted its cultural and aesthetic dimensions." See his *The Aesthetics and Ethics of Faith: A Dialogue Between Liberationist and Pragmatic Thought* (Oxford: Oxford University Press, 2014), 43.

2. See *The Preferential Option for the Poor in Christian Theology*, ed. Daniel Groody and Gustavo Gutiérrez (South Bend, IN: University of Notre Dame Press, 2007), 2.

3. Theodor Adorno, of the Frankfort School of Critical Theory, shared this vision. He considered jazz, for instance, a low product of the culture industry, whose veneer and rhetoric of liberation actually masked its conservatism. See David Bevins, *Spirits Rejoice: Jazz and American Religion* (Oxford: Oxford University Press, 2015), 11.

4. These words are from the last homily of Archbishop Romero, when he was murdered by a right-wing death squad at the altar. The Mass was being offered for the first anniversary of the death of Sara Meardi de Pinto, mother of Jorge Pinto, publisher and editor of *El Independiente*, a small weekly newspaper. Quoted in *America Magazine*, October 12, 2018.

5. Roberto Lovato's searing memoir discusses the work of sanctuary and solidarity among churches in San Francisco back in the 1970s. See his *Unforgetting: A Memoir of Family, Migration, Gangs, and Revolution in the Americas* (New York: Harper Books, 2020), 143.

6. Lauryn Hill, "Everything Is Everything," *The Miseducation of Lauryn Hill* (Ruffhouse/Columbia Records, 1998).

7. Though beyond the scope of this book, I should say that there are important dif-

ferences between Greek and Roman rhapsody, on the one hand, and Hebrew forms of recitation and chanting. For one, a rhapsode was a singer of epic poetry, and since there is no epic poetry in the Bible—the poetry of the Bible is non-narrative and lyrical—it's inappropriate to speak of biblical rhapsodes. In the Bible, moreover, we should distinguish between the poetry and prose: the former was likely chanted and sung, and possibly composed by a singer; the latter, on the other hand, was likely a written composition and not composed by a singer. But even in this case, it was *performed* orally, recited or chanted aloud, as the book of Nehemiah indicates when speaking of Ezra's reading of the Torah (Nehemiah 8:1–8). See Robert Kawashima, *Biblical Narrative and the Death of the Rhapsode* (Bloomington: Indiana University Press, 2004).

8. Anne Carson, *Eros: The Bittersweet* (New York: Dalkey Archive Press, 1998), 50.

9. We can see, in each of these instances, why "breath" is so vital to these cultures: it is the means by which words travel through the air and fall on the ears, the wings that give words their sound, nuance, emotion, and meaning. "For the ancient Greeks," writes Anne Carson, "breath is consciousness, breath is perception, breath is emotion." For the Hebrews of the Bible, too, breath is all of these things, and represented by the single word "soul," *nephesh*: that is, the breath of life and essence of one's being. See Carson, *Eros*, 48.

10. In Plato's *Phaedo*, Socrates tells us that he had been having a series of dreams in which the Muses urge him to write *mousike*. Initially, he takes this command to mean (metaphorically) the practice of philosophy. At this point, however, when he is in prison and awaiting his death, he concludes that it might be "what is ordinarily called *mousike*"; that is, the composition of poetry/music (Phaedo 61 A). In response, he composes metrical versions of Aesop's fables and hymns to Apollo. Given the limits of reason when considering death and the gods, it could be, it seems to me, that Socrates is telling us that poetry/music is a more appropriate medium than philosophy for wrestling with the mysteries of life. For a discussion of Greek *mousike*, see M. S. Silk and J. P. Stern, *Nietzsche on Tragedy* (Cambridge: Cambridge University Press, 1981), 164ff.

11. This is also true in many of the religions of the world. The Rig Veda was an anthology of Vedic hymns, whereby the intoning and chanting of the words themselves had spiritual power; early Chinese scripture such as the *Shijing* was a collection of classic odes; after the death of the Buddha, tradition has it that monks gathered together to chant the *Buddhavacana* (Word of the Buddha), and to eventually codify, via recitation, the official dharma. Without this musical and liturgical context, Karen Armstrong has argued, "an essential dimension of scripture is missing. Contemplating scripture outside a ritualized setting is like reading the lyrics of an aria." See her *The Lost Art of Scripture: Rescuing the Sacred Texts* (London: Penguin Books, 2019), 406.

12. Armstrong, *The Lost Art of Scripture*, 8.

13. The Song of Songs in Hebrew is *shir ha-shirim*. I'm very grateful to Tod Linafelt of Georgetown University for pointing this out to me.

14. See Tod Linafelt, *The Hebrew Bible as Literature* (Oxford: Oxford University Press, 2016), 50-53. Robert Alter also presents many examples of alliteration and sound play in the Hebrew Bible. "My own contention," he suggests, "is that meaning in the bible or in any literary text cannot be reduced to lexical values, that it involves the communication of affect and can never be separated from the nuanced connotation of words and their dynamic interaction as they are joined through sound, through syntax, and through poetic or narrative context." See his *The Art of Bible Translation* (Princeton, NJ: Princeton University Press, 2019), 73-77.

15. Robert Alter, *The Art of Biblical Poetry* (New York: Basic Books, 1985), 111.

16. See George Robinson, *Essential Judaism: A Complete Guide to Beliefs, Customs, and Rituals* (New York: Pocket Books, 2000), 47.

17. Even if the markings of the Masoretic text of the Hebrew Bible date to the sixth to tenth centuries CE, the Masoretes were drawing upon an ancient tradition of recitation. "There was a continuous tradition," writes Robert Alter, "for recitation of the texts on which the Masoretes drew, and anyone who has listened to the Masoretic Text read out loud can attest to its strong rhythmic integrity. . . . Biblical Hebrew, in sum, has a distinctive music, a lovely precision of lexical choice, a meaningful concreteness, and a suppleness of expressive syntax . . ." See his "Introduction," *The Five Books of Moses*, trans. Robert Alter (New York: W.W. Norton, 2004), xliii–xlv.

18. See Friedrich Schleiermacher, *On Religion: Speeches to its Cultured Despisers*, trans. Richard Crouter (Cambridge: Cambridge University Press, 1988), 96ff.

19. See Paula Fredriksen, *Paul, The Pagan's Apostle* (New Haven, CT: Yale University Press, 2017), 48.

20. Quoted in Joshua Jacobson, *Chanting the Hebrew Bible* (Philadelphia: Jewish Publication Society, 2005), 8. Since God's awesome epiphany in Exodus is described as auditory and in no way visual—"The sound of the words you did hear," intones Moses, "but no image did you see except the sound" (Deuteronomy 4:11-12)—it is understandable that this medieval exegete rendered the sound of God's words as the sound of music, the revelation emerging from the burning bush in some enchanting lyrical form.

21. See Timothy Beal, *The Rise and Fall of the Bible* (New York: Houghton Mifflin Harcourt, 2012), 95.

22. Beal, *The Rise and Fall of the Bible*, 95.

23. Carson, *Eros*, 48.

24. Michael Schmidt, *Gilgamesh: The Life of a Poem* (Princeton, NJ: Princeton University Press, 2019), 131.

25. OutKast, "Spottieottiedopaliscious," *Aquemini* (LaFace Records, 1998).

26. Quoted in Ted Gioia, *Music: A Subversive History* (New York: Basic Books, 2019), 433.

27. See Tricia Rose, "Foreword," in *The Hip Hop and Obama Reader*, ed. Travis L. Gosa and Erik Nielson (New York: Oxford University Press, 2015), ix.

28. Nik Cohn, *Triksta: Life and Death of New Orleans Rap* (New York: Vintage Books, 2007).

29. Hanif Abdurraqib, *They Can't Kill Us Until They Kill Us* (New York: Two Dollar Radio, 2017), 195.

30. Rickey Vincent, *Funk: The Music, the People, and the Rhythm of the One* (New York: St. Martin's Griffin, 1996), 164.

31. Quoted in David Blight, *Frederick Douglass: Prophet of Freedom* (New York: Simon and Schuster, 2018), xviii.

32. Friedrich Engels and Karl Marx, *The Communist Manifesto* (New York: Penguin Classics, 2002).

33. Abdurraqib, *They Can't Kill Us Until They Kill Us*, 191.

34. I will discuss many of these figures throughout this study, but Adam Bradley's pioneering work on the poetics of hip-hop is an example; or Joseph Schloss's and Mark Katz's work on deejaying and b-boying; Paul Edwards, Adam Krims, or Loren Kajikawa on musical features; Ben Westhoff and Roni Sarig on Southern rap, et al. Robin D. G. Kelley captures this perspective nicely: "By not acknowledging the deep visceral pleasures black youth derive from making and consuming culture, the stylistic and aesthetic conventions that render the form and performance more attractive than the message, these authors reduce expressive culture to a political text to be read like a less sophisticated version of The Nation or Radical America." See his *Yo' Mama's Disfunktional: Fighting the Culture Wards in Urban America* (Boston: Beacon Press, 1997), 37. A shift away from protest poetry is also evident in the anthology of African American poetry *Angles of Ascent*, ed. Charles Henry Rowell (New York: W.W. Norton, 2013). For distancing itself from social and political poetry, the volume drew the ire of Amiri Baraka.

35. Langston Hughes's story "On the Road" is also in the prophetic vein, and particularly relevant for this study. It tells of a homeless man who, after experiencing racism by the white Christian churches, brings down the doors and pillars of a church. As he wanders away, Christ appears to him and thanks him for setting him free. Christ, the moral is, has been imprisoned by the white churches. Only if you see the world from the perspective of the "road"—"if you'd ever been on the road, if you had ever lived with the homeless and hungry"—only then will you understand the meaning of Christianity.

36. James Baldwin, *The Fire Next Time* (New York: Vintage Books, 1990), 41.

37. I'm recalling here, and slightly tweaking, Ta-Nehisi Coates's metaphor. See his *We Were Eight Years in Power: An American Tragedy* (New York: One World Books, 2017).

38. "While the hip hop generation played an important role in the election of Democratic president Barack Obama in 2008, the global hip hop generation was rejecting traditional politics and politicians, engaged instead in contentious social uprisings and revolts." See the essay by Sujatha Fernandes, "Obama Nation: Hip Hop and Global Protest," in *The Hip Hop and Obama Reader*, ed. Travis Gosa and Erik Nielson (New York: Oxford University Press, 2015), 89.

39. See Ivan Nechepurenko, "Russia's Youth Found Rap. The Kremlin Is Worried," *New York Times*, May 21, 2019.

40. Quoted in Brandon Byrd, "The Black Intellectual Tradition and the Myth of Objectivity," in *Black Perspectives*, August 13, 2016.

41. See Tomoko Masuzawa, "Culture," in *Critical Terms for Religious Studies*, ed. Mark Taylor (Chicago: University of Chicago Press, 1998), 89.

42. Quoted in Francine Du Plessiz Gray, *Simone Weil* (New York: Penguin Books, 2001), 221.

43. Jon Pareles, "Public Enemy: Rap with a Fist in the Air," *New York Times*, July 24, 1988.

44. Shiduri's advice to Gilgamesh is another example of this aesthetic, Epicurean option: "But you, Gilgamesh, let your belly be full, enjoy yourself always by day and by night. Make merry each day, dance and play day and night." Consider how different this vision is from Archbishop Romero's theology of the cross: "If God accepts the sacrifice of my life, may my death be for the freedom of my people . . . If they kill me, I will rise again in the people of El Salvador."

45. John O'Malley emphasizes Constantine's influence in transforming Christian attitudes toward architecture and the arts: "The emperor set in motion a massive redefinition of space, indeed, redefinition of urban landscape, with the concomitant and inevitable redefinition of Christians' relationship to the material culture of Late Antiquity." See his *Four Cultures of the West* (Cambridge, MA: Harvard University Press, 2004), 186.

46. John the Baptist often became the model and inspiration of these eccentric sorts, the desert ascetic preaching repentance and renunciation. Frequently depicted as nude, his nakedness became a parable of a desert-like barrenness and world-renouncing modesty; it symbolized the prophet's repudiation of all cultured and artificial conceptions of beauty; it symbolized his raw and coarse ethics, a vision that called Israel to the return to the desert of Exodus, where God once liberated the nation from slavery in Egypt and led them to a land of milk and honey; it symbolized his passion for justice. In medieval legends, John the Baptist had a counterpart in Mary Magdalene, too. She was also sketched in the nude and shared the Baptist's scathing tongue when it came to the needs of the poor. In the Golden Legend, she rails against the rich and powerful the way Las Casas or Dr. King would years later: "Why," she thundered, "when you are so rich, do you allow the saints of God to die of hunger and cold? . . . You enemy of the cross of Christ . . . You will not escape or go unpunished." See O'Malley, *Four Cultures of the West*, 47.

47. See Tom Piazza, *The Devil Sent the Rain: Music and Writing in Desperate America* (New York: Harper Perennial, 2011), 249.

48. Henry Louis Gates Jr., *The Black Church: This Is Our Story, This Is Our Song* (New York: Penguin Books, 2021), xxi.

49. Gates, *The Black Church*, xix.

50. See Eddie Glaude, *African American Religion: A Very Short Introduction* (Oxford: Oxford University Press, 2014), 115.

51. Pew Research Center, November 13, 2014.

52. Robert Orsi, *History and Presence* (Cambridge, MA: Harvard University Press, 2018), 41–42.

53. For the John Coltrane quote, see Ashley Kahn, *A Love Supreme: The Story of John Coltrane's Signature Album* (New York: Penguin Books, 2002), xvii.

54. Quoted in Eddie Glaude, *Begin Again: James Baldwin's America and Its Urgent Lessons for Our Own* (New York: Crown Books, 2020), 178–79.

55. "Let the blare of Negro jazz bands," writes Langston Hughes, "and the bellowing voice of Bessie Smith singing the blues penetrate the closed ears of . . . intellectuals until they listen and perhaps understand." Quoted in Tracy Fessenden, *Religion Around Billie Holiday* (University Park, PA: Penn State University Press, 2018), 124.

56. "Compared with the other musics available, jazz today is too sophisticated to articulate the lived experience of the ghetto; hip-hop does that better." Geoff Dyer, *But Beautiful: A Book About Jazz* (New York: Picador Books, 1996), 205.

Chapter One

1. For a recent study of *lo cotidiano*, or the everyday, in Latin@ theology, see Jean-Pierre Ruiz, *Revelation in the Vernacular: Disruptive Cartographers: Doing Theology Latinamente* (New York: Orbis Books, 2021).

2. One of the first experts to assess the *Nican mopohua* as a work of classical Nahuatl literature, Ángel María Garibay Kintana, noted four purposes of the new temple to be built in honor of Guadalupe: "to love, to have compassion, to aid, to defend." See Timothy Matovina, *Theologies of Guadalupe: From the Era of the Conquest to Pope Francis* (Oxford: Oxford University Press, 2019), 167.

3. See Matovina, *Theologies of Guadalupe: From the Era of the Conquest to Pope Francis*, 166.

4. Quoted in Matovina, *Theologies of Guadalupe*, 64.

5. The figure of Wisdom is portrayed in prophetic terms in parts of Wisdom literature: Proverbs 22:22: "Do not rob the poor because they are poor . . . For the Lord will defend their cause"; Sirach 34:21: "The bread of the needy is the life of the poor, and whoever deprives them of it is a man of blood." The latter text was decisive, for instance, in the life of Las Casas, prompting a radical conversion that would see him become the "defender of the Indians."

6. David Tracy, *Fragments: The Existential Situation of Our Time* (Chicago: University of Chicago Press, 2020), 45.

7. Angie Thomas, *On the Come Up* (New York: Balzer and Bray, 2019).

8. See my *Wonder and Exile in the New World* (University Park, PA: Penn State University Press, 2013).

9. See Michael Eric Dyson, *Holler If You Hear Me: Searching for Tupac Shakur* (New York: Basic Civitas Books, 2001), 212ff.

10. I wonder if Eckhart knew the parable, related to this theme, of Heraclitus, recounted in Aristotle. Strangers had come, Aristotle reports, to visit Heraclitus, and they paused at the altar of Hestia. Heraclitus, however, invites them to the kitchen stove, for all fire is divine, not only the fire that burns at the altar. The entire universe is sacred. See Pierre Hadot, *What Is Ancient Philosophy?*, trans. Michael Chase (Cambridge, MA: Harvard University Press, 2002), 85.

11. Paul Ricoeur and David Tracy refer to this legacy as "manifestation." The classic account of this tradition is in David Tracy, *The Analogical Imagination: Christian Theology and the Culture of Pluralism* (New York: Crossroads, 1981).

12. See Orsi, *The Madonna of 115th Street*, 219-31. Also see his *Between Heaven and Earth* (Princeton, NJ: Princeton University Press, 2005), 74.

13. Orsi, *Between Heaven and Earth*, 70.

14. Orsi, *The Madonna of 115th Street*, xlvii, 33.

15. Tracy Fessenden's study, *Religion Around Billie Holiday* (University Park, PA: Penn State University Press, 2018), is an excellent example in this vein.

16. See Fischer, "The Catholic Lost Generation," 626-27.

17. Quoted in Rob Kenner, *The Marathon Don't Stop: The Life and Times of Nipsey Hussle* (New York: Atria Books, 2021), 14.

18. Hua Hsu, "Beat Bop: Record of a Moment," in *Writing the Future: Basquiat and the Hip-Hop Generation* (Boston: MFA Publications, 2020), 73.

19. Keith Haring, "Remembering Basquiat," in *The Jean-Michel Basquiat Reader*, ed. Jordana Moore Saggese (Oakland: University of California Press, 2021), 208. The ragpicker was a key figure for Baudelaire and Walter Benjamin. See the discussion of this figure in Howard Eiland and Michael Jennings, *Walter Benjamin: A Critical Life* (Cambridge, MA: Harvard University Press, 2014), 612.

20. See Dave Tompkins, *How to Wreck a Nice Beach: The Vocoder from World War II to Hip-Hop, The Machine Speaks* (New York: Stop Smiling Books, 2011), 271.

21. Langston Hughes, "Christ in Alabama," quoted in Fessenden, *Religion Around Billie Holiday*.

22. Howard Thurman, *Jesus and the Disinherited* (Boston: Beacon Press, 1996).

23. Virginia Woolf, *To The Lighthouse* (New York: Harcourt Brace Jovanovich, 1989).

24. Tracy, *Fragments*, 2. Since the concept of the fragment includes not only texts, but symbols, events, narratives, performances, rituals, music, dance, drama, body, images, and persons, I see it as a development of Tracy's own critique of the dominance of written texts in religious studies. In his essay on "writing," specifically, he warns academics of an overreliance on textual studies: "Writing itself, of course, has

also been used by colonizing powers to dominate those 'others' whose nonliterate and nonalphabetic traditions of writing allow them to be interpreted as lower than cultures with written texts and the writing techniques of the dominant cultures. . . . The central need here," Tracy concludes, "is to study all the physical, material objects (including but not confined to written texts) that different cultural and religious traditions employ." See his "Writing," in *Critical Terms for Religious Studies*, ed. Mark Taylor (Chicago: University of Chicago Press, 1998), 392.

25. See the discussion in *Modern Christian Thought: The 20ᵗʰ Century*, ed. James Livingston and Francis Schussler Fiorenza (Minneapolis: Fortress Press, 2000), 15ff.

26. This principle is central to the work of Jorge Luis Borges, for instance. See, in particular, his "Pierre Menard, Author of the *Quixote*."

27. Robert Alter, "Introduction to Genesis," *The Five Books of Moses*, trans. Robert Alter (New York: W.W. Norton, 2004), 11.

28. One of the clearest examples of the radical potential of apocalypticism is in the life of Nat Turner. His apocalyptic visions inspired a violent rebellion. "I had a vision," he writes, "and I saw white spirits and black spirits engaged in battle, and the sun was darkened." See Henry Louis Gates Jr., *The Black Church: This Is Our Story, This Is Our Song* (New York: Penguin Books, 2021), 58.

29. Tracy, *The Analogical Imagination*, 265–66.

30. I'm thinking here of Walter Benjamin, a writer who also combined the Jewish messianic and apocalyptic traditions with the spirit of tragedy.

31. What Jesse McCarthy has written about Nas's "I Gave You Power"—a song that was written from the point of view of a gun—holds true here as well: "The gun becomes the center of consciousness, while the people caught in its path are treated like fungible objects." See his *Who Will Pay Reparations on My Soul?* (New York: Liveright Publishing, 2021), xix.

32. McCarthy, *Who Will Pay Reparations on My Soul?*, 119–20.

33. Quoted in Loren Kajikawa, *Sounding Race in Rap Songs* (Berkeley: University of California Press, 2015), 60.

34. While N.W.A. and Public Enemy's dense and layered soundscapes swerved widely from Run-DMC's unadorned sounds—the former groups went wild with sampling technology, piling loops on top of loops—they came together in sketching, as Loren Kajikawa has written, an aural cartography of urban life. See Kajikawa, *Sounding Race in Rap Songs*, 87.

35. See Doreen St. Félix, "The Chaos and Carnage of Childish Gambino's 'This Is America,'" *The New Yorker*, May 7, 2018.

36. I'm quoting Phife Dawg here, from "Buggin' Out," A Tribe Called Quest, *The Low End Theory* (Jive Records, 1991).

37. Quoted in Fessenden, *Religion Around Billie Holiday*, 124.

Chapter Two

1. Quoted in Amanda Petrusich, *Do Not Sell at Any Price* (New York: Scribner Books, 2014), 62.

2. "Pythagoras, that grave philosopher," wrote Plutarch about Pythagoras's influence on music, "rejected the judging of music by the senses, affirming that the virtue of music could be appreciated only by the intellect." See Ted Gioia, *A Subversive History* (New York: Basic Books, 2019), 49–50.

3. Jeff Chang, *Can't Stop, Won't Stop: A History of the Hip Hop Generation* (New York: Picador Books, 2005), 179; Adam Bradley and Andrew DuBois, eds., *The Anthology of Rap* (New Haven, CT: Yale University Press, 2010), 13; Loren Kajikawa, *Sounding Race in Rap Songs* (Berkeley: University of California Press, 2015), 59.

4. "They gave rap music its first taste of real power by infusing commercial hip-hop with the honest spirit and look of the streets." See Marcus Reeves, *Somebody Scream: Rap Music's Rise to Prominence in the Aftershock of Black Power* (New York: Farrar, Straus & Giroux, 2009), 60–62.

5. Quoted in Kajikawa, *Sounding Race in Rap Songs*, 63.

6. Gary Jardim, "John Who?," *Village Voice*, June 21, 1983.

7. The Beastie Boys, "The New Style," *Licensed to Ill* (Def Jam/Columbia, 1986).

8. Reeves, *Somebody Scream*, 40.

9. Quoted in Geoff Edgers, *Walk This Way: Run-DMC, Aerosmith, and the Song That Changed American Music Forever* (New York: Blue Rider Press, 2019), 121.

10. See Rakim, *Sweat the Technique* (New York: Amistad Books, 2019), 128–29.

11. See Lamont U-God Hawkins, *My Journey into the Wu-Tang* (New York: Picador, 2018), 36–37.

12. See Rakim, *Sweat the Technique*, 125.

13. "This is the concept," writes Rakim, "that numbers are not simply symbols of quantity as we are taught in school, but instead are qualitative entities with interconnected relationships and higher meanings." See Rakim, *Sweat the Technique*, 214.

14. Hawkins, *My Journey into the Wu-Tang*, 37–38.

15. Rakim, *Sweat the Technique*, 135–36.

16. Kajikawa, *Sounding Race in Rap Songs*, 76.

17. See Peter Shapiro, "Public Enemy," in *Classic Material: The Hip-Hop Album Guide*, ed. Oliver Wang (Toronto: ECW Press, 2003), 137–38.

18. Toni Morrison, *The Source of Self-Regard: Selected Essays, Speeches, and Meditations* (New York: Alfred Knopf, 2019), 151.

19. These statistics come from federal statistics in 2010–2012. The rates would have been higher in the 1980s and 1990s, during the age of N.W.A.'s rise to prominence.

20. See Chang, *Can't Stop, Won't Stop*, 306. Also quoted in Eithne Quinn, *Nuthin' But a "G" Thang*, quoted in Kajikawa, *Sounding Race in Rap Songs*, 96.

21. See Kiese Laymon, *How To Slowly Kill Yourself and Others in America* (New York: Scribner Books, 2020), 11.

22. Quoted in Kajikawa, *Sounding Race in Rap Songs*.

23. RZA, *The Tao of Wu* (New York: Penguin Books, 2005), 73. This passage is also discussed by Will Ashon, *Chamber Music: Wu-Tang and America (In 36 Pieces)* (London: Faber and Faber, 2018), 120-21.

24. RZA, *The Tao of Wu*, with Chris Norris (New York: Riverhead Books, 2009).

25. "Rather than presenting the 'hood as a place of conflict and struggle," writes Loren Kajikawa, "the gangsta experience was offered up as a site of pleasure one might comfortably attempt to re-create within the confines of one's own car or suburban home." See his *Sounding Race in Rap Songs*, 115.

26. Reeves, *Somebody Scream*, 143.

27. As Loren Kajikawa notes, Parliament's "Mothership Connection" echoes various religious narratives: first, the raising of Elijah by the fiery chariot and whirlwind in 2 Kings 2:11; the chariot vision in the book of Ezekiel (known as Merkabah mysticism); the black spirituals; and, finally, the mythology of the Nation of Islam. Though Parliament absorbs bits and pieces of these traditions, the experience of the chariot also includes for them, and this is important for our purposes, the pleasures of music and dance, as it transports its listeners to a state of bodily elation. Not unlike the G-funk of Dr. Dre, Cold 187um, and Warren G, it develops a celebratory ideology of redemption, "a dip in your hip, a bump and hustle," even as it maintains a bond with the era of *Soul Train* and its dreams of equal rights, black power, and festive resistance.

28. Quoted in Chang, *Can't Stop, Won't Stop*, 318.

29. Chang, *Can't Stop, Won't Stop*, 301.

30. Christina Zanfagna has a nice discussion of these tropes in Christian rap. See her *Holy Hip Hop in the City of Angels* (Berkeley: University of California Press, 2017), 16.

31. Ezekiel's chariot vision appears to him in the context of oppression, as the prophet is laboring in exile by the river of Babylon, far from Zion: "In the thirtieth year, on the fifth day of the fourth month, while I was among the exiles by the river Chebar, the heavens opened, and I saw divine visions" (Ezekiel 1:1). Conquered by the Babylonians in the sixth century BCE, Israel and its temple were reduced to ashes, and its surviving people enslaved and exiled. Given this shocking experience of displacement, with the Israelites uprooted from their sacred home, it makes sense that God would come to Ezekiel in the form of a chariot. Proving God's willingness to accompany Israel into the depths of exile, the chariot becomes an ambulatory and mobile symbol of God's solidarity with the dispersed and oppressed nation. His vision of the chariot— with its low-rider-like "wheels that sparkle like yellow topaz"—confirms to Ezekiel the abiding presence of God in situations of apparent abandonment.

32. See Cheo Hodari Coker, *Unbelievable: The Life, Death, and Afterlife of the Notorious BIG* (New York: Vibe Books, 2003), 81ff.

33. Ashon, *Chamber Music*, 249.

34. Quoted in Coker, *Unbelievable*, 192, 224.

35. See Joseph Patel, "Jungle Brothers, De La Soul, and A Tribe Called Quest," in *Classic Material: The Hip-Hop Album Guide*, ed. Oliver Wang (Toronto: ECW Press, 2003), 98.

36. Hanif Abdurraqib, *Go Ahead in the Rain: Notes to A Tribe Called Quest* (Austin: University of Texas Press, 2019), 66.

37. And many others in this alternative stream of rap would complement the work of De La Soul and A Tribe Called Quest, adding their voices to this swelling chorus of creative and eccentric vibes: the Hieroglyphics raided all sorts of 1970s soul and jazz, from trumpeter Freddie Hubbard to the rock group Loading Zone; the Fugees, inspired by Wyclef Jean's Haitian origins, turned to reggae, dub, folk, R&B, jazz, and the blues to complement the social and spiritual contents of their bars; Common's *Resurrection*, produced by No I.D., employed soul scores, jazz/rock fusions, and pop instrumentals to accompany Common's mature and righteous allegories; Mos Def and Talib Kweli delivered albums that were manifestoes of freedom, dreams of artistic license, and anthems of liberation; and Organized Konfusion used organic sounds to strike new chords, combining live instruments, bluesy licks, church choirs, and sung melodies with the intent of busting "a rhyme that might enlighten the mind."

38. Hua Hsu, "How George Clinton Made Funk a Worldview," *The New Yorker*, July 9, 2018.

39. I'm borrowing from Nik Cohn here. See his *Awopbopaloobop Alopbamboom: The Golden Age of Rock* (New York: Grove Press, 2001), 115.

40. Cohn, *Awopbopaloobop Alopbamboom*, 31.

41. Adam Bradley, *The Poetry of Pop* (New Haven, CT: Yale University Press, 2017), 16–17.

42. Bradley, *The Poetry of Pop*, 280.

43. And this was true in Miami as well, where Cuban and Caribbean percussion produced a sound known as Miami bass, a fat, low-down, up-tempo kind of rhythm. "Like Caribbean music," Roni Sarig writes, "Miami styles have always been a bit faster, a little sexier, more concerned with the party than the message." See his *Third Coast: OutKast, Timbaland, and How Hip-Hop Became a Southern Thing* (Boston: Da Capo Press, 2007), 11.

44. See Sarig, *Third Coast*, 313.

45. Neil Strauss, "The Pop Life: Rap Is Slower Around Houston," *New York Times*, April 13, 2017.

46. I'm following Ben Westhoff here. See his *Dirty South: OutKast, Lil Wayne, Soulja Boy, and the Southern Rappers Who Reinvented Hip Hop* (Chicago: Chicago Review Press, 2011), 61ff.

47. Though speaking of the blues, Albert Murray's claim about the prominence of

sound over meaning holds true for a lot of Southern rap: "most of their goose pimples," he noted about a rapt blues audience, "and all of their finger snapping and foot tapping are produced by the sound far more often than by the meanings of the words." See Bradley, *The Poetry of Pop*, 189.

48. Sarig, *Third Coast*, 137.

49. As Adam Krims has noted, the chorus resembles gospel music by the homophonic group singing, the closely spaced harmonies, and the unmelismatic melodies. See Adam Krims, *Rap Music and the Poetics of Identity* (Cambridge: Cambridge University Press, 2000), 127.

50. In P-Funk's mythology, for instance, the character Starchild was responsible for bringing the funk to earth. Prince Paul, from the liner notes of *3 Feet High and Rising*, is described as transporting De La Soul from Mars to earth.

51. See Regina Bradley's book on this topic: *Chronicling Stankonia: The Rise of the Hip-Hop South* (Chapel Hill: University of North Carolina Press, 2021), 28ff.

52. Sarig, *Third Coast*, 172.

53. Laymon, *How to Slowly Kill Yourself and Others in America*, 34.

54. David Foster Wallace's book on hip-hop, written in 1989, registers the insular nature of rap at the time. He spends considerable time and energy reflecting on the exclusive universe of rap music, describing it as a genre that is hermetically sealed from white folks, an expression of a secret folk brotherhood from which outsiders are not welcome. See his *Signifying Rappers* (New York: Back Bay Books, 1990), 25ff.

55. "Rap," writes Adam Bradley, "has become less narrative and less complex in its rhyme structures and metaphors than it was in the time of Eric B. and Rakim's 'Paid in Full,' 1987, Lauryn Hill's 'The Miseducation of Lauryn Hill,' 1998, or Jay-Z's 'The Black Album,' 2003." See his "The Artists Dismantling the Barriers Between Poetry and Rap," *New York Times*, March 4, 2021.

56. Jon Caramanica, "Rappers Are Singers Now: Thank Drake," *New York Times*, November 24, 2019.

57. Michael Eric Dyson discusses this aspect of Drake in his *Jay-Z: Made in America* (New York: St. Martin's Press, 2019), 111.

58. McCarthy, *Who Will Pay Reparations On My Soul?*, 117.

Chapter Three

1. Paula Fredriksen, *Paul: The Pagans' Apostle* (New Haven, CT: Yale University Press, 2017), 21.

2. Biblical prose, by contrast, tended to leave the motives, feelings, and inner lives of biblical characters in the dark, not granting us access within. See Tod Linafelt, *The Hebrew Bible as Literature: A Very Short Introduction* (New York: Oxford University

Press, 2016), 10, 74; Robert Alter, *The Art of Biblical Poetry* (New York: Basic Books 1985), 141ff; and the classic study, Erich Auerbach, *Mimesis: The Representation of Reality in Western Literature*, trans. Willard Trask (Princeton, NJ: Princeton University Press, 2003).

3. See Michael Walzer, *In God's Shadow: Politics in the Hebrew Bible* (New Haven, CT: Yale University Press, 2012), 81ff.

4. The term "ghetto," writes Hisham Aidi about affection for the word among European Muslims, "is embraced by French and Dutch Muslims and used often—sharply, proudly, playfully, tenderly—to refer to the European Muslims' geographic segregation; to embarrass politicians (who hate the term); and to claim kinship transnationally with similar situated people in Brazil's favelas or America's inner cities." See his *Rebel Music: Race, Empire, and the New Muslim Youth Culture* (New York: Pantheon Books, 2014), 66.

5. On the East Coast, DMX was another rapper in this countercultural mold. His debut album, *It's Dark and Hell Is Hot* (1998), introduced a new (ragged and snarling) voice to hip-hop. The rapper represented a return to basics in hip-hop, a stripping away of all the glitter and gloss of the shiny-suit era. Almost an ascetic by the ice-drenched standards of the day, he dressed in jeans, worn jackets, and working-class Timberland boots. The video for "Get at Me Dog," for example, was conspicuous for what it lacked: none of the loud ostentation, flashy cars, sparkling jewels, and half-naked women of other hip-hop videos of the day. And most importantly, in my view, he aimed his lyricism at the poorest and most outcast youth of the streets. His constituency was, as he put it on the song "Ima Bang," the struggling poor of the projects and ghettos: "I speak for the meek and the lonely, weak and the hungry . . ." He understood Christianity, in the final analysis, far better than the more respectable members of middle- and upper-class churches.

6. See Hayden Herrera, *Frida: A Biography of Frida Kahlo* (New York: Harper and Row, 1983), 109.

7. Joan Morgan, *She Begat This: 20 Years of* The Miseducation of Lauryn Hill (New York: Simon and Schuster, 2018), 12.

8. Quoted in Chris Nickson, *Lauryn Hill: She's Got That Thing* (New York: St. Martin's, 1999), 154–55.

9. See Craig Werner, *Higher Ground* (New York: Crown Publishers, 2004), 242.

10. What Narada Michael Walden, Aretha Franklin's producer, once said about the Queen of Soul holds true for Lauryn Hill: "In the voice you feel a lot of gospel roots, it's true. But her expression of the church is very streetwise." See Werner, *Higher Ground*, 259.

11. Quoted in Kathy Iandoli, *God Save the Queens: The Essential History of Women in Hip-Hop* (New York: Dey Street Books, 2019), 190.

12. I'm reminded of what Dorothy Day once said about the birth of her daughter:

"No matter how cynically or casually the worldly may treat the birth of a child, it remains spiritually and physically a tremendous event." See John Loughery and Blythe Randolph, *Dorothy Day: Dissenting Voice of the American Century* (New York: Simon and Schuster, 2020), 192.

13. Ann Powers, "Crossing Back over from Profane to Sacred," *New York Times*, August 23, 1998.

14. Quoted in Werner, *Higher Ground*, 265.

15. In this regard, *Miseducation* fits William James's famous definition of religion: the feelings, acts, and experiences of individuals before what they consider the divine. See Robert Richardson, *William James: In the Maelstrom of American Modernism* (New York: Mariner Books, 2006), 391.

16. Quoted in Vincent Cunningham, "Personal Jesus: What Thomas Jefferson Did to the Gospels," *The New Yorker*, January 4, 2021.

17. Quoted in Geoff Dyer, *But Beautiful: A Book About Jazz* (New York: Picador Books, 1996).

18. Hanif Abdurraqib, *They Can't Kill Us Until They Kill Us* (Columbus, OH: Two Dollar Radio, 2017), 13.

19. Mayfield was sampled by too many artists to count, but these are a few: Big Daddy Kane, LL Cool J, Ice T, N.W.A., Beastie Boys, Eminem, Mary J. Blige, R. Kelly, Too Short, the Geto Boys, Digable Planets, Snoop Dogg, Jay-Z, De La Soul, Brand Nubian, Gang Starr, et al. His very last album, in fact, *New World Order* (1996), fused elements of classic soul with hip-hop, and had the production help of Organized Noize (famous for their work with OutKast), Roger Troutman from Zapp, and Daryl Simmons from Run-DMC.

20. See Craig Werner, *A Change Is Gonna Come: Music, Race, and the Soul of America* (Ann Arbor: University of Michigan Press, 2006), 149.

21. I'm drawing here from Jesse McCarthy's discussion of drill. See his *Who Will Pay Reparation on My Soul?* (New York: Liveright Publishing, 2021), 122.

22. Abdurraqib, *They Can't Kill Us Until They Kill Us*, 15.

23. By way of comparison, Slick Rick comes to mind, especially his famous "Children's Story" (1988), a rap that tells a tragic story in a comedic style. Part jester, part bard, part urban trickster, Slick Rick narrated the dangers and temptations faced by children in the inner city in unexpected pitches and registers, frequently flippant and cartoonish. The theme of the song, stolen innocence, is surely as serious and disastrous as what you might hear in N.W.A. or Tupac, but Slick Rick's storytelling style is much more silly and ironic, striking a dramatic contrast between the innocence of childhood and deadly ghetto realities. These kids, Rick's tale suggests, were never given the chance to be a child.

24. Jill Leovy, *Ghettoside: A True Story of Murder in America* (New York: Spiegel and Grau, 2015).

25. Quoted in Werner, *Higher Ground*, 161. Curtis Mayfield's character in the song has been told all his life that he will amount to nothing: "Been told I can't be nothin' else/ Just a hustler in spite of myself/ I know I can break it/ This life just don't make it/ Lord, Lord, yeah." In this sense, as he comments earlier in the song, he's a "victim of ghetto demands," and only wants to survive the squalor of urban life; he only wants to *be*. Quoted in Werner, *Higher Ground*, 142.

26. Bessie Smith, "Empty Bed Blues" (Naxos Records, 1928).

27. Quoted in Werner, *Higher Ground*, 130.

28. For examples of syntactic inversion in the Hebrew Bible (where the plain and pedestrian word order is inverted to emphasize certain themes), see Robert Alter, *The Art of Biblical Translation* (Princeton, NJ: Princeton University Press, 2019), 32ff.

29. His discography, in this regard, not only samples the Muses of poetry, song, and dance; it also has something of Athena's touch in it: sweet, magnetic, and beguiling, a siren-like voice that esteems persuasion over brute violence, similar to the prayer of Aeschylus in the *Eumenides*: "Let not the dry dust that drinks the black blood of citizens through passion for revenge and bloodshed for bloodshed be given our state to prey upon." Or else, after subjecting the pagan worldview to a Christian and democratic transvaluation, it is similar to Euripides's homage to Dionysus:

The deity, the son of Zeus
in feast, in festival, delights.
He loves the goddess Peace
generous of good,
preserver of the young. . . .
whose simple wisdom shuns the thoughts
of proud, uncommon men and all
their god-encroaching dreams.
But what the common people do,
the things that simple men believe,
I too believe and do. (*The Bacchae*, 416–32)

30. Quoted in Werner, *Higher Ground*, 174.

31. Quoted in Karen Armstrong, *The Lost Art of Scripture* (London: Bodley Books, 2019), 406.

32. William James famously distinguished between a momentous and trivial religious belief, the former existing when the stakes are high, and the latter when there is nothing to lose by not acting. The distinction illuminates, in my view, the difference between Jay Elec and Jay-Z.

33. What's particularly incredible on "The Neverending Story," almost not to be believed, is Jay-Z's battle over religion with his grandmother and mother-in-law, Ms.

Tina Knowles-Lawson. He dismisses their understanding of Christianity, suggesting that they revere a white Jesus. I can't speak for the religious convictions of his grandmother and mother-in-law (do they really believe in a white God, as he suggests, or is it simply because they are committed Christians?), but I recoil at the titanic ego of Saint Hov—he canonizes himself in the song—and have to wonder if they're possibly closer to the truth than he allows. The battle here is revealing of Jay-Z's beliefs: instead of commitment to any one spiritual tradition, seeing such ties as a ball and chain, Jay-Z apparently wants to play the field à la Don Juan, remaining free from the heavy burdens and yokes that bind a devotee to one specific tradition.

34. There was a peculiar Christian preacher in 1927 who took this mythos in a new direction, now fusing the black spirituals with science fiction—the Rev. A. W. Nix of Alabama. One of his sermons, "The White Flyer to Heaven," rhapsodized about a heavenly spaceship piloted by Jesus that would transport his people to the pearly gates, "rising higher and higher. We'll pass on the Second Heaven, the starry big Heaven, and view the flying stars and dashing meteors and then pass on by Mars and Mercury, and Jupiter and Venus and Saturn. . . ." Jonah Weiner dubs these astrophysical imaginings, and subsequent iterations, the Afronaut tradition. Quoted in Jonah Weiner, "Lil Wayne and the Afronaut Invasion," *Slate Magazine*, June 20, 2008.

35. Loren Kajikawa, *Sounding Race in Rap Songs* (Berkeley: University of California Press, 2015), 111.

36. Werner, *Higher Ground*, 7.

37. David Banner's "Cadillacs on 22s," for instance, begins with the strumming of an acoustic guitar and gentle, mournful humming. As the drum and bass lines kick in, the deeply soulful refrain expounds on the plot: "I ain't did nothing in my life but stay true/ pimp my voice and mack these beats, and pray to the Lord for these Mississippi streets." The song, it turns out, has little to do with 'Lacs on 22s; instead, it is a meditation on suffering and the meaning of faith, with the rapper invoking the spirit of Job or Qoheleth: "Sometimes I wish I wasn't born in the first place." Sick of "bouncing" (hustling, pimping, partying), he finds no ultimate satisfaction in the debauched pleasures of his life. On the verge of despondency, the narrator nonetheless discerns traces and footsteps of God in his life: "I don't know if I can take this world right here no more/ 22 inch rims on the 'Lac/ I guess that was your footprint in the sand carrying us on your back." Recall, too, the titles of David Banner's major albums: *Mississippi: The Album* (2003) and *MTA2: Baptized in Dirty Water* (2003). His albums are immediately identifiable as Southern, born in the haunted landscapes of Medgar Evers, the birthplace of Jim Crow, and the place where, he remarks, "my soul still don't feel free." His follow-up album, *MTA2*, continues in this vein, but harps even more on the existential battle being waged for his soul. In "Eternal" and "My Lord," the rapper sketches himself as a divided and conflicted soul, torn between the devil's lures and the desire to please God. Like any number of blues artists in the lineage of Peetie Wheatstraw ("the

devil's son-in-law," "the high sheriff from hell"), he indulges in the devil's music—and the attendant bumping and grinding on the dance floor, the shuffling, bouncing, and jumping in the club and, of course, the pleasures of sex—but he is simultaneously wracked by guilt and unease. Writes Roni Sarig: "David Banner inferred—perhaps subconsciously—a spiritual connection between the pent-up aggression and latent pain of crunk music and the cathartic Mississippi blues." Roni Sarig, *Third Coast: OutKast, Timbaland, and How Hip-Hop Became a Southern Thing* (Boston: Da Capo, 2007), 225.

38. Quoted in Felicia Angelica Viator, *To Live and Defy in LA: How Gangster Rap Changed America* (Cambridge, MA: Harvard University Press, 2020), 231.

39. Quoted in Viator, *To Live and Defy in LA*, 259–60.

40. Marcus Reeves, *Somebody Scream: Rap Music's Rise to Prominence in the Aftershock of Black Power* (New York: Faber and Faber, 2008), 174.

41. See Ben Westhoff, *Original Gangstas* (New York: Hachette Books, 2016), 347.

42. See Westhoff, *Original Gangstas*, 325.

43. See Robert Richardson, *William James: In the Maelstrom of American Modernism* (New York: Mariner Books, 2006), 398ff.

44. Hanif Abdurraqib, *A Little Devil in America* (New York: Random House, 2021), 133.

45. Some of his poems, written between eighteen and twenty years of age, bear this out as well. "When I was alone and had nothing/ I asked 4 a friend 2 help me bear the/ pain no one came except . . . God." See Tupac Shakur, *The Rose That Grew from Concrete* (New York: Pocket Books, 1999), 33.

46. See Michael Eric Dyson, *Holler If You Hear Me: Searching for Tupac Shakur* (New York: Basic Civitas Books, 2001), 209; David Tracy, *Filaments: Theological Profiles* (Chicago: University of Chicago Press, 2020), 140.

47. Quoted in Henry Louis Gates Jr., *The Black Church: This Is Our Story, This Is Our Song* (New York: Penguin Books, 2021), 36.

48. Tupac shared traits with the notion of liberation in Black Theology, but he was finally too cynical and pessimistic about the utopian elements of liberation theologies to fully give himself to social and political struggles. "To be free is to be black—that is, identified with the victims of humiliation in human society and a participant in the liberation of oppressed humanity," writes James Cone. Tupac's work epitomizes the first part of Cone's sentiment, but balks over the second. See his *A Black Theology of Liberation* (New York: Orbis Books, 1990), 101–2. Tupac's thoughts also stretch back to an even older tradition, represented by the AME bishop Henry McNeal Turner. In 1895, Turner argued that since human beings are made in the image and likeness of God, "God is a Negro." Quoted in Gates, *The Black Church*, 97.

49. See the discussion of "Christian Existentialism" in *Modern Christian Thought: The 20th Century*, ed. James Livingston and Francis Schussler Fiorenza (Minneapolis: Fortress Press, 2000), 135.

50. Jack Kerouac, *On The Road* (New York: Penguin Books, 2008).

Chapter Four

1. These lines come from two interviews of Kendrick Lamar: Zane Lowe in *Beats 1*, April 20, 2017; and Joe Coscarelli, *New York Times*, March 16, 2015.

2. Hanif Abdurraqib, *They Can't Kill Us Until They Kill Us* (New York: Two Dollar Radio, 2017), 151.

3. Giovanni Russonello, "Jazz Has Always Been Protest Music. Can It Meet this Moment?," *New York Times*, September 3, 2020.

4. Years earlier, Big Daddy Kane made a similar observation: "So many brothers and sisters are out here listening to rap music," he wrote. "And for those who won't listen to a Farrakhan speech, or won't play a Malcolm X tape, or don't attend any type of Islamic school. . . . they can learn through rappers like myself, KRS-One, Public Enemy, and Rakim." Quoted in Felicia Miyakawa, *Five Percenter Rap: God Hop's Music, Message, and Black Muslim Mission* (Bloomington: Indiana University Press, 2005).

5. See Christina Zanfagna, *Holy Hip Hop in the City of Angels* (Berkeley: University of California Press, 2017).

6. Nelson George describes Compton in these terms: "It felt segregated and forgotten, a self-contained enclave where the imaginations of MCs and the simmering anger of the streets had combined in an unexpected way to turn its limitations into a rebellious, national myth." See Nelson George, *City Kid: A Writer's Memoir of Ghetto Life and Post-Soul Success* (New York: Plume Books, 2009), 225.

7. I'm not saying this religious development struck like lightning, all at once. From 2009 or so, it seems to have been developing and picking up energy in his life. By the time of his studio albums, the question of God was becoming more pronounced. Just before he made the album *DAMN.*, for instance, he complained to the *New York Times Magazine* that God is neglected in our age: "We're in a time where we exclude one major component out of this whole thing called life: God." Quoted in Marcus Moore, *The Butterfly Effect: How Kendrick Lamar Ignited the Soul of Black America* (New York: Atria Books, 2020), 238.

8. See Moore, *The Butterfly Effect*, 116.

9. Jayson Greene, "Good Kid, M.A.A.D City," *Pitchfork*, October 23, 2012.

10. See Michael Eric Dyson, *Holler if You Hear Me: Searching for Tupac Shakur* (New York: Basic Civitas Books, 2001), 265.

11. Quoted in Moore, *The Butterfly Effect*, 114.

12. The song picks up strands not only from Tupac's "Brenda's Got a Baby" and "Keep Ya Head Up" (a song dedicated to Latasha Harlins, a fifteen-year-old killed by a store owner in South Central), but also his own rap on *Section.80*, "Keisha's Song." (Keisha's sister, also a prostitute, is the protagonist of "Sing About Me.")

13. *Classic Material: The Hip Hop Album Guide*, ed. Oliver Wang (Toronto: ECW Press, 2003), 72.

14. See Hua Hsu, "Kendrick Lamar's Holy Spirit," *The New Yorker*, May 1, 2017.

15. See, "Kendrick Lamar Explains 'To Pimp a Butterfly' Album Artwork," YouTube, April 28, 2015.

16. Interview by Joe Coscarelli, "Kendrick Lamar's *To Pimp a Butterfly*," *New York Times*, March 16, 2015.

17. Quoted in David Biale, *Gershom Scholem: Master of the Kabbalah* (New Haven, CT: Yale University Press, 2018), 14.

18. See Moore, *The Butterfly Effect*, 182.

19. Though his vision here resonates with Plato's *Phraedrus* or *Symposium*—where love enables the wings of the soul to sprout and ascend into the heavens—Lamar's butterfly-like soul is constrained not by the human body per se, as in Socrates and Plato, but by the pressures and exigencies of the ghetto. The ghetto is a prison from which he's trying to escape.

20. Quoted in Karen Armstrong, *The Lost Art of Scripture: Rescuing the Sacred Texts* (London: Bodley Head, 2019), 5.

21. Alexis Petridis picks up on the Chi-Lites on "Blood" and Curtis Mayfield on "Pride." See Alexis Petridis, "Kendrick Lamar, *DAMN*," *The Guardian*, April 14, 2017.

22. See Hsu, "Kendrick Lamar's Holy Spirit."

23. Greg Tate, *The Village Voice*, April 25, 2017.

24. In lieu of addressing these legacies of segregation and racism, Geraldo Rivera of Fox News has redirected blame onto black music. Hip-hop, he remarked in a discussion of Kendrick Lamar's "Alright," has done "more damage to young African Americans than the histories of racism." In response to such (idiotic) accusations, Lamar's song here—and elsewhere on "DNA."—flips the focus back onto the sins and failures of Uncle Sam.

25. "The judgement of God," Dr. King wrote, "is upon the church as never before." Quoted in Peniel Joseph, *The Sword and the Shield* (New York: Basic Books, 2020), 136.

26. See *The Jean-Michel Basquiat Reader*, ed. Jordana Moore Saggese (Oakland: University of California Press, 2021), 251ff.

27. Quoted in Eddie Glaude, *African American Religion: A Very Short Introduction* (Oxford: Oxford University Press, 2014), 72.

28. He makes this point clear in an interview with Brian Hiatt in *Rolling Stone*, August 9, 2017. "Everything that I say on that record is from his perspective," Lamar remarks. "That's always been my thing. Always listen to people's history and their background. It may not be like mine, it may not be like yours. It was taking his perspective on the world and life as a people and putting it to where people can listen to it and make their own perspective from it, whether you agree or you don't agree."

29. Jesse McCarthy, *Who Will Pay Reparations on My Soul?* (New York: Liveright Publishing, 2021), 152.

30. On the song "Pray for Me," from the *Black Panther* album, for instance, he specifically speaks of fighting himself and fighting God.

31. Bernard Knox, *The Heroic Temper: Studies in Sophoclean Tragedy* (Berkeley: University of California Press, 1983), 131.

32. Hans Urs von Balthasar, *The Glory of the Lord: A Theological Aesthetics*, vol. 3 (San Francisco: Ignatius Press, 2004), 110. Von Balthasar explains the text thus: "This experience clarifies for John the meaning of the Old Testament, and he quotes in long passages from Job, Jeremiah, and Jonah, whose lot it was to experience the wrath of God, total abandonment by God. . . . The soul feels terrible annihilation in its very substance. She feels a withdrawal, deprivation, emptiness and poverty regarding God's blessings." See von Balthasar, *The Glory of the Lord*, vol. 3, 110.

33. "Here is the real core of the religious problem," wrote William James, "Help! Help!" See Robert Richardson, *William James: In the Maelstrom of American Modernism* (New York: Mariner Books, 2006), 399.

34. "The meaning of the words," writes Karen Armstrong about a mantra, "is not important because the mantra is symbolic and points to something other than itself." See Armstrong, *The Lost Art of Scripture*, 59.

35. Amanda Petrusich, *Do Not Sell at Any Price* (New York: Scribner Books, 2014), 16.

36. Ted Gioia, *How to Listen to Jazz* (New York: Basic Books, 2016), x.

37. Gioia, *How to Listen to Jazz*, 2.

38. While nothing really worthy of God can be said about him, says Augustine, God desires our praise. See *Confessions*, 1.6.6.

39. Quoted in David Tracy, *Filaments: Theological Profiles* (Chicago: University of Chicago Press, 2020), 89.

40. The redemptive atmosphere sets the work apart from classic 1990s New York hip-hop, say, from Mobb Deep's *The Infamous* (1995) or *Hell on Earth* (1996). When contemplating the more distressed and nihilistic moments of *DAMN.*—when the music is a seismograph of the psyche's tremors and tensions—my mind immediately turned to the hard-core rap of the East Coast. Lamar's music shares with Mobb Deep, Wu-Tang, Big Pun, and Nas many of the sounds and tribulations of the toughest blocks in America, but Lamar also belongs to a post-Biggie, post-Drake age where R&B ingredients and melodic crooning are acceptable forms of street-centric hip-hop. This wasn't always the case. Mobb Deep, for example, may have used rich, resonant soul samples, and beautiful—if sinister—pianos and synths, but the verses were bare-boned and unvarnished, devoid of melody. Because the New York streets were wanting in melody, and wanting in mercy and tenderness, the rapping renounced any poetics that rang untrue to these circumstances. They aimed for realism instead, a style of sound and sentiment that gave the impression, writes Hanif Abdurraqib, that they were "playing

over a graveyard on a cloud-filled day while tree branches trembled under the weight of a hundred black birds. . . . The Queens they wrote about was one that was a place merely to survive at all costs. Their music was laced with a type of fear and paranoia that bled through the sonic landscape: an avalanche of drums from each direction; a sharp synth slicing through like a knife; piano loops and distorted bass lines that sounded like they could have been pulled out of a horror film." See Abdurraqib, *They Can't Kill Us Until They Kill Us*, 88.

41. In contrast to the ethereal grace of the angel, or the intellectual stimulus of the muse, Lorca describes the *duende* as more carnal and voluptuous, an experience that ravishes the body and wounds the soul, a wisdom achieved through suffering like Isaiah's encounter with the hidden God, John of the Cross's dark nights of the soul, or Kendrick Lamar's quarrel with damnation. I explored the figure of *duende* in my study *In Search of Soul: Hip Hop, Literature and Religion* (Berkeley: University of California Press, 2017).

42. When he first heard the beats, Lamar remarked in an interview, all he could think about was Marley Marl and the early moments of hip-hop. See the interview by Brian Hiatt, *Rolling Stone*, August 9, 2017.

43. The same thing can be said about the song "i" on *To Pimp a Butterfly*. If taken alone, this song might sound sentimental and self-absorbed (hook: "I love myself"), but in the context of *TPAB* it provides badly needed joy and hope, a moment of self-affirmation in an album of relentless self-criticism.

44. See interview by Jason Parham, *Fader*, April 18, 2017.

45. Since the theme concerns the question of loyalty, Lamar's rap calls to mind the song "Loyal" by Chris Brown, featuring Lil Wayne. In Chris Brown's version, women are portrayed as Medusa-like sorcerers, their heads teeming with deadly charms and poisonous beauty. "These hoes ain't loyal," Brown sings. Needless to say, the song simply remixes the old grievance of rappers concerning "tricks" and "hoes," a motif that goes back to the age of Hesiod if not earlier. Vis-à-vis these tropes, Lamar's consideration of loyalty is drastically different: to whom, or to what, are we loyal, that is the question here. Since Chris Brown's song has been read as a dis of Rihanna (his former girlfriend), it's fitting that Kendrick Lamar invites Rihanna to sing and rap on his song. With the two of them together—Rihanna's badass confidence, syncing with Lamar's philosophical musings—the notion of loyalty is pulled apart and dissected with a keen knife.

46. Paul Tillich, *The Dynamics of Faith* (New York: HarperCollins, 2001), 3.

47. Hanif Abdurraqib, "In Defense of 'Trap Queen' as Our Generation's Greatest Love Song," in *Seven Scribes*, June 5, 2015.

48. I'm paraphrasing Hans Urs von Balthasar here, speaking about John of the Cross's dark night: "The ship lands when it is wrecked, you leap on to firm ground when all the rungs of your ladder break." In giving theological and poetic form to the

dark night of the soul, Balthasar argues that John of the Cross complicates and even rejects the traditional notion of mystical ascent. See von Balthasar, *The Glory of the Lord*, vol. 3, 116.

49. Hsu, "Kendrick Lamar's Holy Spirit."

50. See Clifford Geertz, *The Interpretation of Cultures* (New York: Basic Books, 1973), 412–53. Commenting on Geertz's approach to religion, Robert Orsi describes the role of religion in America in this way: "Religions have provided Americans in the turbulent and distressing circumstances of life in this society over time with a repertoire of feelings and orientations with which to take hold of their world as it takes hold of them." See Robert Orsi, *Between Heaven and Earth* (Princeton, NJ: Princeton University Press, 2005), 169.

51. See Martha Nussbaum, *The Therapy of Desire: Theory and Practice in Hellenistic Ethics* (Princeton, NJ: Princeton University Press, 2013).

52. Quoted in Moore, *The Butterfly Effect*, 240.

Chapter Five

1. Nik Cohn, *Awopbopaloobop Alopbamboom: The Golden Age of Rock* (New York: Grove Press, 2001), 32.

2. Quoted in Jon Pareles, "Spicy Mix of Salsa, Hip-Hop, and Reggae," *New York Times*, August 7, 2003.

3. Hanif Abdurraqib, *A Little Devil in America* (New York: Random House, 2021), 13.

4. Jon Caramanica, "Cardi B Is a New Rap Celebrity Loyal to Rap's Old Rule on 'Invasion of Privacy,'" *New York Times*, April 10, 2018.

5. Pete Rodriguez's "I Like It Like That" was a perfect sample for a Cardi B rap: he was a fellow Bronx native, and famous for forging alliances in the 1960s between Latin and African American musical soundscapes, between timbales and trap drums, Latin percussion and R&B pianos, *gritos* and handclaps, Spanish and English lyrics, and so on. Her song continues, now in a hip-hop idiom, the long legacy of jam sessions, improvisations, and collaborations between African and Latin heritages in the Americas.

6. Ned Sublette, *Cuba and Its Music: From the First Drums to the Mambo* (Chicago: Chicago Review Press, 2004), 3.

7. Sublette, *Cuba and Its Music*, 8.

8. Allen Josephs, *The White Wall of Spain: The Mysteries of Andalusian Culture* (Pensacola: University of West Florida Press, 1990), 70.

9. See Josephs, *The White Wall of Spain*, 68–75.

10. In pre-Roman times, Cádiz traded with a wide variety of peoples: Carthaginians, Africans, Syrians, Israelites, Celts, and others (1 Kings 10:22 reports that King Solomon made an alliance with Hiram, king of Tyre). Following the Roman coloni-

zation of Andalusia (they captured it from Carthage in 206 BCE), Greek and Roman elements—and eventually Visigothic and Muslim cultures—were also thrown into the wild mix of Andalusian culture.

11. Sublette, *Cuba and Its Music*, 78.

12. Sublette, *Cuba and Its Music*, 79.

13. "The musical power of the disenfranchised," Susan McClary writes, "more often resides in their ability to articulate different ways of construing the body, ways that bring along in their wake the potential for different experiential worlds. And the anxious reactions that so often greet new music from such groups indicate that something crucially political is at issue." Quoted in Geoffrey Baker, *Buena Vista in the Club: Rap, Reggaeton, and Revolution in Havana* (Durham, NC: Duke University Press, 2011), 114.

14. "In reality, dance and movement are indispensable to the understanding of hip-hop culture, since physical movement underlies virtually every element of its expression." See Joseph Schloss, *Foundation: B-Boys and B-Girls and Hip-Hop Culture* (Oxford: Oxford University Press, 2009), 9.

15. I've discussed the notion of the soul in Judaism and Christianity in a previous book, *In Search of Soul: Hip-Hop, Literature and Religion* (Berkeley: University of California Press, 2017), 86ff.

16. Adam Bradley, *The Book of Rhymes: The Poetics of Hip-Hop* (New York: Basic Civitas Books, 2009), 39.

17. RZA, *The Tao of Wu* (New York: Riverhead Books, 2009), 60.

18. Tracy points, in particular, to the remarkable male nudes of the Sistine Chapel, the Ignudi. Some popes have defended them as representations of the beauty and dignity of human nature (Pope John Paul II [1978-2005] described them as representing the "theology of the human body"), others criticized their presence in the Chapel as a "stew of nudes" (Adrian VI, 1522-1523), more fitting for a tavern or brothel (Paul IV, 1555-1559); whatever the case, Michelangelo was making a philosophical and theological point: "Michelangelo's critics," writes Tracy again, "failed to appreciate that the nude was an important aspect of his artistic and theological convictions. Even today, the ability to sculpt or paint the female or male nude body is one of the central ways for an artist to depict the movements, the tensions, the twisted rhythms, and thereby the emotions of a distinct human figure." See David Tracy, "Michelangelo and the Catholic Analogical Imagination," in *Filaments: Theological Profiles* (Chicago: University of Chicago Press, 2020), 167–84.

19. Maria Cataldi Gallo, "Sacred Vestments: Color and Form," in *Heavenly Bodies: Fashion and the Catholic Imagination*, ed. Andrew Bolton (New York: Metropolitan Museum of Art, 2018), 16.

20. Gallo, "Sacred Vestments: Color and Form," 17.

21. See "Dance and Religion," in *The Encyclopedia of Religion*, vol. 4, ed. Mircea Eliade (New York: Collier Macmillan, 1987), 203-12.

22. Clement of Alexandria, for example, shared the view of the Talmud that dance is the principal function of the angels, their spins and pirouettes expressing their longing for heaven.

23. Sublette, *Cuba and Its Music*, 235.

24. Alma Guillermoprieto explains the lack of mirrors as both an issue of funding, and an effect of a more general suspicion of the arts in general. Though tolerated and tacitly supported, the Escuela Nacionales de Arte was seen as promoting sensuality and alluding to ideas of cubanidad and Africanness that were unacceptable to the Revolution. See Guillermoprieto, *Dancing with Cuba*, trans. Esther Allen (New York: Vintage Books, 2004), 270.

25. See Guillermoprieto, *Dancing with Cuba*, 59–60.

26. See Guillermoprieto, *Dancing with Cuba*, 57.

27. Gnostic traditions may have incorporated dance into their liturgies, as suggested by the "Round Dance of the Cross" in the Acts of John. The text includes the following lines: "To the universe belongs the dancer. Whoever does not dance does not know what happens."

28. In one of the first articles about the budding genre of hip-hop—from the *Village Voice*—Bones called graffiti, rapping, and b-boying forms of "ghetto street culture," and "flamboyant triumphs of virility, wit, and skill. In short, of style." See Jeff Chang, *Can't Stop, Won't Stop: A History of the Hip-Hop Generation* (New York: St. Martin's Press, 2005), 157.

29. Chang, *Can't Stop, Won't Stop*, 111.

30. Schloss, *Foundation*, 18.

31. Will Ashon, *Chamber Music: Wu-Tang and America (In 36 Pieces)* (New York: Faber and Faber, 2019), 18.

32. Schloss, *Foundation*, 12.

33. I discussed this element of Cuban hip-hop in my book *In Search of Soul*, 227.

34. Chang, *Can't Stop, Won't Stop*, 118.

35. For a classic study of the vocoder's influence on pop music, including hip-hop, see Dave Tompkins, *How To Wreck a Nice Beach: The Vocoder from World War II to Hip-Hop, The Machine Speaks* (New York: Stop Smiling Books, 2011), 238.

36. RZA, *The Wu-Tang Manual* (New York: Penguin Books, 2005), 52.

37. RZA, *The Wu-Tang Manual*, 63.

38. See Tompkins, *How To Wreck a Nice Beach*, 211.

39. Chang, *Can't Stop, Won't Stop*, 172.

40. Wayne Marshall, "From Música Negra to Reggaeton Latino: The Cultural Politics of Nation, Migration, and Commercialization," in *Reggaeton*, ed. Raquel Rivera, Wayne Marshall, and Deborah Pacini Hernandez (Durham, NC: Duke University Press, 2009), 63.

41. See Jon Pareles, "A Caribbean Party with a Hip-Hop Beat," *New York Times*, August 12, 2003; "Spicy Mix of Salsa, Hip-Hop, and Reggae," *New York Times*, August 7, 2003.

42. Wayne Marshall, "From Música Negra to Reggaeton Latino," 25.

43. See Raquel Rivera, "Policing Morality, *Mano Dura Stylee*: The Case of Underground Rap and Reggae in Puerto Rico in the Mid-1990s," in *Reggaeton*, ed. Raquel Rivera, Wayne Marshall, and Deborah Pacini Hernandez (Durham, NC: Duke University Press, 2009), 124.

44. Geoffrey Baker, *Buena Vista in the Club: Rap, Reggaeton, and Revolution in Havana* (Durham, NC: Duke University Press, 2011), 163. Robin Moore has a similar take on the rise of timba in Cuba: "Timba represents movement away from dogmatism and toward 'fun' in a number of senses. As dance repertoire, it represents liberation of the body. . . . Its focus on sexuality, its unabashed embrace of material pleasure, and its avoidance of socialist 'political correctness' constitute a good-natured yet forceful challenge to established values." See Robin Moore, *Music and Revolution: Cultural Change in Socialist Cuba* (Berkeley: University of California Press, 2006), 134.

45. Ned Sublette, *Cuba and Its Music* (Chicago: Chicago Review Press, 2007), 271.

46. Isabelia Herrera, Review of Ivy Queen's, *Diva*, Pitchfork, September 6, 2020.

47. Kiese Laymon, *How To Slowly Kill Yourself and Others in America* (New York: Scribner Books, 2020), 106.

48. "Reggaeton's social moorings among the urban poor," writes Raquel Rivera, "raised uncomfortable problems of class and social inequality virtually absent in other forms of popular music and typically ignored by the cultural elites in Puerto Rico." Quoted in Petra Rivera-Rideau, *Remixing Reggaeton: The Cultural Politics of Race in Puerto Rico* (Durham, NC: Duke University Press, 2015), 28.

49. See Rivera-Rideau, *Remixing Reggaeton*, 17.

50. As the years passed, such sentiments only grew stronger in Vico C's catalog, eventually leading to albums in the area of Christian rap. The career of Héctor "El Father" is a close parallel, too. After finding success in reggaeton by promoting a hardened, ruthless, and nihilistic gangster image, Héctor began to increasingly feel uneasy and troubled by the life he was leading. He felt empty and depressed, and contemplated suicide on numerous occasions. In consequence, he embraced Christianity and became a pastor.

51. Wayne Marshall makes this observations about Daddy Yankee's "Gasolina." See his "From Música Negra to Reggaeton Latino," in *Reggaeton*, ed. Raquel Rivera, Wayne Marshall, and Deborah Pacini Hernandez (Durham, NC: Duke University Press, 2009).

52. See his interview with Leile Cobo, "Reggaeton Star Calderon Goes Back to the Streets," Reuters, February 15, 2008.

53. Sara Corbett, "The King of Reggaeton," *New York Times Magazine*, February 5, 2006.

54. Corbett, "The King of Reggaeton."

55. Quoted in the liner notes for Eddie Palmieri, *Vamonos Pa'l Monte* (Fania/Tico Records, 1971).

56. Paul Edwards, *The Concise Guide to Hip Hop Music* (New York: St. Martin's Griffin, 2015), 31.

57. Bachata was made in this same image: it's known for its irreverence and carnival spirit, its delight in pleasure and dance rhythms. At the same time, Juan Luis Guerra, the "king of bachata," gave it a spiritual and socially conscious flavor. He was deeply Christian and committed to incorporating the sounds and folklore of San Pedro de Macorís—like the triangle and snare drums of the gulolla traditions of the Tortola Islands—into merengue. See Leonardo Padura Fuentes, *Faces of Salsa: A Spoken History of the Music*, trans. Stephen J. Clark (Washington, DC: Smithsonian Books, 2003), 143.

58. See Jessi Roti, "Bad Bunny Anoints Allstate Arena to His 'Nueva Religion' during 'X100Pre Tour' Stop," *Chicago Tribune*, March 25, 2019.

59. Press release for Bad Bunny and J Balvin, *Oasis*, Universal Latin, 2009.

60. Suzy Exposito, "Bad Bunny in Captivity," *Rolling Stone*, May 14, 2020.

61. Paul Lester, writing for *The Guardian*, used the term "original angstas" for these rappers. See his "Original Angstas: Why the Stars of Sad Rap Aren't Afraid to Cry," *The Guardian*, March 5, 2015.

62. In the year that he was assassinated, he delivered a sermon on this topic, "Remaining Awake through a Great Revolution." See Peniel Joseph, *The Sword and the Shield: The Revolutionary Lives of Malcolm X and Martin Luther King, Jr.* (New York: Basic Books, 2020), 299.

Chapter Six

1. Octavio Paz, *The Labyrinth of Solitude* (New York: Grove Press, 1961), 13.

2. Gerard Manley Hopkins, "Pied Beauty."

3. This even holds true for Kendrick Lamar, my favorite rapper. As I see it, *To Pimp a Butterfly* (2015) would have been so much more "real" if he had recognized that butterflies are also symbols of migration. It might have opened his eyes to the migrants in his midst. This short-sightedness is also apparent in the Game, Roddy Ricch, Buddy, MC Eiht, and Vince Staples. The exception has been YG. He has offered a more complete picture of Compton in a lot of his music, and has collaborated with various Latin@ artists.

4. Josh Kun, *Audiotopia: Music, Race, and America* (Berkeley: University of California Press, 2005), 220.

5. To name a few: David Toop, *Rap Attack 2: African Rap to Global Hip Hop* (London:

Serpent's Tail, 1991); Jeff Chang, *Can't Stop Won't Stop: A History of the Hip Hop Generation* (New York: St. Martin's Press, 2005); Nelson George, *Hip Hop America* (New York: Penguin Books, 2005); Tricia Rose, *Black Noise: Rap Music and Black Culture in Contemporary America* (Middletown, CT: Wesleyan University Press, 1994); Cheryl Keyes, *Rap Music and Street Consciousness* (Chicago: University of Illinois Press, 2004); S. H. Fernando, *The New Beats: Exploring the Music, Culture, and Attitudes of Hip-Hop* (New York: Doubleday, 1994); Todd Boyd, *The New H.N.I.C.: The Death of Civil Rights and the Reign of Hip Hop* (New York: New York University Press, 2003); *Droppin' Science: Critical Essays on Rap Music and Hip Hop Culture*, ed. William Eric Perkins (Philadelphia: Temple University Press, 1996); *The Anthology of Rap*, ed. Adam Bradley and Andrew DuBois (New Haven, CT: Yale University Press, 2010); Sohail Daulatzai, *Black Star, Crescent Moon* (Minneapolis: University of Minnesota Press, 2012); Juan Flores, *From Bomba to Hip Hop: Puerto Rican Culture and Latino Identity* (New York: Columbia University Press, 2000); and Raquel Rivera, *New York Ricans from the Hip Hop Zone* (New York: Palgrave Macmillan, 2003).

6. The same street and park settings where the deejays summoned the crowds, moreover, were often dominated by the loud echoing booms and rackets of street drumming, a widespread practice among New York Puerto Ricans and Cubans since the 1940s or so. It's hard to imagine that such a charged percussive atmosphere wouldn't have influenced the aesthetical choices of rap's pioneering deejays. For a discussion of the history of mambo, see Ed Morales, *The Latin Beat: The Rhythms and Roots of Latin Music from Bossa Nova to Salsa and Beyond* (New York: Da Capo Press, 2003), 34ff. For a discussion of breaks in hip-hop, see Joseph Schloss, *Foundation: B-Boys, B-Girls, and Hip Hop in New York* (New York: Oxford University Press, 2009), 19. Also see Marisol Berríos-Miranda, Shannon Dudley, and Michelle Habell-Pallán, *American Sabor: Latinos and Latinas in U.S. Popular Music* (Seattle: University of Washington Press, 2018), 279, for a discussion of the street drumming traditions in New York and San Francisco.

7. This song, "South Bronx Subway Rap," appeared on the soundtrack for *Wild Style* (Animal Records, 1983).

8. See Leonardo Padura Fuentes, *Faces of Salsa: A Spoken History of the Music* trans. Stephen J. Clark (Washington, DC: Smithsonian Books, 2003), 26.

9. Quoted in Frances Aparicio, *Listening to Salsa: Gender, Latin Popular Music, and Puerto Rican Cultures* (Hanover, NH: Wesleyan University Press, 1998), 81.

10. "Salsa emerges as something of our own, which is why it's full of politics and stories from the street. It's a music of the city, and its melodies are essentially urban.... That's the story of salsa: a harmonic blend of all the Latin music of New York." Quoted in Fuentes, *Faces of Salsa*, 29–30. Tales of outlaws and bandits are evident in songs like "Juan Pachanga," "Pedro Navaja," "Juan Gonzalez," "Cipriano Armenteros," and "Pablo Pueblo."

11. Quoted in Berríos-Miranda et al., *American Sabor*, 177.

12. "The Latin American cadence is hard to ignore," writes Josh Kun about the history of Los Angeles, "among the city's most consistent beats, its most influential set of melodies and rhythms, are those that have arrived after traveling through a century or two of cultural contact and musical creativity in the Americas and across the African Diaspora." See his "Introduction," in *The Tide Was Always High: The Music of Latin America in Los Angeles*, ed. Josh Kun (Berkeley: University of California Press, 2017), 7.

13. Lalo Guerrero's polkas with caló lyrics came before Don Tosti's "Pachuco Boogie," but the latter enjoyed greater success and visibility. See Anthony Macias, *Mexican American Mojo* (Durham, NC: Duke University Press, 2008), 124.

14. As a classic in Chicano studies, see Luis Valdez's play *Zoot Suit and Other Plays* (Houston: Arte Publico Press, 1992) about these events.

15. See Anthony Macias, *Mexican American Mojo* (Durham, NC: Duke University Press, 2008), 63.

16. See Kathy Peiss, *Zoot Suit: The Enigmatic Career of an Extreme Style* (Philadelphia: University of Pennsylvania Press, 2011), 37.

17. Quoted in Brad Gooch, *Flannery: A Life of Flannery O'Connor* (New York: Back Bay Books, 2010).

18. Peiss, *Zoot Suit*, 18.

19. Jesuits in Japan, for example, established academies for oil and watercolor painting, copper engraving, sculpture, singing, and the playing of musical instruments; the Roman College in Italy included the study of madrigals, motets, operas, poetry, dance, and drama at the heart of its education (including poetry set to music); in Manila, the love of the arts spilled over the confines of church, school, and royal courts and swamped the lives of ordinary people. "Celebrations," writes John O'Malley, "could last for days, even weeks, as they did with typically baroque exuberance in Manila in the early 1620s after the papacy had approved for the whole church the public observance of the feast of the Immaculate Conception." See O'Malley, *Four Cultures of the West* (Cambridge, MA: Harvard University Press, 2004), 229–30.

20. See Sublette, *Cuba and Its Music*, 86.

21. For a good discussion of the *negros curros* of Havana, see Sublette, *Cuba and Its Music*, 86ff.

22. Peiss, *Zoot Suit*, 3.

23. See the discussion of "Pachuco Boogie" in Berríos-Miranda et al., *American Sabor*, 81–83.

24. See Berríos-Miranda et al., *American Sabor*, 105. Chicano rock 'n' roll groups— Thee Midniters, Cannibal and the Headhunters, Rosie and the Originals, Ritchie Valens, Santana, Los Lobos, Los Illegals, El Chicano, Tierra, Ozomatli, et al.—would channel this spirit, rummaging for beats and rhythms in a variety of places and then piecing them together to speak for the fragmented nature of Chicano identity.

25. George Lipsitz has a nice discussion of these aspects of Chicano rock music and culture. See his *Time Passages: Collective Memory and American Popular Culture* (Minneapolis: University of Minnesota Press, 1990), 153.

26. See Denise Sandoval, "The Politics of Low and Slow/*Bajito y Suavecito*," in *Black and Brown in Los Angeles: Beyond Conflict and Coalition* (Oakland: University of California Press, 2014), 183ff.

27. Quoted in Mandalit Del Barco, "The Story of 'Whittier Blvd,' A Song and Place Where Latino Youth Found Each Other," NPR, November 29, 2018.

28. The Oliver Wang lines were quoted in Jesus Velo and John Rabe, "Gerald Wilson, El Chicano, and 'Viva Tirado,'" *Off-Ramp Radio*, July 11, 2009.

29. See Berríos-Miranda et al., *American Sabor*, 119.

30. Anthony Macias points out that West Coast R&B tended to have a more mellow and smoother flavor. See Macias, *Mexican American Mojo* (Durham, NC: Duke University Press, 2008), 150.

31. Ilan Stavans, *The United States of Mestizo* (Montgomery, AL: New South Books, 2013), 24.

32. See Américo Paredes, *With His Pistol in His Hand: A Border Ballad and Its Hero* (Austin: University of Texas Press, 1958), 3.

33. Quoted in John Storm Roberts, *The Latin Tinge: The Impact of Latin American Music on the United States* (Oxford: Oxford University Press, 1999), 26.

34. See Macias, *Mexican American Mojo*, 170.

35. The image refers to Gorgythion, son of Priam, in the *Iliad*, book 8.

36. I discuss Las Casas in my book *Wonder and Exile in the New World* (University Park, PA: Penn State University Press, 2013), 63.

37. Siqueiros's first painting in Los Angeles was *Street Meeting* (1932), for the Chouinard School of Art, a work that was also painted over. It depicted workers of various ethnicities listening to an angry speech by a husky labor activist, their faces fixed in rapt attention. A black man with his child stands to the right of the orator, a poor white mother and child on the left, and dark-skinned Indians or mestizo laborers crouch on a scaffolding above the speaker, clinging to his words like bread during a famine. The most vulnerable and ostracized of the age, frequently invisible, were its main subjects. Like bright fireflies in the looming darkness, Siqueiros's mural lights up the lives in the shadows of American life.

38. See Marcus Reeves, *Somebody Scream: Rap Music's Rise to Prominence in the Aftershock of Black Power* (New York: Faber and Faber, 2008), 94.

39. "When a black man," James Baldwin writes, "whose destiny and identity have always been controlled by others, decides and states that he will control his own destiny and rejects the identity given to him by others, he is talking revolution." Quoted in Eddie Glaude, *Begin Again: James Baldwin's America and Its Urgent Lessons for Our Own* (New York: Crown Books, 2020), 24.

40. Kid Frost followed up *Hispanic Causing Panic* with *East Side Story* (1992) and *Smile Now, Die Later* (1995). He continued to use elements of Latin music—including other El Chicano samples, "Chachita" and "Look of Love," for instance—while also speaking the musical language of the West Coast, using funk guitars, G-funk's whiny synth lines, hard hand claps, and R&B samples from Sly and the Family Stone, Rick James, Bill Withers, and others. Here and elsewhere, there is no doubt that Frost embraced African American music as much as Mexican music. Pancho McFarland makes this point: "The uses of Black diasporic sounds and the music's development in the multiracial Los Angeles hip-hop scene demonstrate the interracial cultural exchange between Chicana/o and Black youth that begins as early as the 1930s." See his *Chicano Rap: Gender and Violence in the Postindustrial Barrio* (Austin: University of Texas Press, 2008), 39.

41. One of the rappers on the track is a professor of Mexican American studies at the University of Texas at San Antonio, Marco Cervantes, aka Mexican Stepgrandfather or Mexstep. He was raised in Houston, in a neighborhood that was a crossroads of Black and Latin@ cultures, and became interested in hip-hop at an early age: "I wanted to tell my story—the story of the Chicano in Texas—and the best way I knew how was through my music. . . . My solo music has to do with understanding the Chicano experience and politicizing our community." Quoted in Jesus Chavez, "Marco Cervantes," *UTSA Magazine*, May 13, 2015.

42. Quoted in Julyssa Lopez, "When Will Things Change? Niña Dioz, Lido Pimienta, and Ceci Bastida Aren't Waiting," NPR, April 6, 2018.

43. See Glaude, *Begin Again*, 91.

44. Quoted in Glaude, *Begin Again*, 213.

45. Quoted in Glaude, *Begin Again*, 92.

46. This is apparent, for instance, in Alain Locke's essays. See Josef Sorett, *Spirit in the Dark: A Religious History of Racial Aesthetics* (Oxford: Oxford University Press, 2016), 29.

47. Marie Arana, *Silver, Sword, and Stone: Three Crucibles in the Latin American Story* (New York: Simon and Schuster, 2019), 106.

48. Arana, *Silver, Sword, and Stone*, 142.

49. "This is the Blackness I want," writes Vinson Cunningham. "It has its feet on the ground of race and ethnicity and place, and stretches outward, its heart and arms aimed at the rest of the world." See his piece "Freedom and Equality Aren't Enough: A Symposium on *Fratelli tutti*," *Commonweal*, December 2020.

50. Writing for *Remezcla*, about the punk rock group Los Illegals, Michelle Threadgould captures nicely my own experiences with MEChA: "When I attended MEChA meetings at my local junior college, it was at a time when I desperately needed to find like-minded people. Instead, I found a group where male-identified activists led meet-

ings and rarely allowed others to talk. I found a group enamored with the ideal of the 'noble Aztecs' with no reference to their brutal rule of enslavement. I found a group reduced to telling young brown Americans that they were beautiful without a hard look at the oppressive, classist, sexist, and tangled history that makes each of us Chicano." See Threadgould, "Iconic East LA Punk Band Los Illegals on Why Chicano Punk Is an Act of Resistance," *Remezcla*, June 28, 2016.

51. See Glaude, *Begin Again*, 100.

52. The quote is by Edward Said. See Glaude, *Begin Again*, 144.

53. Josh Kun nicely compares these acts to the work of a cross-fader: "The ability of the DJ working in an African American art form to scratch over Mexican music is the ability to be a cultural cross-fader, a DJ who can cut between the cultures he or she lives in. . . . After all, part of the point of the scratch is to transform, to take one musical unit, change its shape, blur its message, reduce it to skeletal percussive noise, then allow it to gather itself and reform and rediscover its code, changed and different, a new sound with new tones." See his "What Is an MC If He Can't Rap to Banda? Making Music in Nuevo L.A.," *American Quarterly* 56, no. 3 (2004): 756.

54. "They pile clapping g-funk beats and Spanish-language rhymes on top of the brassy horns of traditional Mexican regional music, especially the marching oom-pah of *banda sinaloense*." See Kun, "What Is an MC If He Can't Rap to Banda?," 747.

55. Jeff Chang makes this point about Cypress Hill. See Chang, "Cypress Hill," in *Classic Material: The Hip-Hop Album Guide*, ed. Oliver Wang (Toronto: ECW Press, 2003), 52.

56. See Macias, *Mexican American Mojo*, 130.

57. Quoted in Threadgould, "Iconic East LA Punk Band Los Illegals."

58. See Manuel Peña, *The Texas-Mexican Conjunto: History of a Working Class Music* (Austin: University of Texas Press, 1985), 9.

59. See *Cumbia: Scenes of a Migrant Latin American Music Genre*, ed. Héctor Fernández L'Hoeste and Pablo Vila (Durham, NC: Duke University Press, 2013).

60. Mare's quote comes from Walter Thompson-Hernández, "Oaxacan Rap Has a Female Voice, Finally," *New York Times*, October 27, 2018. Chhoti Maa describes her work, moreover, in this way: "I think I have a strong core that I have always worked from, which is dignity, critical thought. My music is part of the Mexican diaspora, it echoes movement, it is made up of many layers." Quoted in "Bruja MC Chhoti Maa Channels the Soul of Her Ancestors Through Hip-Hop," *El Tecolote*, May 17, 2018.

61. For excellent studies of the underground scene in Los Angeles and South Central, see Jooyoung Lee, *Blowin' Up: Rap Dreams in South Central* (Chicago: University of Chicago Press, 2016). Also see Marcyliena Morgan, *The Real Hip Hop: Battling for Knowledge, Power, and Respect in the LA of the Underground* (Durham, NC: Duke University Press, 2009).

62. See Peter L'Official, *Urban Legends: The South Bronx in Representation and Ruin* (Cambridge, MA: Harvard University Press, 2020), 8–9.

63. "Cultural identity," as Stuart Hall reminds us, "is a matter of 'becoming' as well as 'being.' It belongs to the future as much as to the past." See his "Cultural Identity and Diaspora," in *Colonial Discourse and Post-Colonial Theory*, ed. Patrick Williams and Laura Chrisman (New York: Columbia University Press, 1994), 394.

INDEX

Black Star, 13; "Redefinition," 124
black theology, 2, 213n48
Blades, Ruben, 172
Blige, Mary J., 72, 81–82
BlocBoy JB: "Shoot" dance, 39
blues, 20, 23, 32, 41, 57, 65, 71–72, 100;
    Delta blues, 66
Bocafloja, 193
bolero, 194–95
Bolton, Andrew, 146
bomba, 144, 151, 156, 157, 161, 164
Bomb Squad, 49–50, 53, 62–63
boogaloo, 71, 140, 151, 164
Boogie Down Productions, 101
Boogie wit da Hoodie, A, 73
book of Revelation, 36–37, 50, 99
Boom Clap Bachelor: "Tiden Flyver,"
    115
bounce music, 66
Bradley, Adam, 45, 65, 145, 200n34,
    208n55; low end theory, 65
Brand Nubian, 59, 61
Brazil, 157; Carnival in, 13; favelas,
    209n4
breaking, 153; b-boying, 150–51; body,
    as weapon of choice, 153; claiming
    one's territory, 149; and kung fu, 151–
    53; parable, as close to, 153; public
    spaces, 149; transcendence, desire
    for, 149–50
B-Real, 190
Breton, André, 79
Brooks, Gwendolyn, 86
Brown, Chris, 217n45
Brown, James, 33, 61, 64, 87, 115, 152;
    "Give It Up or Turn It Loose," 153;
    and J.B.'s, 49, 61; "Say It Loud," 12;
    "Whole World Needs Liberation,
    The," 12
Brown, Shawn: "Rappin' Duke," 59

Brown Berets, 177
Brownout: "La Raza," 183–85, 188
Brownside, 189
Buber, Martin, 120
Buddha, 198n11
Buddy, 222n3
Buñuel, Luis, 35
Busta Rhymes, 16
Busy Bee Starski, 72

Cádiz (Spain), 143, 218–19n10; singing-
    poets of, 141–42
Calderón, Tego: dembow rhythm, 159–
    60; El Abayarde, 159–60; "El Aba-
    yarde," 160; "Guasa Guasa," 160;
    "Loiza," 160; "Los Difuntos" (The
    Dead), 160; "Pa' Que Retozen,"
    159–60
California, 53, 57, 101, 110, 117, 169, 191,
    194–95
Calle 13, 163; "Atrévete Te, Te," 193
Calloway, Cab: "Minnie the Moocher,"
    160
calypso, 157
Canary Islands, 160
Candomblé, 149
Cannibal and the Headhunters, 224n24
Cano, Eddie, 175–76
cantare, 8
capoeira, 151
Caramanica, Jon, 72, 140
Cardi B, 139, 141, 146, 218n5; "Bodak
    Yellow," 145; collaborations between
    black and Latin American heritage,
    140; hip-hop, as act of prophetic de-
    fiance, 141; "I Do," 141; "I Like It,"
    140–41
carioca, 157
Carr, Anne, 5
Carson, Anne, 7, 198n9